# CITY OF BROTHERLY BLOOD

## MY POLITICAL ADVENTURE OF POWER, CORRUPTION AND REDEMPTION IN PHILADELPHIA

## MICHAEL STACK

**RADIO FREE PRESS**

an imprint of Sunbury Press, Inc.
Mechanicsburg, PA USA

# RADIO FREE PRESS

an imprint of Sunbury Press, Inc.
Mechanicsburg, PA USA

For information about special discounts for bulk purchases, please contact Sunbury Press Orders Dept. at (855) 338-8359 or orders@sunburypress.com.

To request one of our authors for speaking engagements or book signings, please contact Sunbury Press Publicity Dept. at publicity@sunburypress.com.

FIRST RADIO FREE PRESS EDITION: April 2025

Set in Adobe Garamond | Interior design by Crystal Devine | Cover by Victoria Mitchell | Edited by Sarah Peachey.

Publisher's Cataloging-in-Publication Data
Names: Stack, Michael, author.
Title: City of brotherly blood : a walk with my father to political triumph.
Description: First trade paperback edition. | Mechanicsburg, PA : Radio Free Press, 2025.
Summary: Mike Stack comes from a long line of Philadelphia leaders. His father was a ward leader and his grandfather was a former US congressman. Learning from Philadelphia titans, like Senator Vincent Fumo, the Prince of Darkness, and chairman Bob Brady, while combatting union strongman Johnny Doc, guided Stack through his career in politics, which included heartbreaking losses, scandals, and federal probes to win.
Identifiers: ISBN 979-8-88819-266-5 (softcover).
Subjects: BIOGRAPY & AUTOBIOGRAPHY / Memoirs | BIOGRAPHY & AUTOBIOGRAPHY / Political | POLITICAL SCIENCE / American Government / State.

Designed in the USA
0 1 1 2 3 5 8 13 21 34 55

*For the Love of Books!*

# CONTENTS

# INTRODUCTION

The Pennsylvania state senate chamber glittered like the Versailles palace, packed with well-wishers and officials. The gallery was full and the crowd boisterous. The crystal chandeliers and brass rails twinkled from the sunlight that beamed through the stained-glass windows.

My reflection in the mirror of the senate dressing room appeared calm, but I was nervous. What was old seemed new and unexplored. The gavel thumped and thundered, and the baritone voice commanded, "Order!" It was time for the swearing-in of the thirty-third Lieutenant Governor of Pennsylvania. That was the first time I heard the number and found that impressive. Only thirty-two other people had been in my shoes in over two hundred years.

As an army officer, I respected military decorum and was delighted to have soldiers from the First City Troop, the oldest in Philadelphia, escort me to my position at the front of the chamber. They wore dress blues with tassels and gold trim, and several had silver helmets like Patton. I had been around pomp and circumstance more than the average citizen, but this was special. I'd met the guys at the Twenty-Second Street Armory and toured their historical digs. I became an honorary troop member. But today they were all business, and the lead honor guard had a sword encased in a long silver holster with his white-gloved hand upon it.

The gavel banged and shoes snapped. The clang and scrape of steel released from the scabbard created an echo. Suddenly, a violent whoosh whipped by my ear and the hair stood on my neck. Dylan McGarry, an executive staffer who usually blushed, was white as a ghost. His eyes bulged as he stared at the swordsman. A hush enveloped the chamber, but few knew about my brush with death.

I went on to get sworn in by my mother, retired judge Felice Stack, as my beautiful wife, Tonya, held the Bible. I was almost finished before I started. Tom Wolf sat in the second row adjacent to the dais with Katie McGinty, his chief of staff. He would be sworn in after me in the frigid January air. Wolf seemed uncomfortable in the senate, shuffling in his seat.

That was a day of triumph and danger, like many other days in my political career and life. In this book, you will hear about my grandfather and father and their political exploits. But this book is far more than a generational political tale. My genealogy contributed to my journey, but you should imagine as you read that we're on a long car ride up to Happy Valley to watch Penn State play. Imagine you just asked, "So Mike, what's your story?"

I'll tell you.

My journey is about perseverance and survival, not just in politics but life. This is not only a memoir but an adventure story, thriller, self-help guide, a bit of true crime, and finally, of self-discovery.

I went into politics because it seemed natural and familiar, but I needed to learn things Dad and Grandfather Stack never did. I found myself in unanticipated dangerous situations along the way. I got a lot of encouragement and help to advance but eventually had to survive without much help from anybody. I never fully understood why certain adversaries were trying to hurt me, or exactly how they were pulling the strings, but I knew they were. It got terrifying.

My mentors and advisors were clueless, and I had to survive on instinct and prayer. That's what made the voyage so terrifying, interesting, and invigorating, like almost falling off a cliff to a horrible death.

I chose the fiery path of politics for a big chunk of my career. However, I was on a different road at several points to divergent careers. I tried many things and suffered countless disappointments before ever winning an election. I kept getting pulled back into it like Michael Corleone. And that magnetic lore brought me triumph, but didn't solve the riddle of me. Heartbreak awaited. I had to learn new lessons to find my authentic self and lead my best life.

The greatest revelations came through pain, but that suffering would transform into joy. I want my readers to know that, like Forrest Gump, life is like a box of chocolates, ones I found interesting and unpredictable and delicious. The peaks and valleys came and went many times, but ultimately, as Kerouac suggested, the road was like night that blessed the earth—or words to that effect. But just like on his journey and mine, nobody knows what's going to happen to anybody. So I say to the youngsters who have failed and felt sadness acutely, agonizingly, and sometimes suicidally, do not distress. The mystery of your purpose will be revealed if you continue down the road. I have found chocolate-covered strawberries waiting, and you will, too.

The danger of getting my head chopped off wasn't that big of a deal. I came from a tough city and a brutal business. My mother prayed that I wouldn't get badly injured while encouraging me as a young man to walk down the dark alley of family tradition. That alley was treacherous, and my dad and grandfather were assaulted for the public good. But I had a little something more: a dash of charisma and a winning smile. Maybe I could be a contender.

\* \* \*

The Keystone State wasn't just interesting in the late eighties when I tried to bullrush in—it was downright bloody. In 1985, Mayor Wilson Goode dropped a bomb on Osage Avenue in a standoff against a Black liberation movement known as MOVE. Eleven people were killed, two hundred and fifty made homeless, and sixty-one homes were destroyed. Among the dead were six children. The Cobbs Creek neighborhood had been allowed to burn to the ground by Philadelphia's first African American mayor. Philadelphia was known around the world as the city that bombed itself. Mayor Goode later made a formal apology and won reelection against former Mayor Frank Rizzo, who had also used the police as instruments of violence. But things were just warming up.

Two years after that moment, my gaggle of new friends and I took in the icy air as we strolled through the woods as snow fell. A burly former Rutgers tight end named Russ ran toward us, breathing heavily. He'd been a star player before injuring a knee and getting addicted to painkillers. "The treasurer of Pennsylvania just blew his head off on TV!" We didn't know what he was talking about. It sounded ridiculous; over what, balance sheets not adding up? Then we got back to the old Scranton mansion in Wilkes-Barre, Pennsylvania, and saw the carnage on television.

\* \* \*

Budd Dwyer was elected state representative and senator. He seemed like many men I came to know in a rarified world of comradery and competition. An average-looking man with a modified combover, a hearty smile gave him approachability. But apparently, no one got close enough to understand his desperation. He was tall and carried piles of paper under his arms.

What separated him from the hundreds in the state house and dozens in the senate was ambition. This everyman thought he was different. That carried him out of the madhouse and into the gentile confines of the upper chamber, sometimes referred to as the "whore house."[1] Most senators tried to run out the clock to retirement—a better job there never was. But Budd was driven and got elected statewide and then reelected. Former lieutenant governor Mark Singel, who knew Budd from his senate days, found Dwyer's ascent surprising. With

---

1. Former Speaker of the House Robert O'Donnell used to refer to the state house and senate in this way.

each win, Budd probably started thinking about going for the biggest job of them all. Then the anonymous letter arrived.

In 1986, Pennsylvania officials discovered that state employees overpaid millions in FICA taxes due to a technical glitch. Dwyer awarded a contract to the California-based Computer Technology Associates (CTA), owned by Harrisburg native John Torquato Jr., to determine the rebates. But then Governor Richard Thornburgh received a mysterious memorandum a few weeks later, which alleged bribery in the award of the contract and accused Dwyer and others of receiving kickbacks along with Republican committee member Bob Asher and CTA attorney William Smith.

Governor Thornburgh could have shredded the memorandum—anonymous letters were a cowardly tactic used by political enemies—but he passed it on to investigators and effectively sent Dwyer down the road of no return.

No money changed hands, and the contract was canceled two months after it was signed. Nonetheless, prosecutors smelled blood, and public officials made fantastic headlines. The indictments came down fast and hard. The players quickly grabbed deals. William Smith pleaded guilty to offering Dwyer and Asher $300,000 in bribes and received a reduced sentence. Torquato pleaded guilty and received a four-year sentence. Dwyer, however, adamantly proclaimed his innocence and refused a deal of one count and five years. At trial, he doubled down: "I absolutely did nothing wrong." But he must have. Why else would he be in front of a jury with that big stack of papers? He was eventually found guilty on eleven counts, and the judge hinted at a fifty-five-year sentence.

Dwyer ranted against Governor Thornburgh and the prosecutors for months, and was at it again, stuttering and sweating after the verdict. But his press secretary, James Horshock, and deputy treasurer Don Johnson urged Dwyer to be remorseful and plead for mercy. They met with the treasurer on January 15, 1987, in preparation for a press conference. The two aides thought he might resign. They were around the man through it all but claimed they weren't sure what the press event was about.

The media crowded into Dwyer's capitol office to watch the car wreck. One had to beg them to cover press conferences about tax reform or health insurance, but this one was easy. It was a human disaster and public comeuppance. The lunch bell rang, and the mob listened to the rambling, tortured words of a man on a ledge proclaiming innocence and saluting his wife and kids for a wonderful life. Bright the future had been. The only thing missing were the words "Goodbye, cruel world." After half an hour, several reporters began cracking open leather cases and noisily putting away their equipment as if they were dismissing Dwyer for such a boring show. They wanted a resignation or something else that gave them misery to report. But Budd could read an audience.

Dwyer captured their attention by proclaiming, "I am going to die in office." He thought that maybe "the shameful facts, spread out in all their shame, will not burn through our civic shamelessness and set fire to American pride." He asked that the media tell his story on every radio and television station, every newspaper and magazine, in the United States. Then, he was a good guy to the end and urged, "Please leave immediately if you have a weak stomach or mind since I don't want to cause physical or mental distress."

There were no capitol police or state troopers to act even though it was obvious what was about to happen. Budd had the perfect Pennsylvania name. He was a regular guy who believed only good things happen to nice people. He was a nice fellow in a brutal game with imminent potential for blood, but his pride deluded him. He ranted about shame, probably his own, and the notion of some sort of shameful frame-up. It was a fantasy. He thought his death would trigger an investigation, which would expose the plot and exonerate him. He reached for a manila envelope from his briefcase that contained a .357 magnum, the most absurdly violent handgun in the world. Who pulls a gun from a manila envelope besides an accountant in distress?

The people of the media watched like ghosts. Tony Romeo, the KYW radio reporter with a voice that sounded nothing like he looked, was traumatized and needed to take years off from reporting. His portly little figure occupied a front-row seat to tragedy. Interestingly, he got his appetite back and was inches from my face decades later at the biggest press conferences of my career. Maybe he was hoping I'd top Budd Dwyer.

Budd's pride and naïveté were striking. I learned at an early age to never expect fairness from the media or prosecutors. Politics was blood sport and one got cut. My mother prayed that I'd be protected. She knew it was brutal and that I would suffer but felt my talents were needed. In my twenties, I was more rational and less prideful than Budd. Marcellus Wallace understood it best when he advised Butch in *Pulp Fiction* that pride only hurts—it never helps.

# CHAPTER ONE

# POLITICS IS A FAMILY BUSINESS

**W**hy would a nice boy like me walk into a shooting gallery like politics? DNA dictated it over common sense. I had been brought up in the life. Politics was in our house and in our blood. It was tradition and vocation. The people and the players stood toe to toe. But I saw only my parents and mayors and congressmen and committee people of the day. I didn't know about the first Mike Stack and the rumble with Jack Kelly. He was ghost from the ancient battlefield of the other side of the city. That spirit of the past was not revealed until I started running.

*       *       *

The first Mike Stack, my grandfather, came from County Kerry and the town of Listowel, Ireland. He served in World War I and took shrapnel to the chest, and he held on to it for the remainder of his life. He became a realtor and sold houses in his growing West Philadelphia neighborhood. A charming personality endeared him to his neighbors, so there was a natural affinity to a political career with the democratic political organization. Mary was from Armagh in Northern Ireland, which was rebel country. She was selling flowers near Sixtieth and Catherine Street, where he bought a bouquet and handed it back to her. They got married and had three daughters and two sons. As incredible as it sounds, this immigrant ran for the United States Congress and got elected. A New Deal Democrat, he helped pass the first minimum wage in 1932, which was twenty-five cents, and the Fair Labor Standards Act in 1938, which provided a forty-hour work week. He was also an original cosponsor of the first Social Security bill.

Franklin Roosevelt's transformation of America was accomplished with the help of Grandfather Stack's elbow grease. The congressman had an independent streak. He supported his own slate of candidates for city office against the wishes of party chairman Jack Kelly. The father of Princess Grace Kelly of Monaco ran things like a king who wouldn't tolerate insubordination. Kelly ordered Grandfather Stack to stop or be stomped. The Stack tradition of donkey-headed stupidity can be traced at least to 1936. The party kicked back, supporting his opponent and putting Grandfather into the unemployment line he had helped shorten. The congressman helped save America with legislation that pulled us out of the Great Depression, but FDR had his own election to worry about. Philadelphia was crucial, and the president sided with Boss Kelly.

My father and his three sisters and disabled brother rode the roller coaster. Philadelphia's burgeoning population warranted eight congressional seats, compared to the present less than two. The family had an unreliable economic dependence on politics. Grandfather drank at political functions and while away in Washington. He was absent from the family and came home to an ice storm. After he lost, it was worse. Mary practiced both rage and silent scorn, and the kids felt it like a punch in the gut. They walked on eggshells while dinner was served in nerve-wracking quiet. Rather, she was only silent to Grandfather, who complimented her on the flavorless boiled ham, and heard nothing. The kids watched and tried to avoid indigestion.

\* \* \*

My siblings and I didn't know about all this. As children, we thought it was weird that Dad invited people into the house during family dinners. But as a boy, he sought buffers to deflect tension. As a man and father, he welcomed company like a life preserver. The doorbell would ring, and we made it a game to guess which committee person or hanger-on was there. Jack Buck, Bill Malloy, or Joe Afflerbach joined us at the table. Dad fetched some cans of Schmidt's beer, and they watched us and enjoyed mostly happy banter. Dad learned the importance of a buffer from Grandfather. He couldn't seem to stop it in our mostly happy family. Nonetheless, the buffer taught me how to carry on a conversation with anybody.

After graduating from West Catholic High in 1944, Dad got orders to report for duty. The island-hopping strategy in the South Pacific was working, but the fighting was fierce. The experts predicted a million American casualties in an invasion of Tokyo to defeat Japan. Dad and his contemporaries presumed they would soon be dead. When Truman dropped the bomb, Dad was saved. He served instead in the occupying army in Germany.

When a lieutenant was looking for volunteers to bury the countless corpses lying all over Germany, Dad immediately volunteered. Another soldier tipped him off that the job came with an expense account, a jeep, and minimal supervision. The officer paused. "No, not you," he said. "You're too eager."

He was eager for an education, and the GI Bill provided it. He graduated from Saint Joseph's University with a degree in economics. He drove a school bus part time, then went to the University of Pennsylvania for law school because Grandfather advised him that lawyers could always find work. Politicians were often out of work. If Dad wanted to follow in his father's footsteps, he also needed to improve at public speaking. He taught American Government to a night school class at Saint Joseph's to get practice. Even though his voice cracked and he appeared nervous, Felice Rowley liked him as a teacher. She was a Catholic school teacher finishing up her degree. Eventually, she was willing to marry him.

He practiced law at the Obermayer firm and served as a committeeman, a block captain of his precinct. Then he went to Washington on a quest to join the Kennedy Administration. My parents moved to Falls Church, Virginia. Johnson's Great Society enabled Dad to become an administrator of the Poverty Program. Big government was unexciting compared to the call of the wild that brought us back to the cradle of liberty.

In 1962, Philadelphia Mayor Richardson Dilworth resigned to run for governor as required by the city charter. Council president James Tate succeeded to mayor but was eventually opposed by the Democratic Party for reelection. Party bosses didn't like his Kensington accent and felt they deserved more patronage. Perhaps reflecting Grandfather's independent streak, Dad joined the Tate team against the party and encountered a world of scheming and double-crossing. He wrote about it in *Close Personal Friends of the Mayor*, a veiled account of treachery and triumph.

While representing Tate at a meeting of ward leaders, a cigar-chomping, fat-necked boss called for his ejection. The man was not a ward leader and thus lacked exulted standing to be in the room. They still do it today, but the sting was intense. Thus began Dad's quest to become a ward leader.

Philadelphia ward leaders had a mystical lore in the city's political history. They were the backroom bosses in the smoke-filled rooms who controlled things. They were elected by committee people from smaller neighborhood divisions. The leader was then the boss of all those divisions that represented the voters in that part of the city. In this feudal system, before the age of high-tech campaigns and massive television advertising, they decided elections.

Dad literally moved us to the 58th Ward in the Somerton section of Northeast Philadelphia because there was a vacancy. He would eventually recruit lifetime friends and become a kingmaker, but first he had to help Tate win. Legendary South Philadelphia congressman William Barrett became his mentor. Dad became his eyes and ears in the deceitful world of double-dealing by close personal friends of the mayor who were anything but.

Barrett was short and wore a bad toupee. He was late middle-aged and unremarkable but got reelected time and again. A master politician, he cared little about the events of Washington, DC. The intrigues of Philadelphia supplied his oxygen, so he returned to his district office every night, where constituents lined up. Barrett was the secret architect of Tate's campaign.

Barrett ran every meeting by going around the room asking each leader how many votes they would provide for the mayor. He would know their exact totals from the last several elections of each division. When they lied or exaggerated, he called them out politely and sarcastically. Dad learned the importance of making people get specific and to do so in front of witnesses.

I only knew about Bill Barrett from Dad's stories as we drove to political events and polling places. He referred to Barrett as Socrates, and I learned from the Aristotle of Philadelphia politics—my father. If a ward leader said he would support me, Dad asked, "Did he say he would have you on all his ballots, morning, noon, and night? Or did he just say he would vote for you?" Barrett taught him to ask those specific questions, and he taught me.

Tate was a tough Irishman who wasn't big on eloquent speeches, but old ladies knelt when he appeared. They kissed his hand, according to Dad. He won that democratic primary, then beat then-Republican Arlen Specter by only twelve thousand votes in 1968. His detractors continued their perfidy behind the scenes, but Tate called himself a party man throughout. He led Philadelphia through the turbulent 1960s. When African Americans used civil disobedience to gain greater access in the construction unions, Tate helped pass the city's anti-discrimination statutes. He retired to the Jersey shore and died unceremoniously at the age of seventy-three from a heart attack in 1983.

* * *

Dad became the leader of the 58th Ward in 1971. He grew long sideburns to look hip and wore those crazy wide ties. He was over 6'2" and distinguished with thinning black hair and rosy cheeks. His gray eyes were piercing when he took off his thick eyeglasses. His wit was dry as dust, and he could be sarcastic and needling, but he was unusually cheerful most of the time. Being in his presence was educational. His stories were novelesque, and he was like a movie character. When he spoke to strangers, it was an opportunity to brighten a life. Sometimes he'd leave them smiling, other times, scratching their heads.

Dad worked on several statewide campaigns and was on the road often. He'd appear after weeks at the front door in a black tailored suit with a giant bag of toys. We would mob him like a rock star. If he wanted to buy our affection, we were in the market. We sensed he was an important man on the rise.

We kids had arguments but were forbidden to use the silent treatment. Dad believed that was the most hurtful. We learned later about his childhood. Mom expressed her feelings well and explained our father to us when he couldn't.

The house on Richwood Road was 58th Ward headquarters, so operatives, committee people, and local politicians were ubiquitous. Dad's legal clients would mix in and often needed political help. Countless parties flowed onto the front and back lawns. Mayor Frank Rizzo came over more than once. The tough former police commissioner was once photographed in a tuxedo with a blackjack in the cummerbund. His large physical stature bolstered his notorious image.

Rizzo had been James Tate's police commissioner and put down unrest with brutality. "When I'm finished with them, I'll make Attila the Hun look like a faggot," he's reported as saying.[2] Rizzo resigned as police commissioner in 1971 to run for mayor. His relationship with the Black community was volatile; nonetheless, the department had one of the largest percentages of Black officers (20%) among US police departments in 1968. It soon dropped as Rizzo's cops raided the Black Panther office and strip-searched four suspects on camera in broad daylight. The suspects were later cleared, and four people unrelated to the Panthers were found guilty of murder. But the mayhem continued with Rizzo's handling of the first MOVE incident in 1978.

In 1977, members of the group were asked to leave a house in Powellton Village because of compaints from neighbors. By the next year, MOVE members still had not left the property and refused entrance to city inspectors. Mayor Rizzo evicted them with armed police action. Snipers positioned themselves around the house, and one thousand officers blockaded the compound. When police attempted to enter the building, Officer James Ramp was killed, and sixteen other police and firefighters were injured. The MOVE members claimed it hadn't been them, but Delbert Africa was beaten by multiple police officers while leaving the MOVE house with his hands up. The incident was captured by local media, showing Africa being dragged by his hair, struck with an officer's helmet, and kicked in the face and groin while on the ground.

My dad had a mixed relationship with the mayor and was not initially an ally. Richardson Dilworth, the former mayor, accused Rizzo of using the police for political espionage. Dad wrote a veiled account in *The Trouble Squad*, where political enemies were hunted down by thug squads. Future friends conveyed stories of fearing for their lives when they supported Peter Camiel, a Rizzo opponent, for party chair. I recalled these stories every time I drove past the Peter Camiel rest stop on the Pennsylvania Turnpike.

---

2. Jake Blumgart, "The Brutal Legacy of Frank Rizzo, the Most Notorious Cop in Philadelphia History," *Vice*, October 22, 2015, https://www.vice.com/en/article/remembering-frank-rizzo-the-most-notorious-cop-in-philadelphia-history-1022/.

Nonetheless Rizzo got excellent publicity during his first term. He showed appreciation by awarding jobs to two dozen local reporters. The *Philadelphia Inquirer* and *Daily News* changed ownership and his coverage soon got negative. Younger journalists emphasized investigative tactics and were far more critical. Rizzo didn't help his case by endorsing Richard Nixon for president in 1972. He held frequent and bombastic press conferences. Peter Camiel accused Rizzo of offering patronage in exchange for influencing the choice of district attorney and controller candidates. Rizzo called him a liar. Then a media circus ensued like the World Wrestling Federation. A reporter from the *Daily News* asked Rizzo to submit to a polygraph test to prove Camiel was lying. "If this machine says a man lied, he lied," Rizzo said before failing the test. That ended Rizzo's gubernatorial aspirations.

It also led to Dad supporting the independent candidacy of Charles Bowser, a leading Black attorney, in 1975. His charisma was undeniable and his presence in our home made us neighborhood legends. We piled coats on beds, and the girls tried on furs. We took turns diving onto the piles. My friends were fascinated and joined the parties. By twelve or thirteen years old, we were able to join the party with a few beers.

Dad's stature grew. He became known as the man to see if one had political aspirations. His support was crucial to get elected. Like an Irish Don Corleone, he held judges and politicians "in his pocket like so many nickels and dimes." Grownups vied for our attention and urged, "say hello to your father." We knew we were connected. After backing others, Dad sought office in his own right. In 1973, he bucked the party and ran in the primary for district attorney.

Dad was one of the most articulate men on the planet but encountered the same obstacle as many first-time candidates—fear. A large crowd gathered at the Philo Club in Center City for his announcement. We stood next to Dad in suits and dresses as he stepped up to the column of microphones. The bright lights were blinding. The cameras clicked. I couldn't believe what I heard. His voice quivered and squeaked as he struggled through the speech. It was agonizing to watch sweat pour off this sage. Finally, it ended, and he did a better job with questions from the press. I learned a key thing about politics as performance art. Everything changes once the cameras are on.

The campaign became fun, if not misogynistic. The short skirts and fresh faces of the secretaries from Dad's law firm became the Stackettes, the secret weapon to combat the power of the machine. It didn't really work. We assembled a caravan of cars and trucks to honk horns and show enthusiasm while driving around the city. The Stackettes were in the back of a pickup truck decorated with campaign posters, flares, and sparklers. A big speaker was loaded on one of the roofs and played seventies funk as we moved out. The driver of the pickup truck may have been drinking, and his recklessness violently tossed around the Stackettes while the flares burned them. They cursed at the driver when he finally pulled over. They had burn holes in their stockings and stormed off before the rally could complete its disastrous plunge. I watched those young ladies spew such incredible profanity; it was intoxicating.

We Stack kids dressed in all white with green placards that said "BACK STACK FOR DA." At a campaign stop at the Italian Market in South Philly, instead of being cheered like Rocky Balboa, we were berated and implored to leave. My brother and sisters thought this was child abuse, not by the old ladies squeezing cantaloupes and telling us we were ruining their day, but by my parents for dragging us there. They hated it, but I liked the excitement. The acrimony and struggle were part of it.

Dad had guts going against the party, and Mom supported him all the way. They had giant smiles on election night as they headed to his concession speech. Mom embraced me. "We're really happy." She said Dad lost by only three to one.

"How can you be happy if we got killed?"

The look of pride and relief radiated from her face. "We finished the race. We showed them we were serious and got support from people we never expected."

They left me scratching my head as they went out the front door. Little did I know, I'd have too many similar moments in a long losing streak.

The race for district attorney demonstrated the Stack legacy of going on suicide missions. We made them defeat us if they wouldn't join us. I suppose normal people find the idea of defeat appalling. Not us. There's a point to be made. I'll let you know when I find out what it is.

Aspirants continued to visit. Dad introduced me, and I began to handicap candidates. He took me along to meetings and parties. The annual Jefferson Jackson dinner was at the world-famous Bellevue Stratford Hotel in Center City. The party was in its heyday, and the event was packed with players and wannabees, dressed magnificently. People were ebullient because I walked with a sage. There was the energy and aura of celebrity. When I walked into that ballroom filled with balloons and glitter and swirling lights, it felt natural. That's where I wanted to be.

* * *

We eventually moved to Southampton Road into a sizeable Tudor home. Grandmother Stack had been forced out of her West Philadelphia home years before. Dad and his sisters were concerned about increasing crime, so they got the tough Irish immigrant to move to the Northeast. She lived around the corner along with Aunt Betty, Aunt Mary, and Uncle Jimmy, who had cerebral palsy and hydrocephalus.

Aunt Nora married a political consultant named Tom Williams, who worked for the governor of Ohio. They were killed in an auto accident and that's how I got my sister Carol, who was in the backseat and survived. Aunt Mary died on the operating table before her fiftieth birthday during heart surgery. My parents planned to move Mom's stepmother, Rita Rowley, and the rest of Dad's family into the new home in one fell swoop. Getting Grandmother Stack to go along was heart-pounding. She was more bunkered in than the MOVE compound. I still have nightmares recalling her angry face as we drove past her on Southampton Road. Aunt Betty drove the bursting Ford Maverick, barely able to see over the dashboard, looking terrified. As she shook her fist, Dad, who was steering the Lincoln as if in slow motion, went pale.

Uncle Jimmy was prone to violent seizures, which involved blood-curdling screams that echoed through the house. Aunt Betty cared for Jimmy and became the night watchman. She carried a flashlight and inspected every corner of the house, sometimes finding necking teenagers and underage drinking. She was 4'8" and had a piercing, nasally voice that made you jump. She was bullied by Grandmom Stack for surviving birth defects and being short and hunchbacked, which resulted in Betty being authoritarian with us. We were young teenagers with our own problems. She would let us off with warnings and ended up being an extra shoulder to cry on. She insisted our friends call her Aunt Betty. Once we added the committee people and political types and mixed them with all our friends, the household was a spicy jambalaya of love and dysfunction.

Mom was appointed to the Board of Education by Mayor Rizzo. The route was circuitous. Dad evolved into a Rizzo ally after beginning as an enemy. The newly elected mayor tried to eliminate all the Northeast ward leaders because they were Irish and untrustworthy. Only one survived. A reporter called my old man the night of the election and asked how he won. He said, "Well, the mayor must have been for me. Otherwise, I would have lost." Rizzo thought that was good sportsmanship and told Dad to name the city job he wanted. Dad became counsel to the Parking Authority. Later, Rizzo fired him for not agreeing to become his personal attorney. It was tough to keep track, but they ended up friends.

Philadelphia had one of America's largest public education systems in the early seventies. There were three board members who had to balance racial tensions, failing schools, and fiscal crises. The compensation package consisted of nothing except a driver and the use of a city-owned Ford LTD. Mom's driver was a former cop with a handsome face and snappy wit. Lou Frangipanni had black hair and dark suits and became part of the family. He was forced to retire from the cops after getting shot in the face, and he still had a scar between his nose and lip. He called me Moe and asked if I'd gotten my end wet yet. I was going on thirteen. He would sometimes pick me up at school and take me to the dentist or eye doctor. Mom worked hard, visited hundreds of schools, and advocated for reform and equal funding. She participated at forums across the state and had to evacuate from a conference near Three Mile Island. Nonetheless, the media condemned the "free drivers" and the cushy offices. Lou drove on and shared wisdom that helped guide my life. I appreciated having an extra adult ear.

\* \* \*

Dyslexia caused massive confusion in my childhood. The special education teacher at Saint Christopher's ended up being my mother, a rescuer. I remember feeling lost and terrified, unable to see letters clearly. School was a nightmare, and teachers and other kids rebuked my unruliness. I found ways to cover up and conceal my confusion by using humor. Repeating first grade was a shameful event I tried to conceal. Kids teased me about how stupid one had to be to flunk first grade. To this day, the heat of humiliation comes over me when my school years don't match my date of birth when someone confronts me.

I was lucky to transfer to Pen Ryn in Cornwells Heights, which had small classes and focused teachers. Years later, fellow lieutenant governor Jim Cawley mentioned his son was attending a new school, and Jim was nervous about it. He was relieved when I told him that was my school. "Oh, thank God. I can't wait to tell Suzanne you went there." Even though I washed out in Catholic school, the extra attention was a relief. I performed better. The embarrassment dissipated, but I still felt different riding the short bus instead of walking to school with my friends.

I carried the emotional baggage of my learning disability into law school and the United States Army Legal Center at the University of Virginia. Words jumbled with stress, making it impossible to read. The shame was suffocating. But my teachers were patient and encouraged me to keep on trying. I took that to heart and never stopped trying. In politics and life, perseverance has been my strength. At some point, after running away in frustration from my schoolwork, I decided to return and try again.

\* \* \*

The newspaper columnist Tom Fox quoted my dad, the politico, often. His wit made great copy. Those columns enhanced Dad's mystique. He delivered for countless judicial candidates, which made him an even more formidable lawyer. Clients valued his judicial connections, but the judges would recuse themselves when they could most help. Nonetheless, lawyers joined the firm as a road to the bench. The law firm parties were filled with aspirants. The energy was palpable, and 1600 Locust became an epicenter.

The four-story red brick building formally belonged to the Breyer ice cream family. The iconic briar bush leaf logo appeared on different metal encasings on the windows and garden. Dad's office looked presidential and even had a Resolute desk. The fireplace crackled and glowed, even in summer. The classical furnishings were the residue of estates he had helped administer. He disappeared behind a high-back leather chair, with only the Dictaphone cord visible, but swung around when called. He had the aura of a pope or Don, where lines formed to seek his counsel.

John Glenn, Ted Kennedy, and Jerry Brown were among the presidential candidates who attended a reception hosted by Ronrico's, the rum distillery. The building was packed to the gills on that June evening in 1979. All the beautiful people pushed into each other and maneuvered through the hallway to reach Dad's office. Everyone was ridiculously tan and delighted. I couldn't keep track of all the elected people I'd only read about or seen on television. The governor of Puerto Rico recommended our place for the event, and Dad claimed to have never met him. The old man was mysteriously powerful. His Cheshire cat smile was familiar. His hair was grayer, but his eyes even more intense.

Before all that competition, Jimmy Carter asked for a meeting in 1974. Dad had never heard of the Georgia peanut farmer and threw his card away after their chat. "That guy's got the same chance as me of becoming president," he told Tom Fox. He didn't know how Carter found him but didn't hear from him again until after the president's reelection was in jeopardy. Carter brought him along in the big black car as the president made desperate campaign stops in Philadelphia. Carter's son Chip was in his thirties and became friendly. He hung out and spoke at the 58th Ward meetings in the basement of our home.

The ward meetings were held at a variety of interesting places, including DiGiacomo's funeral parlor. Committee people leaned against metal caskets and chuckled about ghost voting. Philadelphia's famous tradition of voting the dead to maximize results gained new irony. Louie DiGiacomo joined the State Undertakers Board with Dad's assistance. The rent at the funeral home was cheap, but our basement was free. Inevitably, committee people and candidates ended up at the kitchen table and all over the house.

Dad was delighted to have the home as the nerve center of ward politics. Unendorsed candidates tried to crash meetings but were easier to rebuff. "This is my home, and you are not invited," he told numerous interlopers. Rizzo once showed up with a candidate the ward wasn't supporting, and Mom told him to leave. That may have been the gesture that made him appoint her to the school board.

The 58th Ward was the second largest in the city and half Jewish. Thus, it was the largest Jewish ward. We attended many seders, shivas, synagogues, and countless funerals, and celebrated Jewish culture. Most of these folks were public school teachers or principals. Later, I became a prominent advocate for Jewish causes and traveled to the Holy Land multiple times.

I met political players all the time, so it was only logical to consider a career in politics. My siblings didn't feel the same. I enjoyed shaking hands and remembering names and trying to be charming. I wore suits and worked a polling station as a preteen. The Republicans were polite but subtly hostile. This was empowering. They were threatened by a kid because of his dad.

However, Dad bet on the wrong horse regularly. This was true in politics and at the racetrack. A self-described horse degenerate, Dad lost money on horses and credibility in elections. He bet on Bob Casey in three straight losses. He became a horse owner with Captain Tevo, who won his first race, then took Dad's shirt, progressively dropping places until finishing consistently last.

Chuck Feldman, an irascible committeeman, needled, "Who's your dad backing in the election?" I'd ask why. "I need to know so I can back the other guy." Later, Chuck backed me blindly. He was a chalk player but believed in luck. He had a salt-and-pepper beard and wore a suit uncomfortably. He was sarcastic and deadpan, working countless hours greeting commuters at the crack of dawn with me. We would tell each other stories about the old man while picking up my handouts that had been thrown on the ground.

* * *

I went to LaSalle High School in Springfield, where I played on the freshman and JV football teams before taking a wrong turn. I loved playing sports. We grew up on a block with tons of kids, and we were always playing something without thinking about it. One never worried about getting picked for basketball or baseball because another kid was always needed. I wanted sporting goods for every birthday.

I had a good pitching arm, and Dad regularly threw me a glove and said, "Let's go. Throw me three innings." Winter or summer, I threw. One year, on a family trip to Ireland, I threw him pitches near an eight-hundred-year-old stone wall that partially collapsed on him. No matter when we were throwing a ball, he would show me his beet-red hand when we finished. I pitched in the Stone Harbor summer league and got the nickname Rocket Arm. He was delighted. Kids would yell it out to me as I walked with him down Ninety-Sixth Street. That may have been his favorite title of all the ones I was privileged to have.

My misspent youth was a combination of bad decisions, too much drinking, and learning struggles. I could hang with burnouts or the jocks, the smart kids or the idiots. A coach once pulled me aside after a scrimmage. "You can play on this team. You've got the ability, but you're hanging with the wrong people and going down the wrong road."

He was right.

In my junior year, I got asked to run for vice president of student council. My friend Gregg Melinson was a national merit scholar who thought I could help the ticket. I would attract the rabble and denizens with my misdirected charisma. I entered the race late but was practiced at shaking hands and asking for votes. We hurdled several other tickets and finished a close third out of ten. The vice principal, Brother Frank, was a ginger-haired autocrat who quipped, "I feared we'd have the inauguration in The Pit." This was the designated smoking section outside the lower-level cafeteria. Yes, our high school had a smoking section. My respectable electoral performance foreshadowed the future despite Brother Frank's fears.

Doctor Jack Seydow encouraged my writing at LaSalle University. He was a challenging instructor who assigned weekly papers on broad topics such as "Machine or Car." I got the hang of it and used rhetoric and humor to create several quality papers. He directed me to enter a national writing contest. The letter informing me that I hadn't won urged continued effort. Doctor Jack later told me that he had only given eleven A's in his career and I was a recipient. I contemplated becoming a writer but chickened out.

My parents supported whatever career path I might discover, but politics was the family business. I accompanied Dad to City Committee and met the ward leaders and party operatives regularly.

I was being groomed and dressed like a politician. Dad would ask me what I thought about a candidate. If his tie was crooked and didn't match, he would probably lose. It was a game of first impressions. You didn't get a second chance at one.

* * *

The Republicans had taken over Northeast Philadelphia one seat at a time. There were a variety of reasons. The Democratic electorate had grown more African

American, and Rizzo was banned from running again. He tried to change the charter through a referendum, but it was soundly defeated. Mayor William Green was the son of a party chairman but didn't like the rough and tumble. He was handsome, with dark hair reminiscent of Tyrone Power. The criticism came and he prepared to go. The schools were failing, and he needed relief. He met with my mom and fellow school board members and praised their loyalty and excellence. He then asked for their resignations. She was incredulous, but my dad advised, "When the mayor asks for your resignation, you give it."

The divisions in the city gave way to our first Black mayor, Wilson Goode. The acrimony was intense as Rizzo attempted a comeback, but the brutality of the past was highlighted. Nervous whites in Northeast Philadelphia leaned Republican. When Rizzo ran, they switched registrations to vote for him in the Democratic Primary. These closet Republicans didn't show up on the registration sheets, only on election day.

It got worse in 1985 with the police standoff against MOVE, a Black liberation organization bunkered down in a row house on Osage Avenue. The African American neighbors demanded Mayor Goode act against the group that blared speeches on a bullhorn all day. The MOVE members had dreadlocks and were shirtless, and the Cobbs Creek folks called them unsanitary. The police had a violent history with the group and were worried about escalation. Under Goode's orders, a police helicopter dropped two explosive devices onto the roof of the MOVE compound. The police allowed the resulting fire to burn out, destroying sixty-one previously evacuated homes over two blocks and leaving 250 people homeless. Six adults and five children were killed, with one adult and one child surviving. It was an incredible disaster that surpassed all the police violence of the Rizzo era. After televised hearings captivated the city, no one was held accountable. Years later there would be a civil suit and other developments. For the purposes of our story, the city was combustible.

Frank Salvatore was an old-school state representative who owned a beer distributorship. He exploited racial tensions by proposing legislation allowing Northeast Philadelphia to secede and create "Liberty County." The separate suburban municipality would ostensibly address taxpayer demands for improved city services. The primary interest was to stoke racial anxieties. Supporters of secession pressed for independence from the city. Rizzo stoked fears in his two races against Goode in 1983 and 1987 and used the words "vote white." Salvatore proposed the bill again in the aftermath of the MOVE disaster.

Following the botched effort, Northeast residents spoke fearfully that the mayor might drop explosives on their neighborhood if they failed to comply with executive authority. Goode campaigned hard in Northeast Philadelphia and appeared in our basement. He proposed a satellite City Hall so that Northeast residents wouldn't have to drive downtown. But the animosity continued, and Salvatore clambered for Liberty County. Some idiots called him a latter-day Patrick Henry who would save Northeast Philly from the perceived tyranny of King Wilson the First. All this insanity didn't get Salvatore his own county, but it did get him a state senate seat in 1984. He rode with Reagan to beat rising star Jim Lloyd.

Bob Borski was elected to Congress with the support of the 58th Ward. He was young and already in hot water. He had a Polish name but Irish roots, and made some public statements in Northern Ireland while on a family trip there. He offended everyone. Charles Dougherty, the congressman he had defeated, accused Borski of supporting terrorism by recognizing the legitimacy of the Irish Republican Army. The headlines forced him to take cover, but the steam was running out of the controversy when I arrived on the hill in 1985 as an intern. It was exciting to see John Lewis, Maxine Waters, Ted Kennedy, and Tip O'Neill up close. Reagan was still riding high, and the tide was conservative. Borski was trying to stay to the center while our party went even farther left. I attended White House briefings and saw former actors pitching for the free market. They were much better dressed than the Democrats. The simple message of self-sufficiency and smaller government sounded good, but they increased spending to record levels.

Borski paced nervously on the sidewalk of Frankford Avenue. A budget vote was scheduled for later that night in the capitol, but there he was. Dad shook his hand as he entered O'Malley's saloon, where the caucus of leaders gathered to decide Borski's fate. Marge Tartaglione's towering beehive coiffure was surrounded by clouds of smoke from her habitual extra-long cigarette. After a tortuous period of negotiation and groveling by Borski, Tartaglione withdrew her opposition to an endorsement. Although Borski "thinks he's better than us," she said, he committed to finding more patronage for them. Marge's ward met in her basement, where the committee people faced abuse and ridicule if their numbers were bad. Nonetheless, bruised egos were nursed to health by access to the beermeister. She didn't have the biggest ward but the most traumatized. Her disdain for my father stemmed from when he'd allegedly called her "Marge Tarantula."

There were other tough women Borski had to deal with before being permitted to go to Washington to vote on national legislation. One of them was his former ward chairwoman.

Borski had once been a ward leader. One fall day while doing home repairs, he hammered a rusty nail that shot into his eye. Peg Ripski, his petite assistant, visited him as he waited for emergency surgery. She took his hand and caressed it with with the firmness of fortitude. She pledged she would handle the election at the ward's upcoming meeting. He would have nothing to worry about. The surgery went well, and when Peg showed up with flowers and a relieved tear in her eye, it was as the newly elected ward leader. At least that's how Dad told the story.

* * *

In the early eighties, we Stacks discovered our relationship with a rising politician from Ireland. Seamus Mallon was the deputy leader of the Social Democratic and Labor Party (SDLP) from Armagh, Northern Ireland. He was related to Grandmother Stack and was a cousin of my father's. When Seamus was in the States to raise money for his party, he couldn't believe his good luck in discovering Mike Stack, the insider. He began visiting us around Saint Patrick's Day. Every year he was a regular lodger on tour to promote reconciliation in the North at a time when Sinn Féin and others advocated violence. Anyone for peace was a target, and Seamus and his family lived in a house with bulletproof glass. He frequently attended Brehon Law Society events, drank with them, and marched in the parades. Once or twice he engaged in energetic debates with Irish American journalists like Jack McKinney of the *Philadelphia Daily News*. Seamus once proclaimed that McKinney threw the first punch, but it wasn't the last.

Seamus shocked the world when he was elected to the British Parliament in 1986. The election was called because Unionist incumbents resigned in protest over Margaret Thatcher's signing of the Anglo-Irish agreement. They did not expect Seamus to win. He was a Catholic in a largely protestant district, but his credibility with his protestant neighbors led to victory. British conservatives were nervous about the new SDLP member in Parliament at a time of violence and instability. Seamus arrived in London to a snafu over office space, which he and future Nobel Peace Prize winner John Hume called an intentional act of bigotry and abuse. I arrived that summer as a research assistant with a lot of excitement. Seamus admitted the office fiasco may have been an honest mistake but couldn't pass up the chance for political points.

The official receptionist at the gothic Westminster structure wore cobalt blue tails, a top hat, and a handlebar mustache. I was jetlagged and lugging an overstuffed suitcase. I had only sketchy details on how to find Seamus. But once I mentioned a member of Parliament, he transitioned from gruff and suspicious to friendly. "Welcome to you, Mister Stack from America." Seamus joined me after being paged and escorted me to the Stranger's Café along the Thames. We joined John Hume and a handful of members and staff who spoke in thick, incomprehensible brogue. Seamus gave instructions on how to get an identification card and arranged lodging at a convalescent home in South London. I received free rent in exchange for helping with the residents, and rode the double-decker bus and the tube to Westminster.

Several days later, with proper credentials, I encountered the same receptionist. He seemed impressed. His voice thundered off the cathedral-esque walls. "Well, Mister Stack from America. You've decided to join us for a while." Dad loved that story. He adored the idea that I worked in Parliament. His version of how I got the job was that Seamus received a thousand applications. After careful review, he chose his cousin.

I watched Margaret Thatcher beat down the cries for sanctions against South Africa from close range. Apartheid was still in effect, and Nelson Mandela was the light of justice. In the cramped gallery, I watched the raucous debate and pinched myself. At around the same time, a crisis was building in Northern Ireland that also involved a kind of apartheid. An investigation into a shoot-to-kill policy of government opponents by paramilitaries controlled by the police had been uncovered. An investigator named John Stocker was dispatched from London to Belfast. He compiled a scrupulously documented report that exposed the conspiracy. The report was shelved, and Stocker slandered, derided, and dismissed. The roof of indignity was about to blow off when the new MP went to work.

I accompanied Seamus to TV interviews with BBC and SKY, where he criticized the British government for whitewashing the investigation. Death squads were targeting people who hadn't received due process. A policy of reprisal was exposed whereby tit-for-tat revenge killings were authorized by the Northern Ireland government, which Great Britain supported. We visited with families and officials in the North, and I quickly saw how dangerous politics were there. We encountered heavily armed British soldiers at countless checkpoints.

Years later, in 1998, the Good Friday Agreement led to actual peace. A Northern Ireland assembly created a power-sharing executive branch. Seamus was elected deputy first minister of Northern Ireland and served alongside Ulster Unionist Party Leader David Trimble. This was the result of negotiations by President Bill Clinton and his special envoy, George Mitchell. Seamus called injustice by its name and remained an opponent of IRA violence. Martin Luther King and the civil rights movement in America influenced him. Peaceful non-resistance was the only path to conciliation. My family would visit with Seamus again on a family trip after I became lieutenant governor. His baritone was nicotine-raspy, and he was forced to shuttle his coffee for Bushmills as he regaled us with tales of political intrigue. His retirement was not a happy one. Without the arena, his life was missing something vital. As a politician, I understood it better than anyone.

I returned home in 1987 just in time to volunteer for Bob Casey Sr.'s fourth run for governor. He was hesitant to do it. Philadelphia lawyer John Elliott implored Casey to go one more time. Maybe the fourth time would be the charm. Dad met Elliott while teaching Pennsylvania civil procedure at George-town University Law School, and he became a significant presence in our lives. John was a relentless, workaholic cheerleader. He was part motivational speaker, part fascist coach. He even dressed aggressively. I had never seen a man with more pinstripes. He wore striped suits and shirts that somehow matched with striped silk ties. Slicked-back brown hair and wire-rimmed glasses were attached to a stocky, athletic body. Not a day went by without a story about college base-ball days at Saint Vincent. Once, when I was a boy minding my own business by our shore house, he took a bite of my apple, leaving only the core. Then he encouraged me to go across the street and throw my best fastball, which he launched onto the beach. He violently patted me on the back and cheered, "That's my man! Good pitching." That was Elliott's greeting for the next thirty years. His hello sounded like, "CHARGE!"

The Casey campaign office was located on Walnut Street across from City Committee in a large basement space. Casey had lost in many bizarre ways, with treachery from other Democrats. He probably wanted to keep an eye on the Philadelphians who made side deals when the right ones came along. He defeated Philadelphian Ed Rendell in the primary and was focused on Bill Scranton Jr. in the general. I remember staffers pointing out the neophyte media consultant from Louisiana named James Carville. Experts predicted Casey would lose again. His defeats should've been in the Guinness Book under "world's most excruciating." An ice cream vendor named Robert M. Casey once siphoned off enough votes in the auditor general's race to defeat Casey for gov-ernor—voters had the wrong Casey. Another Bob Casey won the nomination for lieutenant governor on Pete Flaherty's ticket. Casey's dark hair and brushy eyebrows were now gray. His youthful optimism had hardened into grizzled determination. I admired his grit and hoped to work for his administration.

Bill Scranton was the young son of a former governor. His position as lieu-tenant governor made him recognizable and electable. Casey trailed most of the race, but Carville had innovative ideas. He produced a commercial that portrayed Scranton as an eccentric radical in the Guru Ad. The commercial highlighted Scranton's experimentation with marijuana and transcendental meditation. Grainy black-and-white photos of hippies and flag burners that unsettled Pennsylvania's conservative voters joined images of a long-haired, bearded Bill Scranton. The commercial was lightning in a bottle, but Casey hesitated to unleash the distortions. John Elliott implored him to pull the trigger or suffer the ruination of another defeat.

I watched the commercial at headquarters before it aired and liked it. The Democrats usually got murdered because of their high ideals and principled restraint. Republicans did what was necessary and used a baseball bat. Carville said that politics was a substitute for armed conflict. All was fair in love and war—plus, I needed a job. The election was nip and tuck until the final days, and the commercial put us over the top by 79,000 votes.

I was invited to fly out to Scranton on a private plane with some other staffers. When I arrived at the airport, a silver-haired pilot in a leather jacket met me near the runway at Northeast airport.

"They sent a plane just for you?" he asked. "Who are you?"

I said I was just a volunteer. He asked me my age and I told him twenty-three.

"What are you trying to be . . . emperor?"

# CHAPTER TWO

# THROW SOME WATER ON HIM

F rank Salvatore had been charming the ladies at the polling places since I was twelve. I couldn't stand that he was beating Dad and our party. He wasn't young and dynamic but old and folksy. The men liked him too. He was a Marine veteran and a former boxer who seemed to know their uncles. He'd pull out a wad of cash and grease all the Republicans for working the polls. Sometimes he'd put his arm around a Democrat and walk off. Then he'd get into his shiny black Cadillac and wave like he was in a parade, blowing kisses and winking.

In 1984, Salvatore announced a run for the state senate against Jim Lloyd. It seemed like a reach. Lloyd was young and articulate. His star was bright enough to garner a nomination for lieutenant governor. The incumbent was intelligent and liberal, but the district was blue-collar and turning conservative. Reagan's landslide helped Salvatore pummel principled Jim Lloyd. It was a brutal, personal campaign that the Republicans specialized in. Lloyd couldn't account for his pro-welfare and high tax positions that state Democrats were taking. They blew him up for having staffers that weren't from the district. The GOP were masters at magnifying petty little missteps into epic scandals. Once Lloyd became defensive, he was in trouble. Salvatore was brilliant with a whispering campaign that highlighted horrible, untrue things about Lloyd and his family. They were never publicized but included incest, child abuse, and depraved sex. Salvatore won by a thousand votes, and Lloyd's fresh face went from incredulous shock to a dull stare interrupted only by incessant blinking.

This wasn't the first time Republicans had done a number on our leaders. They'd beaten Dad's good friend Mel Greenberg for council a few years earlier by running a young candidate named Brian O'Neill, who used similar attacks as those against Lloyd. Greenberg's support for social programs was characterized as "helping downtown" or supporting Black people at the expense of the Northeast. We had nothing left except for Bob Borski in Congress. Northeast

Philadelphia was now a Republican bastion with simmering racial animosity. When asked if I would consider running for office, I didn't feel ready to run as a Democrat in such hostile territory.

Billy Meehan, the GOP boss, liked Dad, and they worked deals out together. I was friends with the Meehan girls, Maggie and Lizzie. They were more my sister Eileen's comrades, but we got along great as young adults in a crew. The Meehans were some of the top Republicans, and we held the fort in the Northeast for the Dems. We occasionally had heated debates about politics, but that was rare. Meehan praised my father as a gentleman and partner.

Governor Casey appointed Jim Lloyd as special assistant for Southeastern Pennsylvania in 1987. He helped Lloyd retain a public profile in anticipation of a rematch with Salvatore. Lloyd seemed in no hurry. His full head of auburn hair had become prematurely gray, and his boyish face had deep wrinkles.

I interviewed for the position of economic policy analyst in Harrisburg but didn't want to leave Philadelphia and my comfort zone. I graduated from LaSalle on fumes and worked as a probation officer. The job was not glamorous. All my grooming and experience amounted to monitoring non-violent criminals who committed fraud or theft. They'd bring me money orders as restitution. Occasionally, I would do home visits in bad neighborhoods and tell the probationer to report to my office with a check or be violated and sent to jail. Most people presumed I was armed. Either that or I was crazy. I needed a change.

Whenever I drove with Dad in his giant Lincoln, I felt like a little kid. We had heart-to-heart conversations about our family and politics. One dreary winter night in 1987, he turned to me as we crawled down I-95 and said, "We still don't have anyone to challenge Salvatore." Then it was quiet as a snow drift for what seemed like an hour. "You might be an attractive candidate if you got your act together." This was an allusion to excessive drinking. "But I can't take a chance of you making a fool of me." Then he made a proposition that would change my life: "If you can do something about your struggle with the Irish curse, I can probably get you the support of the ward leaders to run for senate."

I wanted change and this was dramatic. Fear crept in and I tried to escort it out. "I think I can," I offered. Nonetheless, he wanted to wait and told me I had a couple of months to show him. It's hard to believe that an opportunity to run in what would likely be a kamikaze mission was the catalyst to save my life. But it was.

The old man liked what he saw. I would put what I learned to work. We agreed I'd run against Salvatore, but first I had to resign from my city job under the charter. Then we needed to assemble a campaign and line up support. The general election was a year away, and a person needed to be twenty-five to run for senator, so I might have to wait to be sworn in. I'd be happy to cross that bridge later. We put together a policy committee that would meet in the basement at Southampton Road. Then we met with the Fifth District Ward Leaders Caucus about getting endorsed.

Dad invited the nine ward leaders to dinner at an Italian restaurant in Foxchase, one of the many neighborhoods that used to be small towns. My dark suit, starched white shirt, and red silk tie demonstrated I could look like a candidate, but could I sound like one? Dad was chairman of the caucus and knew the ward leaders would show up for the free dinner. Everyone was in business attire, and the toughest looking one was councilwoman Joan Krajewsk, the leader of the 65th Ward and a friend of that other cage fighter, Marge Tartaglione.

I admired the hard-scrapple ladies who elbowed out male rivals but were also intimidated by them. Joan's deep, gravelly voice softened after a few minutes, and she called me sweetie. After initially kicking the tires, the leaders perked up. They asked about my background and my campaign plan. They became conspicuously friendly out of respect for the other Stack. He caught my eye and nodded like he was about to call a trick play. "Pass the bread, please, Joan," he said, then motioned for an endorsement like it was butter. It was unanimous, and everybody ordered dessert and more drinks as Dad smiled and held up his credit card.

"Why was that so easy?" I asked as we walked to the parking lot later.

The old man grinned. "Because you've made their life easier. It's a suicide mission, but they needed someone to run." I was a little insulted as I came to be quite often in my career. "Most of them are calling Salvatore right now, telling him they got him a patsy." He assuaged my indignity that we didn't care. We just needed that endorsement.

Campaigns like that first one were smoke and mirrors. We recruited friends and ward leaders for our policy committee so they would report to the world how great we were. If there was a committee, there had to be a viable campaign nearby. Suspicious and gruff, Frank Conaway was the leader of the 57th Ward and didn't like many people. "I'd like to punch that one in the nose," he would say of countless politicos and union leaders. He was happy to serve on the committee and gather more targets for his punches. Patricia and Jim McGinley were my parents' friends who became much more. They would become tireless boosters who would never let me quit. We included several appointees of ward leaders who enjoyed the coffee, pastries, and inside scoop. Every week, we emphasized how many doors I was knocking on and the great speeches I was making. Dad stepped back. "I want these people to see you as leading the way, not relying on me."

If I started saying negative things about the campaign, like that we didn't have any money or endorsements, he cut me down. "Stop it. We don't sell rotten fish here. We leave that to our opponent." Congressman Barrett had taught him how to sell.

Neil Oxman was the political consultant who created Ed Rendell, America's Mayor. He also happened to rent office space in Dad's office and was treated so well by Dad and Pat McGinley that he offered free advice. I wished they hadn't been so nice. Oxman's volcanic temper and spiteful manner ignited more campaign anxiety. He berated me for "dressing like an idiot in pinstripes" and ordered me to wear plain suits like "a normal fucking human being." He was bear-like and lunged with rage. His wavy brown hair and wire-rimmed glasses gave him the appearance of a frightening law professor. He happened to be a lawyer that didn't practice. But he knew exactly what editorial boards wanted to hear and how they wanted to hear it. He could be charming and funny when taking his medication, and hilariously bitchy about other public officials. I heard him condemning Rendell's eating habits on the phone as I waited to be tortured. The mayor had dipped his fingers into a tub of butter that looked like an ice cream scoop and lapped it up. The mayor did this while regaling an aghast constituent with a story. I shared the anecdote many times, which probably contributed to Rendell's secret disapproval. This is only my recollection of how Oxman was during my first anxiety-filled political campaign. He may have been a teddy bear, and I may have misunderstood his descriptions of Rendell.

Oxman formulated my campaign themes of "fresh ideas" and "a new approach." When I used these words, voters rarely asked for examples. They highlighted my youth, which people found refreshing. I had something *new* to say. My policy group wrangled for weeks as to what a senator did and why I was running. One day, Conaway offered that a senator's duty was to vote on bills in Harrisburg. That was it. That was the job, and Salvatore wasn't doing it. He'd missed dozens of votes. We surmised he was busy at the beer business. Now my mission had clarified—I would show up and vote and do it well.

Once I got elected.

\* \* \*

The campaign didn't feel like a suicide mission. People were emotionally involved. The inscrutable staffers from the Democratic Senate Campaign Committee visited the compound to see what we had cooking. Mark McKillop was a husky, ginger-haired Scotsman without a trace of guile, and Laura Schonberg was a younger, friendlier version of good cop, bad cop. Short, dark hair and a black pantsuit gave her the appearance of an accountant. They were auditors and listened keenly to the policy committee discussions. Their cynical air revealed that Philadelphia was an evil place. But our vaudeville act had cheered their spirits. Our plucky group sounded expert. This neophyte evolved into the second coming of Bobby Kennedy, and they invited us to Harrisburg to "meet the senators."

We drove up to the capitol like we were in clown cars with the McGinleys, Mom, and assorted other affiliates of our paper tiger campaign, including my cousin Molly, a former reporter, and Matt Nardi, an unemployed Wall Street broker, who was living across the street with my sister while going through a divorce. But on our ragtag team, everyone had a fancy title, such as communications director, operations manager, constituent outreach director, and campaign manager. We slid into the leather seats around the mahogany conference table in the Democratic leader's splendid office, and the cool air turned warm with Senator Mellow's affection.

Bob Mellow, a Scranton native, had been elected to the state senate at the age of twenty-seven and was encouraged by my youth. He was an avid runner like me with a trim figure, and wore a loose tie with rolled-up sleeves in a blue-collar style. Unbeknownst to us, many of the other candidates SDCC had interviewed were disasters. We knew how to put on a show, and they liked it. Mellow wanted to win more Democratic seats and win the majority. He needed more than warm bodies, and we were full of hot air. Mark McKillop gushed that they had never witnessed a more prepared campaign team, and we looked behind us. One doesn't get a second chance at a first impression, but I wished we were as good as we looked. Maybe we would be. We were in line to get a lot of money as a targeted race.

Campaign workers were often like orphans looking for homes. McKillop and Schonberg became adopted children of my family and spent a lot of time at the house. McKillip grew very fond of Pat McGinley, and it was a relationship that lasted for years. The Democratic campaign committee was looking at only two other races ahead of us. About two weeks later, I received a terse-sounding summons from a secretary in Mellow's office, noting that my presence was required in Harrisburg immediately. I drove up with Chuck Feldman, who worried the senators would be antisemitic, the next day. Chuck's neuroticism calmed me down. He envisioned a room full of silver-haired Gentiles in country club blazers who would be suspicious of him. Chuck had spent too much time shaking hands with grumpy commuters in the early morning. He was one of the few people I could count on to join me in that task. His enjoyment of it was baffling. I needed to get him out of the Northeast for his own good—plus, no one else could go on short notice.

We strolled into that fancy conference room, oblivious that the Silver Streak was speeding down the tunnel. Accusations flew like doves at the Olympics. Mellow and Democratic Whip Bill Lincoln snapped at me to take a seat in front of the room. Other senators leered from the conference table or stood, arms folded, against the walls. The inquiry began with Mellow and Lincoln grilling me like Spanish Inquisitors about Dad's suspicious relationship with Billy Meehan, the Republican chair. Wasn't it true that Billy Meehan and Frank Salvatore were Dad's good friends? And wasn't I a sacrificial lamb to ensure reelection for Salvatore? I was indignant and began to stutter. My father was friendly with Meehan, but they were competitors. We all disliked Salvatore and wanted to beat him.

But I paused to think about it. Would the old man serve me up as a patsy, or did someone else poison the well? The lie was plausible, like something out of a Salvatore whisper campaign. That's how they lied in Philadelphia. Just a shred of truth made the whole thing sound authentic. I felt gaslighted, surveyed the room for a clue, and found one, the only senator who wasn't facing me.

The shrewd-looking gentleman from South Philly peered at a document like it told his future, pretending to be oblivious to the radiation fallout. The snow-drift silence melted when Senator Vincent J. Fumo, the Prince of Darkness, met my eye, then returned to his fake reading with a subtle smirk.

I had found the poison pill.

I didn't want to appear a paranoid maniac and accuse the most powerful Democratic senator in the state of perfidy. I played it cool and defended my legitimacy, effectively explaining the relationships as the teapot simmered. The relief was therapeutic. The senators seemed to like me even more once we were all breathing calmly after that rollercoaster ride. Chuck Feldman's mouth had been hanging open since the initial shocking accusation, and his glasses were fogged, but Mellow and Lincoln shook his hand so enthusiastically that Chuck's snug jacket almost ripped. They grabbed the "Back Stack" T-shirts, dangling from their wrists like a waiter's handkerchief, and squeezed into them like SCUBA gear. We hugged and laughed and felt our pulses. We had leaped another hurdle, but the chairman who had slipped out would be a problem.

Only two other races stood in the way of one million bucks. One was the typical preference of SDCC, an elegant liberal woman from western Pennsylvania adorned in a pantsuit and scarf, the official feminist uniform against a conservative male incumbent in a right-wing district. She was vehemently pro-choice, anti-gun, and anti-victory. Naturally she was target number one.

The other race involved a liberal Democrat in a district that was proud to be American. We were ranked third because of the Fumo taint. But that enabled us to get some help against a powerful incumbent with a big bank account.

I just wanted some rocks for my slingshot.

I knocked on thousands of doors and made speeches all over the district. Volunteers appeared out of nowhere. The *Philadelphia Inquirer* sent a reporter to follow me, and they did an amazing story on the family legacy. Reporter Bill Miller spent hours in our living room. He walked around the house and went through photo albums. A great shot of Dad and me sitting together accompanied the story: "Another Stack Enters the Arena." Dad quoted Grandfather as saying, "Politics is a great game, but don't get down because you will get kicked." I had learned more about my grandfather and my father and their journey along the public service road than ever.

Dad's friend Charlie Garuffe loaned us his Eagles bus that often appeared at tailgate parties. The horn was loud and festive, and the speaker blared string band music or Motown. Literature drop squads jumped from the bus and put flyers on doors or in neighbors' hands. I flew off the bus to greet voters like Elvis. The neighbors treated me like the King, but Salvatore thought I was a turkey. He had plenty of name recognition but wasn't hungry. He didn't hit the campaign trail until the last month because he thought it was in the bank. But his complacency worked to our advantage. There were spies in both camps, and we liked knowing he was asleep.

Double agents made sure they were with the winner, just like in Dad's book, *Close Personal Friends of The Mayor*. Spies were part of the game. If I was worthy of being spied on, it was respect. But I learned to be careful of what I said in order to give false information to the right spy.

The Senate Democratic Campaign Committee came through with ten mailings in the last two weeks of the race, and Salvatore didn't know what hit him. The mailings were creative and funny. We were delighted as each bomb dropped. There was even a scratch-off card asking, "Who is Captain Mysterious?" The preceding mailings launched single attacks about missed key votes, votes against Philadelphia, big pay raises, free cars, and auto insurance. Then we put it all in one grand indictment where Salvatore's smiling face was a penny scratch away. I was going door to door, worried voters might be turned off by the razor-edged mail. But one young voter gushed that he ran to his mailbox every day. "I can't wait to see the next one. I love it!" We did too, but the scratch-off was exquisite.

Denny O'Brien, the Republican state representative who later became Speaker, passed on the gleeful gossip. He called the scratch-off "Gloria in The

Kitchen." Fred the mailman reported watching Salvatore's wife, Gloria, go to the box and walk back into the house. A crash and scream joined a chorus of breaking dishes. Fred kept walking.

Some of the fun was perilous because Salvatore had some dangerous associates with blood on their hands. On December 16, 1980, John McCullough, the tough union boss of Roofers Local 30, arrived at his split-level twin on Foster Street in Bustleton. He was talking business on the phone as his wife, Audrey, prepared dinner. She answered the doorbell to receive a poinsettia delivery from a plain-looking man with a knit hat. "I've got another one," the delivery man said and returned to his truck. Before she knew it, he was standing in the kitchen and fired six shots into her husband's head and face using a .22-caliber automatic with a silencer.

Poor Audrey had been searching her purse for a tip when the delivery man opened fire. But why? McCullough was making major moves in Atlantic City with the opening of casinos. Big John had links to Philadelphia mafia boss Angelo Bruno, who had been assassinated a year before. But McCullough's clout was diminishing with the loss of Bruno, and other gangsters and unions wanted his territory. In this dark world of violence and corruption, there was room for politicians like Salvatore.

I knocked on doors on Foster Street, oblivious that it had been a street of blood or that my opponent might be linked.

McCullough had a full head of silver hair that was styled like Bruno's, blow-dried on top, combed neatly on the sides. But could a local union head be worthy of a Hoffa-type hit? It wasn't that efficient. One veteran detective quipped, "It was the most unprofessional hit I've ever witnessed." Hours later, the gunman's van was found in a parking lot at Roosevelt Boulevard and Red Lion Road, a half mile from McCullough's home, poinsettia petals and leaves on the floor and keys still in it. They never found the killer, but Dad said his nickname was "Frankie Flowers" because he handed them to the victims and pulled the trigger.

How did he know that?

The next Roofer leader ran opposed. Former boxer Steve Traitz orchestrated an ambitious program to win back turf by bribing a large portion of the Philadelphia judiciary. Two judges eventually went to jail and thirteen were removed for taking cash in the notorious scandal. A union man delivered envelopes stamped "Seasons Greetings" containing $300-500 in cash in 1985. Most of the judges incomprehensively kept the loot. The bribes were so small, FBI agent John Tamm called Philadelphia "the Kmart of political corruption," adding, "they wanna just put a blue light on at City Hall." Dad hired two of the disgraced judges out of sympathy for their terrible misjudgments. They were disbarred and disgraced but had families to feed. I passed them on the way up the steps to see Oxman.

Steve Traitz didn't just send Christmas gifts. He sent messages. His union guys would throw scabs off roofs. If you weren't Local 30, you'd better sprout wings. And Traitz had more diverse mob connections than his predecessor. His sons became union officers and eventually went to prison for trafficking in methamphetamine with the Mexican cartel. The father died in prison.

I took my own life in my hands when I okayed a negative mailing against Salvatore for being the "sole elected official to accept a $500 contribution from the notorious Roofers Union." It was the simple truth. Nonetheless, when I walked into crowded rooms, I felt icy stares and heard cracking knuckles from burly labor men. For the first time, the feeling was palpable that my life was in jeopardy. But I was too naive to grasp it, and my parents surmised I'd survive. The mailing incensed Salvatore and his followers and probably contributed to the hazy accusation that I was anti-labor. Interestingly, Jim Lloyd had passed on an FBI wiretap transcript in which Salvatore said, "Tell Stevie I'm his guy." I didn't use it, and maybe that's why I'm alive to write about it.

All the fun and danger brought only 44% of the vote. The pundits thought that was a miracle, but I was crestfallen. A real politician never thinks he'll lose. When the numbers came in on election night, I had trouble accepting it. Our victory party was in the basement at Southampton Road, and it was packed with people who were proud of our fight. I didn't want to face the crowd.

The old man chastised, "Get out there and thank those people who helped you for free." His twinkle turned steely. "They don't care you lost. They just want to see you."

He told me about other candidates over the years who couldn't concede or blamed everyone but themselves. One senator didn't thank anyone after winning a tough election. The same senator had beaten Fumo for appropriations chair by one vote, but Vince later got revenge.

I stepped in front of the crowd after Dad yelled for their attention. He said the words I heard too many times. "Tonight is not our night." I gave an energized concession speech and proclaimed, "We'll be back!" I thanked dozens of people by name. They didn't want money but to know they were appreciated. Conversely, they burned for years when you forgot. Mom cried gingerly and Pat McGinley wept prodigiously. Jim McGinley was disgusted but hopeful for my future. Frank Conaway wanted to punch other ward leaders in the nose. The loss was a wound that festered and throbbed.

I couldn't shake my depression. Three days later, Dad asked, "Why are you moping around?"

I shook my head. "I can't believe we lost. Those ward leaders across the boulevard cut me." They had strategically left my name off certain ballots.

"Who are you disgusted with?" He didn't wait for an answer. "Make a list of who you're mad at and start writing them thank-you notes. You're going to need them in four years."

I did it with a shaking hand, acid in my stomach. The gracious notes were effusive and nauseating. That's the difference between an idiot like me and a sensible person—I was willing to suffer. Dad presumed correctly that this was just the beginning. We didn't need to discuss it. I spent every day of the next three years reliving the loss and thinking about a rematch.

* * *

I am so glad to get through telling you about that 1988 campaign. It defined my life in that I knew I could take a licking and keep on ticking. The bleakness diminished, and I remembered other wonders during the quest. Upon reflection, many amazing things happened. During the race, Governor Casey came to the district to tour a future addiction treatment facility. He pulled me to his side. "Hook your belt to mine, Mike, and we'll show them you're on the rise." Casey was a popular governor at the time and didn't have to help me. I was a twenty-four-year-old neophyte who appeared on all the TV news stations with the big man. Bob Borski called me "savvy" for my ability to get photographed and make it into the papers. That was "a rare skill" for politicians. I squeezed into shots without being obvious with my sharp elbows. I was endorsed by the *Daily News* because of Neil's drilling. The editorial praised the "fresh new voice," even though "he's no Daniel Webster." Oxman was the toughest coach I ever had, but he brought out the best in me. His thundering voice guided me through the media minefield, and the PTSD faded.

Another pertinent recollection was seeing presidential candidate Michael Dukakis up close. He was the Democratic frontrunner for president and gave a speech at the Hershey Hotel. One of the elites, he gave shoutouts to colleges like Swarthmore and Haverford while Dad and I stood aghast. Dad was a Saint Joe Hawk, and I was a LaSalle Explorer, and this was a blue-collar town. National Democrats had forgotten who made them. I liked Al Gore better.

Oxman's client decided to end his presidential bid if he didn't win the New York primary. The disappointing loss gave him extra time to come to Philadelphia to endorse a certain little neophyte.

* * *

We planned a blockbuster event in the reception area of the law firm. Steam floated above Neil Oxman's head when he saw only a handful of mangy volunteers and a few tumbleweeds with Gore's arrival only minutes away. Pat McGinley sprung into panic mode and frantically summoned all the usual suspects. We ran to the banks, restaurants, and other offices, offering free food and a big party. Lawyers and secretaries hustled in and suddenly friends and well-wishers poured in like that Jimmy Stewart movie. From vapor, a packed house waited for Senator Al Gore. Oxman morphed into an unrecognizable pod person who was calm and magnanimous. He pulled me into a tiny adjacent office. Gore was broad-shouldered and spectacular, looking younger than his photograph and model-like in his dark suit. "Tell me about your race." They were big and we were cramped. The future vice president was a foot from my face. "Tell me about yourself."

Oxman said, "Do it fast. We have fifteen seconds."

I told Gore about Grandfather Stack being an original sponsor of Social Security and the minimum wage, and I was fighting for lower auto insurance rates.

"Perfect! I got it," Gore snapped.

The crowd was raucous, and Gore set them on fire. He just had to come to Philadelphia to help his friend. I was fighting for him and America and the little guy against big insurance companies. He'd lit candles in church for my grandfather and prayed I'd raise the minimum wage in carrying on the sacred legacy. I nodded in agreement about how awesome I was. They were blown away. All this time, they thought I was a lightweight. Joe Cullen, a young Yale Law graduate, was suddenly impressed. He never knew that Gore and I were Batman and Robin, fighting for truth and justice. Years later, I met Vice President Gore at the White House, and he didn't remember any of it.

Yes, I lost in 1988, but it was so much fun.

* * *

When Grandfather Stack advised Dad to go to law school, he said, "If you're going to be in politics, you'll likely be out of work." Lawyers often had gainful employment in between elections. Dad gave me the same advice, and I applied to Villanova Law, hoping for a miracle. In late August 1989, the admissions office called. I was working in Rosemont as a claims examiner for the Medical Catastrophe Loss Fund, a state agency.

"Would you be able to come up to Villanova?" the assistant dean asked.

"For what?"

She cleared her throat. "To attend law school."

Before she hung up, I was in the parking lot. I got accepted from the waiting list on the first day of classes.

Diane Merlino was the Democratic Chair for Delaware County and my boss. I told her the good news and regretted I'd have to leave. "Don't leave, sweetie. Find out your schedule and you'll work part time. Then you'll go back to full time in the summer."

I had an office and a paycheck. Diane was a tough, gritty leader. Later, she was one of the subjects of an inspector general's investigation that threw the agency into turmoil and scandal. She was terminated and slandered. I never understood the necessity of the investigation or the precise charges. It hurt Diane, who was the first female chair of Delaware County Democrats. It was unclear what the Casey administration's political motivations were in investigating another Democrat. Years later, I mentioned her name to Mark Singel, and he blurted out, "She screwed us." I could never understand why Democrats were willing to do each other in. Republicans rarely did.

Law school reignited my learning disability anxieties, but I worked twice as hard to keep up. Our class was the first to have more women than men. The atmosphere was collegial, not cutthroat. I don't think I would've been comfortable in any other school than Villanova. At other places, books were hidden or pages torn out in frenzied competition. We shared outlines and helped each other.

I had the advantage that Mom graduated from the law school in 1985. She raised us, then went back to school. She was the second-oldest in the class and eventually won the National Moot Court competition with her partner. She advised me of the professors to avoid. I didn't want to get roughed up by the Socratic method from some Paper Chase wannabe. The tides turned. My mom was pretty, blond, and effervescent and had become a lawyer. Now all the professors urged, "Say hello to your mother for me."

I never worried about joining a top law firm or getting an elite clerkship. Frankly, I didn't think I could. I knew I wanted to get elected to the state senate. That was my mission in life. I was satisfied going to law school while preparing myself, but I also wanted to have adventures. I loved international affairs and believed I could one day be secretary of state or some kind of ambassador. Dad's friend Richard Kryzanowski lived in our garage apartment and traveled the world as Crown Cork and Seal's attorney. At breakfast one morning, I mentioned I wanted to speak Spanish better. He suggested I spend part of my summer living with an Ecuadorian family. He arranged for me to work in the law firm of Jaime Roldos in Guayaquil.

I knew flying to a strange country would stress me out, but this had become my habit. Anything that made me nervous, I had to do. Jaime Roldos held a sign with my name on it, like in the movies. The airport was crowded and raucous, and Jaime tried to carry my overstuffed duffel. His English was as rudimentary as my Spanish, and we had a tedious and challenging conversation. He had a twenty-three-year-old daughter named Gigi living at home, a troubled older son, Jaime Jr., and a welcoming wife, Mariana. He arranged for me to live in a hotel near the law office, but I often ate meals and took siestas at the family home.

Gigi and I became friends. She was on a breakup with her boyfriend Santiago, and the rumor got around that there was a new gringo in town. We were walking around the mall one Sunday when a bunch of twenty-something girls ran up to Gigi, speaking rapid, incomprehensible Spanish. Something dramatic was happening. I couldn't comprehend much other than that Santiago was around and there might be a showdown. It was a Latin soap opera, but there was something innocent and ridiculous about it. I was the older man and the exotic foreigner. I surmised Santiago wouldn't show up, but if he did, I'd be the friendly, clueless foreigner who didn't understand anything.

I really liked being the clueless foreigner. It was refreshing to say a simple sentence, like "pass the bread," in Spanish at a family dinner and receive applause. This was before globalization and English-speaking TV. Every morning I figured out what conversations I might have and practiced the words. I changed American dollars on the street, because it was a better exchange rate, and became a familiar face around Guayaquil. I returned to the hotel one day to find Gigi berating the front desk clerk. She demanded to know where Señor Stack was. The clerk pleaded he didn't know. I ducked around the corner to avoid her temper. I wasn't up to any intrigue, but the clerk admired my romantic prowess. He handed me a love letter that she demanded he "deliver personally." Under her signature, she wrote, "Perhaps you will give me a little kiss."

My Spanish improved and I made wonderful friends. Jaime wrote to Richard, commending my "gentleness." He raved about how kind I was. I took it awkwardly. I felt vulnerable in that setting and just tried to be myself. The Roldos family thought I was making it up about running for the senate because I was too nice for politics. They were right.

Governor Bob Casey was our Villanova Law commencement speaker, notwithstanding some pushback about his position on abortion. It was 1992, and I was successfully nominated for a second shot at Salvatore. Our student speaker surprised me by saluting my public service spirit in running for office. Casey grinned when it was his turn. He looked at me in the audience and said, "She stole my thunder."

I spent the summer preparing for the bar exam and trying to campaign. I was stretched thin but took the exam and hit the trail hard. Salvatore was ready for me this time. He went negative right off the bat, questioning my "ghost job" at the Medical Catastrophe Loss Fund. The negative mailings landed before we were ready. They even cracked at Grandfather Stack's association with radio star Father Coughlin for being antisemitic.

I tried one more time to persuade Vince Fumo to help. I finally got a meeting at the Bunker after months of evasion. His courtesy felt rude. But chief of staff and future mayor of Philadelphia Jim Kenney was bitter. They took turns highlighting my shortcomings and arrogance, not to mention the impossibility of the campaign. Fumo threw Dad into it, claiming he had been insolent or obstructive against him at City Committee.

"Ever heard of sins of the father?" he asked.

"Let's put that aside, Senator, and beat the Republican," I said. But my plea fell dead. It was all pretext. Democratic senators were a dime a dozen, but Salvatore was a rare jewel.

Neil Oxman agreed to be my media consultant and anticipated I would receive $500,000 as a targeted race. With three weeks left, the SDCC and Fumo dodged my phone calls. Oxman was infuriated the money wasn't coming and roared into the phone, "You are not getting funded, and you are going to LOSE!" After the click, I gazed out the back window of our family home into a gray and rainy sky and knew this was worse than 1988. I was a sucker this time. I didn't surprise anyone, and the chalk was against me. The senators paid for some homogenous mailings that lacked the humor and edge of four years before.

Dad was older and more stressed. He had almost engaged in fisticuffs with Salvatore at a polling place. Salvatore's whisper machine spewed lies about my supposed heroin addiction and crazy, sexual depravity. The old rumor about Dad being in bed with Salvatore was enraging. Our spies reported sightings of Democratic Chairman Bob Brady dining with Salvatore and Billy Meehan at the Cottage Green. The rumors grew to include Fumo and Ed Rendell and many other Democratic leaders, and all were screwing me. In the terrible darkness of sleepless nights, it all seemed plausible.

I encountered more negative comments from voters than before. I picked up less than 3% from 1988. Bill Clinton won the district but had no coattails. Pat McGinley, who had served as my campaign manager, blamed herself. Frank Conaway plunged into a depression so deep he didn't even want to punch anybody in the nose. I made another stellar concession speech while contemplating tying a noose. My mother was a lover of Catholic martyrdom and raved that we should have recorded it like the one years earlier, which also wasn't recorded. I wanted to throw up.

When the going got tough, the Stacks moved furniture, lots of it, and it didn't matter where. Dad was pale and sweaty as we slogged patio furniture from the basement to the garage. We were disgusted by the loss, and Dad was on a rampage of passive-aggressive, sarcastic rage. The sky was like tar, and drizzle hit like salt in wounds. My sister Eileen suddenly blurted, "Dad fell!" Soon an ambulance was taking him away. He'd had a serious heart attack. He underwent open heart surgery that day, and it was touch and go the next week. I blamed it on Salvatore. My dad might die over a stupid senate seat.

The following week, Mom and Eileen waited outside Dad's room at the University of Pennsylvania hospital. They were tired but relieved. He would survive but have a long rehabilitation. I was terrified about Dad dying and worried about failing the bar exam. When I reached the hospital, my phone rang. A friend from law school went to City Hall, where the bar exam results had just been posted.

"Hang up if it's bad news," I said. I couldn't bear another disappointment. She stayed on. I'd passed by one point.

Once I heard Dad was okay, I said, "We lost the election; we almost lost Dad, but I passed the bar." The accomplishment provided little joy.

The second loss had other highlights. Although Jim and Pat McGinley were inconsolable, I realized they were more than friends and had evolved into another set of parents. When the notion of quitting emerged, they dismissed it. I couldn't let them down.

Dad had met the McGinleys in 1970 while going door-to-door, recruiting new committee people. They were educators and helped Dad win, then became part of our family from that point on. We hung out with the McGinley kids and attended family events. Pat became my campaign manager, Dad's office manager, and later Mom's judicial staff manager. In short, she was a manager of people and feelings. She had dark hair and black Irish features and could be restrained and sensible. Jim had rosy cheeks, fair skin, and an Irish temper. But it was all about loyalty. Jim battled weight and wore a skintight "STACK FOR SENATE" T-shirt that gave him the appearance of an agitated Michelin Man. He was sixty-three and had thick eyeglasses, untied sneakers, and violent conviction.

He nearly pummeled brawny Mike McGuigan on the front lawn of an ornery constituent. Jim ordered hothead McGuigan, a LaSalle classmate, to stop debating George H.W. Bush with voters. "We are here for Michael Stack and no one else. Do it again and we're going at it!"

McGuigan, a former bricklayer who became a dysfunctional lawyer, chuckled. I heard the words "voodoo economics, my ass!" and just shook my head.

The crack of Jim's clipboard hitting the sidewalk was like gunfire. "Let's go!" Jim bellowed with frightening belligerency. He lunged at McGuigan, who was initially frozen in shock.

"Try it, Jim," he quivered unconvincingly. Had volunteers not jumped in, Jim would have sent McGuigan to the hospital.

Years later, Jim developed Alzheimer's disease. When Mom and I visited him in a community living home, he thought it was 1972 and wanted to come to the next ward meeting. He was ready to go to war for the fighting 58th Ward and me no matter what year it was.

* * *

World champion boxer Bernard Hopkins said that he learned more from his defeats than from his wins. After my 1988 loss, I received several handwritten notes commending my effort. They were from people I hardly knew. One of them pointed out the strong qualities of Abraham Lincoln, who had suffered many losses and always persevered. He failed in business in 1831 and was defeated for the Illinois legislature in 1832. He tried another business in 1833 and failed. His fiancée died in 1835. He had a nervous breakdown in 1836. In 1843, he ran for Congress and was defeated. He tried again in 1848 and lost again. He tried running for the US Senate in 1855. He lost. The next year, he ran for vice president and lost. In 1859 he ran for the Senate again and was defeated. In 1860, the man who signed his name A. Lincoln, the man whose unflagging faith in himself seemed to grow with every failure, was elected the sixteenth president of the United States. This motivational story was sent to me with a picture of Lincoln's perseverance poster.

I didn't get as many letters in 1992, but one reminded me that when Lincoln took the oath of office in 1861, it was not a sudden moment in time. It was the culmination of a long, difficult journey filled with disappointments, setbacks, failures, and ultimate success. It was an incredible testament to the power of faith and perseverance. "Damn you, Lincoln!" I thought again. Most people would have walked away. I wrote thank-you notes again and practiced law with my parents.

Had Mayor Greene not asked her to resign from the board of education, my mother may have never gone to law school. Instead, she practiced family law for five years, during which time she got emotionally involved with her clients. She was a rescuer and saved women and families through her advocacy. She ran for common pleas court judge and didn't get endorsed by the bar association because she allegedly didn't have enough experience. Raising five kids and serving on the board of education was insufficient. She suspected her pro-life stance on abortion agitated the liberal-leaning organization. Her 1991 campaign was unsuccessful. She got cut by ward leaders and had poor ballot position, but a vacancy appeared on municipal court. There was only one problem: the judiciary committee of the state senate had to approve it.

The rumor that Dad was in cahoots with Salvatore still stung. Once gas-lighted, always gaslighted. My mother was nominated for the bench in 1992 but needed senate approval. Suddenly Mom was in the capitol, appearing before the judiciary committee. And who, of all people, rushed in to sit next to her? Frank frigging Salvatore! The bane of my existence introduced her to the committee in gushing terms. She was the best mother, the smartest lady, and would be the best judge in the world. He was uncharacteristically gracious, and I felt my hair igniting. When my father argued, "But he's our senator," I was in flames. My parents proclaimed I was "too sensitive."

They always said I was too sensitive. What was the trauma that led me to mistrust the people who loved me the most? I could trace it back to my dyslexic childhood. Father Joe and Sister Julia Mary whispered and pointed at the problem child. What were they going to do about the disruptive one? Then Mom and Dad huddled and tried to figure out what was wrong. I was at the center of some kind of shameful scandal. They started monitoring my failures and making decisions without explaining. I didn't know what the hell was going on and wanted answers. Gosh darn right I was sensitive! When my mom was practically sitting on Salvatore's lap, I was more than mildly perturbed.

Nonetheless, she became a wonderful jurist. She was like Judge Judy, but with compassion and empathy. She was patient with stumbling lawyers yet wise to bull slingers. She listened as only a mother can to cops and prosecutors as well as defendants. Soon countless folks would ask me to "say hello to the judge for me."

My old boss at the Medical Catastrophe Loss Fund got fired and left a vacancy. Governor Casey's Secretary of Administration was Joe Zazyczny, a for-mer Philadelphia city councilman who could pull a string. He was easy to talk to and knew my dad, but he told me to forget about him. "I'm talking to you, not him. We're discussing this job because you're qualified." I threw a long bomb and tried to apply for director, but Joe helped me become deputy director. He was emphatic. "You got this job on your own merits. This has nothing to do with your father. We need someone smart and political to keep the director out of trouble." This was one of the first times someone emphasized my skills solely. The old man had cast a large shadow, and I was climbing out of it.

Most of my colleagues at the Medical Catastrophe Loss Fund were happy to see me back as a boss, but some felt threatened. I tried to be sensitive to their feelings. I steered the new director through political landmines and learned how to be an executive of the state-run medical malpractice insurance company. I went out to McDonald's with my old claims rep buddies and tossed the Frisbee around the field across Lancaster Avenue. But another campaign was coming.

I loved Mark Singel, but his gubernatorial quest in 1994 seemed unlikely. As a young lieutenant governor, he joined me in northeast Philadelphia for some memorable campaigning. We heard he was looking for things to do. I didn't know what to expect when his black SUV drove up, but he was ready to have fun. He looked too young to be a lieutenant governor, and his state trooper driver seemed amused at the novelty. His energetic personality was like that of a fraternity president. He clapped his hands. "Where are we going? Let's meet some people." We went everywhere, including an aerobics class, where we shook hands with women as they jumped around like Jane Fonda or stretched out in awkward poses. "I love this! This is how to campaign," Singel raved.

Singel's relationship with Governor Casey was strained. Casey hadn't blessed Singel's run for the US Senate in 1992 because of his shift on abortion. Key supporters sat on the fence waiting for the nod from Casey, which never came. Mark lost the election to southeastern Pennsylvania liberal Lynn Yeakel, who was the only candidate who could lose to incumbent Arlen Specter. Mark appeared to be all washed up but somehow made a comeback two years later and was poised to beat Tom Ridge. I dreamed of becoming Governor Singel's insurance commissioner. Mark's perseverance would help make him a great governor. He had overcome the sneers and doubters and was poised for victory. But he had a knack for the bad break.

Mark had an eleven-point lead in the polls, and Republicans were already sending emissaries. Delaware County Republican Chairman Tom Judge was allegedly negotiating a deal for a piece of the pie in the next administration. While the fat lady cleared her throat, a paroled prisoner named Gerald McFadden went on a rape and murder spree. He had been sentenced to life in prison in 1974 for robbery and homicide. In 1992, the Pennsylvania Board of Pardons incomprehensibly voted to release him. At the time, Singel served on the board and voted in favor of the release. Governor Casey signed the commutation papers, and soon after his release, McFadden murdered two people and kidnapped and raped a third within ninety days of hitting the streets. When the news of the murders broke, Tom Ridge turned it into a decisive issue. The race flipped in one weekend. At a hastily arranged press conference, Singel took the blame for his mistake without consulting his advisers. He calculated that voters would appreciate his candor. He calculated wrong. Tom Ridge won. After that, a chill in the pardons process would last for decades and was still there when I became chairman of the board. Mark never really shook that loss. Over lunch in 2019, he revealed that McFadden had written him from prison, claiming the whole thing was a setup. Mark seemed to believe they were both patsies.

Dad imitated Marlon Brando in his role from *On the Waterfront*: "I could have been a contender." Usually, this was after I brought up my senate losses. He did it after Singel lost. He would point out homeless guys pushing shopping carts. "Another failed candidate." It was an exquisite needle. He rarely yelled but could be so sarcastic I wished he did. Nonetheless, he was urging me on.

* * *

In my last year of law school, my then-girlfriend nudged me into joining the cast of *Arsenic and Old Lace*. The acting bug led to several roles with community theater groups. Theater was more fun than politics. Many people attributed Reagan's success to being an actor. He had an amazing ability to project optimism and inspire confidence. That wasn't on my mind when I started acting, but it was certainly a skill that helped my career later on. At the time, I thought politics was fruitless. I wasn't just getting bad reviews but experiencing crushing defeats. The 1996 election was coming up fast. I couldn't imagine taking a third consecutive loss to Salvatore. Dad implored me to snap out of my silly thinking and get ready to run. Then I received a call from Tom Leonard.

Leonard had been a rising star in the late 1970s. He became city controller in his thirties, then ran for mayor as an independent. Only one ward leader supported him—my father. John Elliot was Leonard's law partner at Dilworth Paxson and convinced him to go on the suicide run. Leonard's quixotic run failed miserably. Later he finished way back for lieutenant governor. Then he disappeared like a mob informant, not only from politics but sight.

We were in the stands on a beautiful October day in South Philadelphia for the Clinton rally in the plaza next to Pat's Steaks. We spotted Leonard as he strolled onto the stage just before the president. A mischievous grin expressed poetic justice. He eyed many in the audience who had worked for his opponents. Leonard's brown, curly hair had a reddish tint from fresh coloring. The expensive tailored suit must have been from Boyd's, the only high-end clothier in the city. His rosy cheeks and bright, azure eyes gave him the appearance of a much younger man. Indeed, he had been reborn as a presidential money man, an elite of national politics, miles above the clawing denizens of grubby little crabs.

The Clinton reelection was underway, and the national campaign needed help in Pennsylvania. Leonard thought of me. Sometimes people just think of you. He asked me to come to his law office and meet one of the neophytes who worked for the president. The towering young man Leonard introduced me to had a neatly trimmed beard, was nearly seven feet tall, and didn't have a clue about Philadelphia politics. He was the future mayor of New York City, Bill DeBlasio.

The Clinton folks needed delegates to get on the ballot. Their candidates had difficulty figuring out paperwork and a variety of fundamentals for running. The national campaign had already alienated Chairman Bob Brady by inviting him to the White House for a reception but leaving his name off the guest list. Brady suffered the humiliation of standing in the rain as the other guests passed contemptuously by. When I called Brady to inform him where I was, he ignited. "You're with those idiots?!"

After I lost in 1992, I spent less time at party events and fell out of touch. "You're one of us." He was glad. "Tell them I'm not talking to anybody but you." He had a warm, buttery relationship with Salvatore, but that was the past. "This is going to be good. I'm going to bust their balls for a while. Then we'll build it up and you'll deliver me just in time." Brady chuckled like the call was to tell him he won the lottery.

Tom Mills was a sixty-something former member of the board of education with a following among public school advocates. Dad thought I'd regret not running. But Mills was taking on Salvatore, and witnessing it was excruciating. Although he disagreed with my decision, Dad was intrigued by the dynamics of national campaigns. He predicted the staffers would come from all over the country and hate us backroom locals. Inevitably they would falter and blame it on the most powerful machine in America.

Our team was small during the primary. DeBlasio talked to the big shots in DC and took credit for everything I did. I knew how to get petitions executed because I'd done it since I was a kid. No one ever got elected who wasn't on the ballot. You didn't get on the ballot unless you got signatures on your petitions. These people were babes in the woods. Karen Patricelli served as DeBlasio's lieutenant and got a kick out of how many insiders I knew. Later she became chief of staff for New York Governor Kathy Hockul. The three of us worked well together and got the Clinton campaign organized; all the delegates got on the ballot. I enjoyed helping folks instead of begging for their assistance. I didn't feel any knives in my back, but they were forthcoming. Tom Leonard urged me to attend the Democratic National Convention in Chicago and protect my new stature as a key Clinton staffer.

I arrived at the Four Seasons every afternoon to get credential even though I stayed at the Holiday Inn. Leonard promised to try to secure the treasured floor pass, but sometimes I waited in suspense. The Pennsylvania delegation had landed in hot water at other conventions for using counterfeit floor passes. The Philly people were usually behind the fraud. One wasn't in the loop unless on the floor, so it was worth the fallout.

Each day I encountered a different celebrity, like Kevin Costner, who thought we were lifetime friends.

"Kevin?" I blurted. "It's Mike Stack. How have you been?"

He bearhugged me after I told him I loved *Field of Dreams*. "Mike, I've been very lucky."

I thought to myself, *this guy has really, really blue eyes.*

Ted Danson and I waited for the elevator, but he glared with suspicion after I said I wasn't a fan of *Cheers*.

JFK Jr. stood next to me at the urinal but only nodded; protocol required not speaking. A big feeling of superiority came over me, knowing I passed the bar on my first try. It had taken him three, not withstanding everything else he had going for him.

DeBlasio was pessimistic about my chances of joining the fall campaign. He said I did a great job, but they didn't need any more white males. Ed Rendell said the same thing. The former mayor and national campaign chairman was sitting on a park bench by Lake Michigan. I was amazed he was all alone. I said, "Mayor, I don't want to bother you, but can you help me with the Clinton folks?" He committed to call the state chair, Tony Podesta.

The next day I saw him at the delegation breakfast. Once again, he was sitting by himself at a table reading a newspaper. I poured a cup of coffee and sat down. "Hi, Ed."

He folded the paper. "You're a great guy, Mike, but it's not going to happen. I really tried, but they don't need any more white males. That's directly from Podesta."

I stumbled away in disbelief and reported the disappointing news to Leonard. He said he would call Podesta to try again. Fifteen minutes later he directed, "Podesta is going to call you to tell you you're on board. Rendell never talked to him." The former mayor never learned to be less specific when lying. He should've just said he couldn't get him on the phone.

I acquired a new title, chairman of Ethnic Americans for Clinton-Gore, and became the point man for ethnic events at the White House. The most fun was the Irish Americans because I knew so many. I made lists of "prominent" Irish people to be invited to St. Patrick's Day at the White House. The top Germans and Poles were easy to find and unlike the Irish, there weren't countless grudges to maneuver. Interestingly, they were all from our social circle. I transferred attendees at Dad's office parties to the White House list. He kept adding friends and cronies, and I thought we'd get caught. I couldn't believe White House receptions happened like that. Knuckleheads like me made a list of all his friends and—*voila*—the White House. By the Steinway where Truman played "Auld Lang Syne," Frank Moran, an ambulance chaser, chatted with Senator Ted Kennedy. Nearby, Tom Darcy, a sporadically employed accountant, discussed peace negotiations with special envoy George Mitchell, who helped bring peace to Northern Ireland working closely with Seamus Mallon, our family's member of Parliament.

The national campaign staffers were suspicious of the most effective Democratic machine in America and my connections to it. Nonetheless, Congressman Chaka Fattah became influential, and his chief of staff Greg Naylor became a point man for the Clintonites. Naylor was alarmed when I walked into the big staff meeting as a full-fledged member of the team. Nonetheless he was savvy enough to act cordially and convey his regards to my father. The Fattah Camp vied for supremacy and abhorred other locals.

Philadelphia was a fractious, treacherous crab trap that shunned unity at all costs. Our politics was the opposite of inclusion. Fattah and others considered me an ally of Bob Brady and thus aligned with the white faction. I didn't have any real allies other than those short-term, transactional alliances where I was a long shot worthy of a bet. But the parochial thinking would be an obstacle in my career and prevent the city from becoming great and made me work harder to win.

I shared an office with a middle-aged woman named Berle from Washington, DC. A forced Texas accent betrayed saccharine-sweet passive aggressiveness. I smiled sympathetically when she directed I go fetch coffee. Then she turned clandestine and kept me out of the loop. But I freelanced and aided committee people or ward leaders looking for campaign literature.

College kids were ignored until I helped coordinate on campuses like Temple and Penn. DeBlasio called in a special mission to sneak into a closed Bob Dole event. I used Dad's press credentials by taping my photo onto it. He wrote an anonymous political column under the pseudonym "City Hall Sam" and took the initiative to register as a legitimate journalist. I took over the column in later years and after his death. I followed his lead discussing politicians and their activities. The topics were light and breezy but still managed to offend Johnny Doc, the powerhouse union boss who would take over the city. The tough guy had the thinnest skin. He demanded more than one retraction, threatening to pull "all union advertising." After that, City Hall Sam felt compelled to report every Doc defeat at the building trades council all in the name of freedom of the press and to send that guy into the stratosphere.

The old man wrote an amusing column, and I imitated his breezy, irreverent style of describing candidates and officials like movie stars walking the red carpet. He could have been a journalist like his award-winning buddy Tom Fox, who quoted Dad on Philly politics. Dad was also great at espionage, like in the Ludlum books he read. He coached me on how to penetrate security at a press-only national speech by Senator Bob Dole. He suggested doctoring credentials to gain access and hide a tape recorder inside my coat. I wore dark glasses and a fedora hat and leaned against the wall while the presidential nominee castigated Clinton. My heart raced and sweat dripped as I stood near the stage at the Convention Center. The recording was poor, but the Clinton brass admired my cunning.

While working on the Clinton campaign, I rehearsed a play at King of Prussia players called *Dangerous Corners*. The opening soundtrack was "Would I Lie to You" by Eurhythmics. I played a closeted, affluent gay guy who may have committed murder. I was amazed how well it worked out. I did both jobs, staffer and actor, well. But the new director of the campaign tried to send me to Erie, Pennsylvania, in the last week. Clinton had Philly locked up and this bright thirty-year-old wanted me to freeze my buns off helping a congressional candidate near Canada.

I said to the kid, "I'm from Philadelphia. I'm the lead in a play. The other actors are counting on me. I'm not going to Erie." The conversation wasn't heated.

He said, "You've got to decide whether you're an actor or a Clinton staffer. And if you can't, maybe it's best that we part ways."

I responded with a smile. That was an easy one. "Then let us part ways." I spread my arms apart in a theatrical gesture.

The acting career didn't prevent Tony Podesta, the state chair, from recognizing my value. The Washington insider invited me to the reunion party at his fancy Georgetown digs. Berle and the other catty staffers nearly fainted when I strutted in, chest out and grinning. I drove down there just to get that look. I ate some hors d'oeuvres, drank a couple of Cokes, let Podesta show me his masterpiece paintings, then got the hell out of there, dropping a figurative microphone.

Salvatore thumped Tom Mills by thirteen thousand votes. I was glad I didn't run. Fumo and Salvatore were still buddies, an evil alliance. Fumo used Salvatore to get Republican votes for budget deals. I admired Vince's brilliance in hiring the best fiscal people and always finding the leverage. From him came reward and punishment, success and failure, smiles or tears. He spent nearly his whole career in the minority party and was inexplicably integral. As excruciating as it was, the reality that I could never penetrate his black wall settled in. I was done running for the state senate. It was time to change my future. I would be an actor, lawyer, or a staffer. I didn't need to get kicked in the privates or get stabbed in the back by Democratic politicians. Darth Vader Fumo was against me, therefore the Force wasn't with me.

\* \* \*

I met Tonya at a picnic around this time. We both had bouquets of people gathered around listening to our adventures. I noticed she had taken some of my audience and wanted to meet her. She had never seen me as a candidate but thought my acting was cool.

I took classes at Kathy Wickline Casting and Walnut Street Theater. *How to Be a Standup Comedian* by Paul Solari was alluring. I was amazed that one could learn such a thing. My brother Patrick and I used to fall asleep listening to records of Steve Martin, Richard Pryor, and George Carlin. Participants were required to perform at a comedy club to graduate. It was both terrifying and exhilarating. My political training helped with poise and precision. After my first performance, Solari recruited me for the master's course. About five weeks later, I was the middle comic in a five-act bill at a packed Laff House in Delaware County. Tonya was part of the sellout crowd that was raucous and inebriated.

The two comics in front of me, who I thought were funnier, bombed. But I went out there, determined to get laughs. I treated the audience like a room full of committee people and won them over. Foolishly, I invited my drunken hairdresser, who heckled me. Tonya was in the audience and tried to muffle her. It was exhilarating watching my new girlfriend tussle with hecklers while I executed jokes on stage. That night I seriously considered a career in show biz.

Dad surmised I was having some kind of breakdown. He watched my acting and comedy with bewilderment, followed closely by alarm that I was veering from the political plan. The 1999 race for council at-large was wide open. The Northeast ward leaders did not have a preferred horse because of their habit of blocking each out of jealousy. But if they could coalesce behind one candidate, however unlikely, my father surmised victory was almost certain. Thirty-one candidates vied like clowns in a three-ring circus for just five at-large seats. Over a Reuben sandwich at the deli on Chestnut Street near our office, Dad made the case.

I wasn't convinced. "Haven't I been a good son to you?".

He thought it was worth doing. "You could win." Then, after a pause, he said, "The only problem is you'd need to be in that nuthouse." Council president and future mayor John Street had a fistfight with Councilman Franny Rafferty. Two grown men crashed into desks and wrestled on the floor as horrified screams mixed with encouraging cheers.

Franny's wife had sent a note after my 1988 loss, mentioning Lincoln. I didn't want to waste my Lincoln energy on that shit show. But what could I say? My dad was the coach and I listened. He alerted the Northeast hoodlums to expect a call.

"He's running again?! What is it this time?" Frank Dillon, the silver-haired, red-nosed half of Frank and Jesse, (because they held you up) quipped. The fresh face with new ideas had evolved into a desperate office-seeking political hack. Fifty-second ward leader Tim Savage, who became a federal judge, was smarter than the average bear. He pulled me aside at a beef and beer at Bridesburg American Legion Hall like a CIA operative. "Your dad is right," he whispered. "If all those Northeast ward leaders support you, it's a slam dunk." He rubbed his chin. "Sadly, my guess is they won't. Marge hates your dad, and others will be envious." He chuckled acerbically, "But I think you got to try."

Marge Tartaglione was tougher than Margaret Thatcher and sported an iron, ivory hairdo and black, hateful eyes. She had demeaned Bob Borski and punched a few guys in the nose over the years. But her rattler tongue caused tears. She was hard as nails but also opportunistic, flipping her registration from Republican to become Frank Rizzo's pick for city commissioner. Later, her daughter Tina triumphed in a tumultuous state senate race and became a friend. But Margie spewed poison, so Tina became an enemy, then eventually a friend again on the love-hate rollercoaster of the City of Brotherly Love.

Where many found Dad's humor witty, Marge charged it was condescending. Her abuse could nonetheless be endured, he felt, on the way to an alliance. He coached me to go to mental case leaders, hat in hand, and beg their forgiveness.

"But I didn't do anything!" I said.

He dismissed this naiveté. "Do it anyway. We've got a campaign to win!"

After I apologized for my dad's offenses dating back to the seventies and my own terrible accident of birth, our bare bones, city-wide campaign began. We made some deals in South Philly with other ward leaders, including Fumo's cousin, former senator Buddy Cianfrani, and got on half the promised ballots. We also got lied to by dozens of operators and ward leaders, which was better than most candidates. On election day, Tonya rode around to polling places and pretended to be a voter. She waived the ballot, smiling if my name was on it or nodding disappointingly. Our slogan was "the Only Northeast Candidate."

Tim Savage had the prescience of a soothsayer. We performed well in most of the Northeast but got "cut" in key wards, including Tartaglione's. Maybe I hadn't been convincing in my contriteness. I came in seventh out of thirty-one, even though early news reports had me in the top five. Savage delivered his ward, then later was the only Philadelphia ward leader to join the federal bench without serving on a lower court. Our chairman made that happen. Bob Brady must have owed Tim big. Fumo underestimated Bob, saying that he was only useful "getting you over the goal line." I watched Brady perform miracles countless times for people he really liked.

My growing list of detractors claimed I ran for council to set up another shot at the state senate. That was ridiculous. I lost three races and was done with it. If anyone mentioned Lincoln, we were going to tussle. Three strikes and you're out. I could take a hint.

\* \* \*

I finished another play and was enjoying acting classes. One teacher encouraged me to go to New York and get into soap operas. He recognized my overdramatic style. I set out my clothes on the bed and unzipped my Samsonite. Then the old man came pacing around. "People want to know if you're running for the senate."

What people? The ward leaders who sold me down the river? We were in the basement just after what I thought was one of my last ward meetings. Framed posters from my losing campaigns decorated the walls. "You need to make up your mind." Nothing had changed from my last state senate run in 1992. No problem, Dad, I'm out.

Dad had been screwed in politics more times than a Kansas City hooker, but he had an incurable virus of hope, or perhaps delusion. Maybe I represented redemption. Back in the day, he had been promised the party chair when he was the right age. Then they said he was too old. He'd lost for public office and been passed over. Time marched on, he often said. He wanted me to take all my shots. Hadn't I? Why would leaders recruit a failed candidate for another brutal race? He thought I could take it. He was a mystery. He had suffered so much heartbreak in the darkness and disappointment of the Congressman's losses in that family home on Catherine Street filled with ice and tears. Then he traveled his own road of broken dreams, dragging us along in white shoes. Now he was pushing me down that broken, glass-strewn path using an emotional cattle prod. This festering family wound had to be treated. Did he see my gifts or was he desperate, or both? He wouldn't let me escape. The ease of my youth was over. He had once encouraged me to stay home to avoid a bully. Now he was deaf. He would be in my corner, but as far as he was concerned, I was going into that ring.

"I can't do it again. I won't." I knew Vince Fumo and Salvatore played patty cake with Representative Mike McGeehan, the influential leader of Mayfair's 41st Ward. McGeehan had been rumored to be eyeing the state senate for years as he rolled up landslides in his house district.

"How will you feel if someone else runs and wins?"

Jimmy could crack corn and I didn't care. "No one else could win but me or perhaps McGeehan."

Dad stared like I was on drugs. "McGeehan is the one who wants you to run!"

I dismissed that notion until he handed me the phone.

McGeehan was cheerful. "We need you, Michael. You've got a name and could beat this old bastard."

Previously, on our show back in 1992, I peered into his steely eyes and saw contempt. His warm relationship with the senator was like chocolate pudding. I scrapped out a ninety-vote win while he cruised by five hundred in his ward. But that was almost a decade ago, which is like a century in politics. "I'll get those hoodlums in line."

If he meant it, the others would think twice before sticking it to the pincushion. "I'll call you back." I looked at my father. "You believe him?"

He slid into a leather chair at the long table. Those gray eyes turned twinkly. "As much as no one can really be trusted in this business . . ." He cleared his throat. "I think he's reliable."

I sat facing him, piles of blank petitions and registration lists in front of me. "Do you think that's good enough?"

He cracked a salty smile. "It's about all you can expect."

I asked him to get McGeehan back on the phone.

I hadn't really run for office in the true sense since 1992. The council race was spur of the moment and superficial. Running for the state senate was a mythical blood-and-guts quest. The fire-breathing demons of the past and the glimmering hope for the future wrestled on a tightrope. I couldn't imagine putting myself and the people who loved me through the disappointment again . . . unless I could envision a different outcome.

Pat and Jim McGinley were predictably ready to drop everything. They clapped and pounded feet at our kitchen table. "Thank God, Michael. We were praying," said the lady who blamed herself for my losses.

Frank Conaway had endured the eight years to nurse his incredulity. "Are you sure it wasn't four years ago? It seems like it was only yesterday." He had kept an endless list of all the people that failed us. The other leaders were surprisingly enthusiastic. This campaign seemed like a fresh start. Once they knew McGeehan was on board, they smelled something cooking. The special momentum, like lightning in a bottle, was already there.

Any aspirant who was talking to the right people asked, "How are you with Bob?" If she answered, "I think good," she was in trouble. In Philadelphia, one had better know. Candidates for judge or congress would beg Dad to take them to see Brady. He took me before I asked. We were on that worn leather sofa in the rickety old building once again, two big men sandwiching me in, talking like I was inanimate.

Everyone called Brady a street guy, but his custom, French-cuffed shirts cost more than my Buick. When I complimented Brady on his presidential cufflinks, he gave them to me as a gift. His thick, curly brown hair had flecks of silver but was lush like Gorgeous George. The tailor needed extra tape to get all the way around that barrel chest. He regularly benched three hundred to break the thread. He was light on his feet, coming from behind the oak desk to hug my old man. "My guy!" he gushed. Then the smile fell like rain when he caught my eye. Dad served a purpose for the chairman, steering the policy committee and controlling other ward leaders in the interest of city committee. What purpose did I serve other than upsetting the apple cart?

Dad sat at the armrest, and I fell into the center and couldn't lift up to get with the adults. "He's taking another shot at the senate."

Brady sighed. "What's different?"

Dad extended his arm along the rest. "We've got Michael McGeehan, and the district is better." The two warhorses seemed to agree on something—Bob had been talked to. Kissing the ring garnered a riddle.

"Let's see what happens. Sure, go ahead and take a shot."

How was I with Bob? Ask Einstein. Three years ago, I had been "one of us." Now, sort of.

Even with the positive momentum, there were plenty of unreturned calls and dismissals. I was a political hack who perennially sought office. I had already taken my best shot and failed. I still had to convince myself I could do this. It was difficult to imgaine myself running from door to door. I didn't feel physically fit and had flashbacks of my face bouncing off the canvas. When I was twelve years old, I appeared in the movie *Rocky II* as one of the kids who chased Stallone through the Italian Market. You'll see me gaining just before Rocky leaves us in the dust. I hoped that kind of adrenaline would come. We still had something vital missing. Out of nowhere, I received the phone call that changed everything.

If Salvatore was my nemesis, Vincent J. Fumo was the archvillain. He was Darth Vader, who ruled the Philadelphia galaxy with cold brutality and bravado from the time of my boyhood. He was the central figure in Harrisburg battles and always in the papers and on TV, usually playing the villain. Scowling and scornful, Fumo wore dark suits like a gangster. Blunt gestures, wagging fingers, and waving arms telegraphed defiance and contempt, preferring to be feared

than loved. At the Jefferson Jackson dinner, groupies fawned and aspirants grov-
eled as his grim-faced capos blocked interlopers. They would step aside for senators like Tina Tartaglione, who kissed his hands like the Pope. He bankrolled
her state senate campaign, owned her adoration, and handed her a check for six
figures more than once, gesturing, "Let me know if you need more, sweetheart."

I wasn't his sweetheart. I tried to get his attention at that dinner for years
and he turned away like I was a vagrant with a cup. He sabotaged me in 1988
and 1992 with clandestine treachery. I despised my desperation and begged for
a chance to kiss his ring. He'd moved heaven and hell with ease like arranging
the chess board to win the 1993 budget battle. Fumo had Senator Frank Lynch
wheeled from the hospital onto the state senate floor, IV bottle and oxygen in
tow, to cast the tie-breaking vote. He giggled slyly at Republican leader Bob
Jubelirer, savoring his ingenuity. Lynch's heart monitor flattened at the finish
line. But Fumo held the purse strings and could write checks to the world.
Money was no object if he needed you. And he needed a replacement for Lynch.

The state senate was locked in a 24 to 24 tie, so Fumo bankrolled the candidacy of jeweler William Stinson to break it. Stinson's pocked complexion and
thinning black hair made him look seedy and suspicious. He was a very nice
guy but hardly the ideal candidate. It seemed incomprehensible watching the
power players and money people stand behind Fumo and Stinson on television.
Eventually they would head for the mountains. The election came down to a
handful of votes and tons of acrimony. Stinson was declared the winner and
seated as Republicans threatened violence. Federal judge Clarence Newcomer,
a Republican mouthpiece, declared the result fraudulent and ordered Republican Bruce Marx installed in April 1994. The action was unconstitutional and
unprecedented and upheld. But Fumo wouldn't take it sitting down. After the
indictments had passed and it was safe to come back to work, Fumo whistled to
the money folks and power players that he was starting a new band.

Tina Tartaglione captured the seat. But the Democrats held a majority
for only eighteen months. It didn't matter that much to Fumo. He was great,
even in the minority. He was a genius at the legislative business that required
brass knuckles. When he bought a senator's loyalty, they usually stayed bought.
And he could usually count on the kindness of strangers, even if they were
Republican.

# CHAPTER THREE

# A NEW CAMPAIGN

I tried to put a Fumo out of my mind, but he kept showing up on my TV, like during a Sixers game in 1995. A news report broke in that the senator had fainted and was rushed to the hospital for emergency brain surgery. Maybe he'll die or become an invalid, I'd pathetically hoped. But he recovered and was running things once more with a new mystique, and his evil invincibility continued. Nonetheless, I admired the way he held up President Clinton's appointment of Legrome Davis to the federal bench. The prince told the president how it would be. Fumo hated Judge Davis for opposing him on some parochial issue a decade before. But he never forgot. Clinton was almost speechless when Fumo told him, he could have Davis, his guy, once Bob Scandone, Fumo's guy, got confirmed. The leader of the free world stuttered, turned red, and promised it would be done. Fumo's relationship with Republican US Senator Rick Santorum enabled him to put a hold on Davis. Bubba later reneged.

Vince had allies everywhere, and his political slogan was "We Get Shit Done." It could've also been "We stop shit from happening." His formula was "brains, balls, loyalty, and leverage."[3]

I had been brought up to believe that Democrats helped other Democrats. Fumo lived in the world where everyone is competition. I thought I was tough and smart, but compared to him I was a babe in the woods. Senators went to Harrisburg and voted on groundbreaking legislation in story books. Legislation was the lead pipe he used to bash opponents over the head. The longer I thought about the South Philly senator and his tactics, the more I questioned ever going into politics. I didn't know if I could ever play it like him, or would want to. He seemed to fuction in a netherworld. But there was a big part of me that was attracted to his brutal mastery.

I lit candles at Saint Christopher's church and prayed the rosary that something special would happen. The events of the early spring of 2000 made divine intervention seem likely.

---

3. Ralph Cipriani, *Target the Senator: A Story about Power and Abuse of Power* (CreateSpace, 2017).

"Senator Fumo wants to see you in his office tomorrow morning," the tough-sounding lady instructed. "And the senator said to bring your father." The delivery was clipped and the tone expectant. Dad juggled his schedule and showed surprising skill in parking the humongous Lincoln into a minuscule parking spot on Tasker Street.

I had visited the "bunker" in 1992 and was slapped with opprobrium and rejection. The converted row house with iron bars on the windows looked the same in 2000, except for the addition of bulletproof glass, surveillance equipment, and reinforced steel doors.

"Please don't say anything sarcastic," I pleaded as we descended the concrete steps.

Surprisingly, Mike McGeehan was seated on a wooden chair next to the bulletproof glass. His dark hair was now silver, and he'd put on a few donuts and beer pounds. "Your Grace," he greeted Dad.

He was gracious, but his crimson cheeks revealed nervousness. "I got the call so here I am."

McGeehan looked around the room suspiciously, then leaned in to whisper, "The man has helped me for years. Not many people know that." A violent buzz broke the silence and released the heavy door. Ruth Arneo, who would later be indicted with Fumo, escorted us from the reception. The long, dark hallway seemed to get longer and darker as we pushed each other ahead.

The sourpuss of before had evolved into a sugary grin. There was no Jim Kenny or anybody else this time, just Vincent. Fumo's beige khakis and blue oxford shirt with the sleeves rolled up were his work uniform. He was friendly but distracted, anxious to do serious business.

We were barely seated when he blurted, "Today is the luckiest fucking day of your life!" His stare was like a laser. He drummed a pen. "If you came here last week, I would've told you to forget it."

Dad sat on the slippery leather sofa against the wall behind me. McGeehan was seated uncomfortably on a velour chair at the adjacent wall, and I was in front of Fumo's desk, close enough to smell his sweat.

Fumo's grin fell apart at the seams. His eyes turned to flames. "That son of a bitch Salvatore convinced Ridge to appoint him to the Delaware River Port Authority." This was interesting. It seemed like somebody had made a big mistake. "In my fucking seat!" he boomed. Governor Ridge, future homeland security secretary, was "Dudley Fucking Do Right who don't know shit about Philadelphia." Fumo let out a contemptuous laugh. Then stopped it on a dime. "Well, I'm going to fuck that old bastard Salvatore . . . and I'm going to fuck him"—the ethereal drumbeat rolled—"WITH YOU!"

After pinching my thigh to make sure I was awake, my participation in the conversation wasn't needed. I became an inanimate object in the center of the room. Fumo questioned and gave instructions to Dad and McGeehan like a drill sergeant. I heard only garbled sounds as oxygen tried to return to my brain. Could Dad deliver the 58th Ward? When Dad equivocated, "I think so," Fumo shot, "You better know so! Do you want to make your kid a senator or not?" It was a dream. I couldn't believe what I was hearing. In a blink, the chief personification of evil became my pivotal political pal, my new best friend, and the best guy in the world.

Fumo went to Wharton and was a lawyer and a member of Mensa. He inherited a bank, and lived in a five-story brownstone mansion near the art museum. He wintered at homes in Florida. His thick hair was perfectly styled, and his skin was smooth and moist from expensive facials. His nails were mani-cured, and a hired driver steered him around in a Mercedes. I wanted to be like him: a master of the universe, free of the backbiting rivalries of ward politics. But once I got behind the curtain with the wizard, I discovered he had his own problems. The exterior elegance, wealth, and education were but subterfuge that concealed his enflamed foundation.

Within days of the meeting, the truth of Fumo's crumbling empire emerged. Confidantes like Charles Hoffman, a tall ex-ward leader who had helped wheel the dying Frank Lynch to the state senate floor, remarked, "It's great he's with you, but you should've seen him five years ago when he was powerful." The bespeckled, thoughtful Hoffman added, "Now he needs you as much as you need him. Salvatore's making him look like a punk."

It wasn't a bowl of cherries after all. My fourth race was the first where I was authentically armed with real weapons of campaign war, but my sustainability was inextricably linked to Fumo's survivability. My quixotic voyage evolved into paddling through storming seas with each of us holding an oar. From my perspective, the races he lost were amorphous and forgettable. But his rivals saw blood in the water. One of them was an emerging labor leader with a dangerous borderline personality disorder and hateful jealousy named John Dougherty.

Johnny Doc was Fumo's bitter enemy and became mine. He was ubiq-uitous whenever mischief and scandal lurked. And I had hardly even known he existed. He seemed like such a nice guy that I had no idea he wanted me destroyed. I had stumbled nonchalantly into a blood feud that would erupt into Armageddon and ruination for the most talented politicians in our city.

* * *

Like everyone with fingers crossed, Vince's word was his bond. You couldn't trust anyone. It was all about self-interest, first and last. His predecessor, Buddy

Cianfrani, had the same loyalty. To aspirants, he promised, "I'm with you one hundred percent . . . unless something changes." Buddy came out of federal prison on a bribery pinch and became a highly successful political consultant. The most respected felons were the most coveted. One of his new clients was the incumbent senator from the Fifth District.

When I brought my incredulity to Fumo, he shrugged. "Buddy knows I'll choke the shit out of him if he tries anything." Politics made strange bedfellows and that made for sleepless nights.

Most of the Philadelphia Democratic big shots had Republican bed buddies. Having Republican sway set you apart. The association was a form of psychological warfare, used to torture rivals into insecurity. The ruthless, experienced politicians used mind games to confuse or freeze opponents. It became feasible that Fumo's support of Mike Stack was for show or negotiation. No one knew for sure it was rock solid. Everybody was winking and nodding as I walked the ledge, not knowing who was lying or telling the truth, or even what language they were speaking.

I decided to focus on what was real and controllable. All that South Philly nonsense was a sideshow because our campaign clicked like a Geiger counter. Volunteers joined in droves from unlikely places. Local 1824 of the United Carpenters Union joined my team because they were oblivious that the rest of its union endorsed Salvatore. They didn't figure it out until the last week of the campaign and were among the most industrious workers we had. Volunteers from other campaigns swept in, and people who had never heard of me wanted to be a part of a potential upset. My fundraising went to a new level. Investors recognized I had a puncher's chance and were ready to be asked. They liked the long shot. I got good at the dialing for dollars most candidates abhorred. The labor-intensive task required humility and audacity to ask people straight out to write checks as though I was granting a favor. I got them on the phone or on their front step. I stalked and hounded them for money and support. Then I ran around neighborhoods, pleading for votes. We knocked on doors every day and attended every conceivable community event. Soon we were getting noticed by voters and dangerous enemies.

Evil was not always obvious, even when before our eyes. I was still naive to Johnny Doc's megalomania when I met him in the mayor's reception room in 2000. All the potato eaters at the Saint Patrick's Day Parade party surrounded him like a rock star. Doc stood near the podium as Mayor Street gushed about his generosity. Local 98 had written another big check to fund the parade. All the Irish people that I had referred to the White House weren't invited. The room was filled with brawny construction workers and electricians wearing green Local 98 Hoodies. The change had come. Doc was a man on the rise.

Johnny Doc's hyper disposition gave him a nervous tick that made him blink and shuffle. He was tall, with salt-and-pepper hair and rosy cheeks. When I reached him through the crowd, he quickly introduced Pat Gillespie, the president of the Allied Building Trades, who gave a soft handshake and avoided eye contact. Gillespie had a perfect record of opposing me in every race.

Doc knew what I wanted before I said anything. He put both hands on my shoulders like my big brother. "Look, you're going to do okay, pal." In a cheery, conspiratorial tone, he confessed that his guys "kind of like the other guy." But not to worry. He loved my dad and my mother. He was a big fan of me. "You're Irish-Catholic—how can I not like you?" Then he made a promise like many he would make over the years. "I'm not going to hurt you. I'm giving the other guy money and some manpower, and that's it, okay? Nobody will bust your chops. I guarantee it."

Dougherty had a kind of street charisma that made him seem believeable. That's what made him so duplicituous and dangerous. He pretended to like you when he actually wanted to kill you. He explained that Fumo wasn't his cup of tea. He sounded like a diplomat. Later I found out what that meant. But Johnny Doc would find a way to contribute financially "under the radar" and, in the end, surpass his aid to Salvatore. Who was I to look a gift horse in the mouth? The key labor boss in one of the biggest Democratic towns in America admitted to my face that he was supporting the Republican, but crumbs were forthcoming.

Why would Dougherty hate Vince? Fumo had been Dougherty's faithful mentor eight years earlier and giving him his illustrious start. Vince had been a high school teacher before elected office and was skilled at recruiting youth to participate in politics. He taught chemistry and gave extra credit for working a polling place. Dougherty and Jim Kenney were Fumo's young guns. They were classmates at St. Joseph Preparatory School, Fumo's alma mater. He encouraged Dougherty's involvement in Local 98 to increase his own political power, and Doc's rapid ascent transformed the union into a powerhouse. He repaid his mentor's kindness by turning on him. No one knew what happened. Envy was the usual suspect. Jimmy Kenny hated Dougherty for his disloyalty to Fumo until decades later when he allowed Dougherty to bankroll his mayoral quest.

Our policy meetings grew in attendees and energy. People sensed an upset. Dad upgraded the pastries and coffee to full breakfast. He coached me harder on our narrative. I was human and had moments of doubt. The building trades were against us. "Don't say that. Keep it positive." There were always plenty of negative people in our campaigns who enjoyed the attention of being a Debbie Downer. Pat and Jim figured out who might want to rain on our parade and hit them with a firehose first. They strategically talked over them, drowning out their negativity. They were also highly effective Catholics who delivered shame like the Sunday paper. If you didn't believe we would win, there was something wrong with you. They were just so disappointed in you.

We were forced to fictionalize our own polling to head off hysteria. Our support was fragile, and anything could cause a stampede out of our camp. If news of a disturbing poll was circulating, we trumped it with our own exciting survey of a surging four-point lead. No one ever asked to see the poll. But they repeated our fantasy numbers, and days later, we received congratulations and additional contributions from folks who heard about the poll.

Sadly, there was authentic polling that had me trailing by seventy-eight points. I'm not kidding—seventy-eight freaking points! And even worse, it came from our pollster, Howard Cain, a trusted Fumo advisor. But his methodology was unique and kept me off the ledge. He constructed issue-oriented polls with push points and tabs that measured voter reaction to nuanced issues. If we could deliver our message surgically, there was a road to victory.

Howard Cain was short on personality but long on intelligence. His gloomy disposition turned sunny when he showed a potential spike in our favor. He carried charts and surveys around like uranium in a bulky, worn leather case. His slumped shoulders and sparsely covered head accompanied a nasal voice that went from nails on a chalkboard to the sound of music with good news. If we attacked Salvatore on guns, education, and votes against Philadelphia, we could reach the margin of error by election day. But everything had to go right, and in campaigns, they never did. We had to be mistake-free, and we wouldn't.

Fumo didn't like Mayor John Street. He had invested sizeable capital behind former Rizzo advisor Marty Weinberg. The same cast of clout from the ill-fated Senator Stinson jaunt was rounded up. Tonya's reaction was "a guy named Marty will never become mayor of Philadelphia. He might own a deli."

John Street had a better name, like out of the movies—he came from the streets. Street had been a hot dog vendor outside Temple University in North Philadelphia when a guy named Carl encouraged him to go to law school. Eventually he became council president. Weinberg was savvy, friendly, and knew everyone. But Marty was unpolished and always had mustard on his tie. All the money in the world couldn't create a connection to the voters like John Street. Fumo didn't take the loss well and got even by poaching staff. When Mayor Street fired smart, young Ken Snyder as communications director, Fumo hired him immediately.

Snyder immediately told his new boss that he should pull out of my race. His shaved head glistened with sweat and pessimism as he paced the office with compact strides. His voice was whinier than Cain's, and their debates were like waterboarding. Senator Fumo's ears bled for six months. "Why are we doing this?" Snyder protested. Cain's analytics predicted a dead heat, but Snyder thought it was poppycock.

Snyder wasn't the only one who thought I was a dead duck. The chief editor of the *Northeast News Gleaner*, Don Brennan, got an urgent call from Salvatore urging him to come right to his office for a scoop. In the spring of 2000, Salvatore was as giddy as a teen with a crush as he pulled out a chair for Brennan.

"You're not going to believe it!" he chuckled. "It's all done. I'm getting reelected. Brady is helping me out." Brennan leaned forward in suspense. "He's giving me that turkey Stack again." He clapped his hands. "I'm all set!"

Fumo hosted lavish dinners at his favorite restaurant, La Veranda, on the Delaware River. His strategy of "ward leader management" enabled us to keep an eye on them as they stuffed their gullets. The bosses sang our praises, watching Vince sign the check. Fumo followed the same rule as my dad. "We don't sell rotten fish." Trouble was brought up in private. Amusingly, Salvatore dined in the next room and was delighted when the ward leaders paraded by. "Hi, Senator!" Hank's millionaire host, Peter DePaul, was impressed by the affectionate response. I missed that kind of fun because I was knocking on doors and dodging dog attacks.

\* \* \*

I thought cash would fall from the sky, but Vince made me work. "You raise one hundred grand by June 30, and I'll match it." I asked everyone I could think of for an exact dollar amount as opposed to saying I would really appreciate their support. It wasn't easy. I asked for the business card of every new person I met so I could call them. Soon, folks claimed they didn't have one. I pulled out a pen and paper and asked for their number. They could run, but they couldn't hide. Nobody enjoyed getting touched for money, but people appreciated my directness. My stomach churned during interminable silences at the other end of the line. But in that silence, I found my manhood. I wouldn't interrupt it. The answer would be yes. Most candidates couldn't do that. The game of cat and mouse was unnerving, but every call session came with surprises.

Al Dragon, a distinguished trial attorney and friend of my parents, sounded aloof.

"Would you be willing to contribute $250, Al?" I asked. "I'd really appreciate it."

Silence, deep, dark, and pulsating. "No, I will not." Now it was his pause to master. "But I will contribute $1,000." That was crazy money for me in those days.

I sniffled and wiped my eyes. "I love you, Al."

Tonya was new to politics but great at handling people, including me. I was transitioning from normal civilian life to the fire and ice of the game of thrones. Movies and dinners and sleeping late were replaced by neurosis and workaholism. Happy Mike was in the wind. When I told her that was politics, she said, "You're just saying that because you're afraid of a commitment." The poor girl had no idea. But she was game and helped the fundraising operation. She deposited the checks as the June 30 deadline approached and couldn't understand my mania. On June 28, she returned from the bank and joined me in the basement, where I was chained to the phone.

"I don't want to show you this." She held up the deposit slip. It was good news, but I wouldn't think so "because you're a psycho." She was right. I couldn't accept good news. The slip read $99,704.71, and I should've been ecstatic. We were still short of the goal, but it was *a fait accompli*. On June 30, it read $101,300.13. I phoned Vince.

"Great job, pal." Vince was like an old friend.

"Don't you want to see the receipt?"

I couldn't believe we did it. That was chicken feed in today's game, but in 2000, for little ol' me, it was splendid. The watershed moment inspired more confidence in me. I could play the big boy game and raise the loot. People amazed me with their generosity and their cheapness. Friends who couldn't afford much wrote the biggest checks. Vivid memories remain of the fat cat lawyers who rebuffed me with "I will not contribute" above their signatures of the request letters. They're in my scrapbook. I remember all the folks who said no as I fall off to sleep decades later.

Dyslexia compelled memorization to avoid humiliation. I developed association techniques that sealed information in my brain ad infinitum. The exact tone of someone's voice from a conversation long ago, the look in their eye, the scent of the room, their wardrobe, it's all indelible. It's a great skill to have as a politician but a bad one to have as a human. I worked hard to forget unpleasant exchanges with people. But I found it mindblowing that detractors would actually put it in writing that they were against me. They were absolutely positive I would amount to nothing.

The campaign was a mental and physical battle of knocking on doors through the sweltering summer. The task required organization and execution, and we had an All-American football player to run it. Gene McAleer was the

son of Mike, the reinvented ward leader of 66A, a recipient of thank-you letters from the past, and half of "Frank and Jesse." Gene had tree trunk arms,
a clipboard, and a whistle. He assembled packs of young volunteers eager to
play on our team. They executed canvassing missions like commandos. Our
machine-like efficiency was measured with pins on maps and sweat on brows.
Dozens of people gathered with clipboards and smiles every hot night. New
strategies enabled us to cover both sides of the street with split crews. I darted
from house to house, crossing back and forth in my Nike Air black loafers,
gasping for air as they laughed. Gene was disappointed when I wasn't winded or
puking. He chastised me once for my soaking blue Oxford. "I don't want to see
that shirt ever again unless you're wearing an undershirt. That's unacceptable."
He stomped off, disgusted, shaking his head.

Leaves fluttered gently down and cool breezes caressed faces as Labor
Day subtly passed. Fumo prohibited me from attending another dinner at La
Veranda. The ward leaders drank rarer vintages and added lobster. "I don't want
you doing anything but knocking on doors." He wasn't being nice about it. In
Philly, elections were won on the pavement. Personal contact gained you two
or three points if you were lucky. It seemed meager, but it was a game of inches.
All the money and technology couldn't get those extra votes. We pounded doors
and treated each voter like gold. All the betrayal scenarios about who was meeting with Brady and what the polls revealed were none of our business. There
were a ton of excruciating betrayal rumors, but with cotton in my ears, I plowed
the fields.

Senator Fumo didn't want me dialing for dollars anymore. He would raise
the funds along with Senator Mellow and the SDCC. The last call I made was
to Tom Previc, the top lobbyist for the Philadelphia Trial Lawyers. Previc was
bearded, balding, and bespeckled, with an air of cynicism and superiority that
made me want to get Frank Conaway to punch him in the nose. I was a trial
lawyer and a Democrat, and I'd always heard that got you the support of the
alleged victims' advocates. The most powerful senator was my patrician. Yet this
supercilious jokester was treating me like a chump.

"Is Fumo for you? Or is he *for* you?"

I was practically stuttering. What kind of doublespeak was this? He was *for*
me, I think. Previc's political action committee did little to help because of a
warm relationship with Dougherty. Doc and his friends in Labor referred their
injured workers to trial lawyers. Once again, a premier Democratic booster was
for the Republican.

Fumo's steely helmsmanship was the centerpiece of my flowery future. But
I couldn't help but be insecure with the innuendo and history of perfidy. Cain's

recent poll had me down a mere thirty points in early fall. Nonetheless Snyder begged, "Why are we doing this?"

I continued to stalk voters just short of being weird. "Hey, honey, it's Mike Stack again."

Big Jim in the Eagles jersey yelled. His wife came to the door with the dog, Shamrock, panting happily instead of snarling.

"We got you, Mike!" I heard everywhere. The polls couldn't be right. Dogs like Shamrock had shifted into my column.

A *Daily News* columnist hosted a stand-up comedy night to benefit the Variety Club. In early October, I appeared before a packed house at Finnigan's Wake. Most of the audience were candidates and their followers having fun. I worked the crowd and handed out "Mike Stack for Senate" nail files, which were a hit with a group of beautiful dancers from Delilah's Den. The strippers cheered and laughed the loudest, but the stone-faced lugs with big necks leered. Salvatore and his henchmen guzzled beer and punched their open hands from the front row.

Dad got a fresh round of calls from Billy Meehan and other Republicans. "This time they're really going to hurt your son." The friendly warnings about my checkered past becoming public threats were clear. I had some addiction issues and preferred to keep them private, but I wouldn't be intimidated. They could take their best shot.

The shame that came with a learning disability was an amorphous black cloud that hovered throughout my life. Whenever political opponents threatened to expose my secrets, like addiction, I was mortified that there was something much worse, more shameful, than I could remember or grasp. I was always in trouble as a little kid in school. And I could never quite figure out what I had done. My real skeletons were not immense. Nonetheless, the feeling that they had something on me was always there.

In October, we ran a cable TV commercial where I saluted Bobby Kennedy. Howard Cain thought I resembled him and liked connecting me with the Kennedy legacy of service. I wasn't the biggest fan of Bobby, who had bullied and badgered, doing his brother's dirty work, but he became a heavyweight after Martin Luther King's assassination when he put out a fire of rage in Indianapolis.

Bobby quoted Aeschylus: "Even in our sleep, pain which cannot forget, falls drop by drop upon the heart, until, in our despair, against our will, comes wisdom through the awful grace of God." Bobby became a true man of peace with those words. There is such an agonizing truth about God's mysterious plans. We don't know why bad things happen to good people. I've been a beneficiary of that awful grace through the down-times in politics and life.

In retrospect, the answers have often appeared at exactly the right time, not necessarily in my time.

After the Bobby Kennedy commercial, we launched the surgical mail campaign that would move those poll numbers like moutains and put us in contention. We were mind readers who understood nuance. The district had a lot of cops who liked guns, but they didn't want criminals with assault weapons on the streets. But Hank was adamant that there should be no new gun laws. Cops and their families felt differently, particularly with increasing police deaths. We rapidly picked up support from soccer moms, a key demographic. Nonetheless, Salvatore still thought he had a turkey on his hands, so he went to Harrisburg and made deals and took a pass on debates and joint appearances. I wasn't insulted. I just ripped into his dismal record on education and guns and people, nodded, and cheered. I demanded to know why he didn't care enough to join us.

Salvatore's ethical problems were getting exposure in the *Philadelphia Inquirer*. I became cozy with their reporter and invited him to our protest of L and M Beverage. About twenty of us drove up in the Eagles bus and used a bullhorn to ask how Salvatore could chair the committee that regulated the beer industry. He was the fox guarding the henhouse and had made millions. *Inquirer* reporter Ken Dilanian wrote several hard-hitting articles and won awards. "I'll take care of you if you take care of me," he promised. We did.

Later, state representative Denny O'Brien quipped that we had "only touched the tip of the iceberg." But Northeast voters didn't care that much about ethics; bread-and-butter issues like guns and education dollars were paramount. Nonetheless the articles propelled Dilanian to the big time at NBC. He currently serves as a national security commentator for one of the national networks.

The chalk players still favored Salvatore. Most of the unions loved him and found my challenge disrespectful. The Teamsters hauled his beer, and the trades guys needed his clout with parking tickets and red tape. The Harrisburg lobbyists didn't even know he had an opponent. Fumo was astonished when Salvatore posted a $500,000 pickup in his finance report. When I heard the news, I pretended not to care. But I couldn't help but feel this was weakening my hold on the prince.

It wasn't as easy for Fumo to pull in cash as in previous years. His stock dropped, and Dougherty threatened Fumo's supporters, promising repercussions upon his imminent downfall. Fear had risen like morning mist then exploded like broken valves. The developments had been Shakespearean, and Fumo was Macbeth. They were taking it all. Salvatore grabbed the Delaware River Port Authority like a kid's ice cream cone. Governor Ridge wasn't concerned. Johnny

Doc backed Salvatore with the temerity of a slap in the face. Brady liked Salvatore and dined with him freely in public. Mayor Street needed Republican support in Harrisburg, and Salvatore was a somebody. The noose tightened. The kingdom was crumbling. Would Fumo let me hang to save himself? After all, it was just business.

I had never knocked on every door in the district in my previous campaigns. When I promised to do it in the 2000 campaign, it was mostly wishful thinking. But by mid-October, everything was like déjà vu. The cul-de-sacs looked the same, and I had petted that dog Shamrock three times. John Del Ricci drove a Ford pickup slowly down the middle of narrow streets like a combat Humvee while canvassers unloaded lawn signs and literature. The lawn signs indicated captured territory, and our flag was everywhere. Salvatore's union henchmen in Local 98 hoodies were enraged by the sight and tore posters down and stole lawn signs. We replaced them like lightning. The Hoodies wanted to fight, but my guys were smarter. They saved their energy until election eve.

Campaigns were never predictable except in their unpredictability. Robert Harris, in his historical novel *Imperium*, about Roman political intrigues, called an election like a living thing with brains and limbs and eyes. He believed it wiggled and twisted and turned just to prove it could. He had it right. My irresponsibility came home to roost in just such an unpredicatable way and nearly killed our chances.

Salvatore landed a surprising shot with a mailing that called me an insurance cheat. The grainy photo of my blotchy face on a bad hair day was superimposed over a crook in handcuffs. The mailing charged that I committed insurance fraud by registering my car in Montgomery County to avoid astronomical rates. My blue-collar neighbors of cops, firefighters, and teachers hated hypocrisy, so I had flames to run through. I'd worked in Rosemont and lived in an apartment in Ardmore but neglected to change my insurance. Fumo and Cain teetered like boxers caught by a blow. Snyder had new fodder and Neil Oxman, my former consultant, diagnosed a mortal wound. We were too far along for wholesale abandonment. Instead, the team worked on an effective response but thought the next few days were "existential." I would hear that word later in my career when it was even more bloodcurdling.

Salvatore's campaign smacked us again with an even shadier portrayal of me behind bars, cigarette between my fingers. The local media lunged in to roast me. The *Inquirer*, *Daily News*, and TV stations weren't focused on my campaign until the scandal erupted. Pat McGinley had been replaced by Cindy Mariela as campaign manager because Cindy was a war horse of countless South Philly conflicts. She had been executive director of the Parking Authority and was a lucky pickup for our campaign. She constructed an election-day operation that rivaled the D-Day invasion. She was yet another surrogate mother who contained my unraveling. Her demeanor was fearless, unlike the drama queen men. She believed Salvatore's attacks lacked authenticity and that people wouldn't buy them. Men like Snyder and Oxman ignored the common sense of voters. This had become a matter of will for me, like all the best leaders. I had to believe in myself, she insisted. "If you don't, you won't win. You can't worry about yesterday." Then she quoted Maxim Gorky but thought it was Lincoln. "In carriages of the past you can't go anywhere." The woman they called "Tombstone," because she always buried her enemies, sent me back to the frying pan with a smile on my face.

Three days later we were ready with the best response in show business. No response. We wanted it to die of its own accord and not fan flames. We resorted to Old Time politics, pure, exquisite vintage, and called Salvatore a damn liar, portraying him in our mailers as Pinocchio with a growing nose. He didn't want voters to know how bad he was on guns and education, so he lied about me to distract them. It was razzle dazzle misdirection but stopped the bleeding. Oxman was surprised that Salvatore abandoned the issue instead of doubling down. He was breaking my ribs like Apollo Creed but mysteriously made the tactical error to stop. I thought I was a dead man and had blown the race. But after a few days, voters started joking at the Acme in Morrell Park that they didn't recognize me without handcuffs. They busted my chops big time. If they weren't busting them, I had something to worry about.

That same day, Dad performed vintage campaign dirty work by disposing of evidence. He appeared at the supermarket, looking like a tall Barry Fitzgerald from *The Quiet Man*, in a wool jeff cap, Irish sweater, and mischievous grin. He bent down to tie his white sneakers and said, "Give me the keys."

I kept shaking hands with soccer moms and firefighters. "What keys?"

"To the Buick," he said tersely. "Vince wants us to get rid of it." He looked over at Gene Mac, who wagged his head with contempt toward me. Dad was no stranger to Bay of Pig tactics. The metallic blue Buick LeSabre from Salvatore's dirty mailing disappeared like Jimmy Hoffa. Simultaneously, the voters acted like I was the courageous underdog battling through the punches. I may have dodged the bullet but still needed a miracle. Two days later, we got one.

Laura Schonberg and Mark McKillop analyzed Salvatore's voting record like crime scene investigators. They discovered an unlikely pearl deep in an omnibus budget bill. Insanely, Salvatore was the only vote *against* a bill to ban sex offenders from working in public schools. Howard Cain's mouth watered as he drafted a radio commercial that spelled P.A.I.N for Salvatore. Days later, producer Hank Shankoff played it for me. The narrator was high-priced New York talent with a rich, leathery voice that stuck in the knife.

"Sex offenders in our schools?" he asked incredulously. "Are you kidding me?!" It was fantastic. The silence was deafening until Shankoff asked, "Did you just hear that?" I shrugged. "The sound of Hank's career . . . going down the drain." Fumo couldn't believe the vote was real. He didn't want to get sued for slander and asked that we double-check. After that he tripled the order for radio spots.

Salvatore's office was overwhelmed with angry phone calls. He couldn't explain it. The budget bills moved fast that day, but he claimed to be thinking straight. Allegedly, Salvatore hated the anti-gun language and wanted to show the NRA his loyalty. The Republican leadership implored him to change the vote, but he had been blindingly, perfectly confident. He worshiped that Second Amendment so much he didn't grasp the sex offender language. His staff should have used chloroform. Thank God we found that obscure vote. It was another example of divine intervention. And it was a lesson that Salvatore forgot: Every single vote is a potential negative campaign commercial. I was happy to remind him.

Gene Mac handed me the phone while we pounded doors. The troops carried on while I sat on a concrete step and took the call. "Please take a breath and don't be offended," Joe Steward said. He was the operations manager who met with Fumo and the consultants while I campaigned. "I need to ask you a personal question. It's imperative that you tell me the truth." The swirling rumors of campaigns past had regenerated. "Do you have an addiction issue? Fumo wants to know." Steward was accusatory. They were upset with me for keeping secrets. I had completed a program and was sober for years, and it was my damned business. There was a brief silence followed by a joyous yelp. "Fucking A! If those bastards bring it up, we'll kill them!" Then Joe conveyed that Fumo supported me and thought Salvatore was reprehensible. But he hoped for an attack "so we could shove it up their asses." I confess I was mortified. My emotional baggage related to childhood trauma and dyslexia gave me the feeling that I was always to blame. I didn't want any credit for dealing with addiction, but I sure didn't want to be condemned for it.

After all this, Salvatore still wasn't alarmed. Howard Cain was encouraged that our polling numbers kept improving, but Snyder was only slightly less skeptical. I was sixteen points down with thirteen days to go but didn't know it. I didn't want to hear anything about polling. It only made me nervous and less effective as a candidate. Vince told everyone we were coming up fast and the political stock market went crazy. Chalk players were coming over to our side.

Unbeknownst to me, Vince had almost fallen under Snyder's pessimistic spell. It was during one moment of weakness that he almost pulled out. But the numbers just kept improving so he couldn't drop me. Instead, he pushed the intercom button to his secretary and said, "Ruthie, it's time to send in the Fumocrats. Call everyone and get them to the Northeast stat."

We were swinging axes and swords with blood and guts everywhere and measuring territory by muddy inches. My ragtag team was fighting hard, but I admit the sound of those thundering hooves charging down the hill was beautiful. The savvy staffers and elected officials loyal to Fumo bolstered our flank. They hadn't known my name weeks back but now smelled an upset. Donna Gentile O'Donnell, the wife of former state house Speaker Bob O'Donnell, meant to help but ruined one of my days. Her energy and tenacity made her too chatty. She hadn't gotten the memo about polling. After a speech at Casino Deli on Sunday morning, she blurted, "We need to do something drastic. We're down by twelve points!" The words slogged like a dying vinyl record. *Twellllvvah poooinnttsah*. With ten days left, at that exact moment I knew I would suffer the horror of a fourth and final loss.

This was a watershed moment because I was so convinced. It was based on irrational fear and trauma but welcome to my life. Opinions didn't matter, the cynics and scoffers, the dweebs, the dickheads, they all loved Ferris Bueller. But nobody knew anything about what was in my heart—relentless, grim death. I knew that no matter what happened, I would try my hardest. There was nowhere to run except forward. All the money and polling and canvassing and psychological warfare was a pitter-patter, fiddle-faddle waste of air. I'd heard countless stories about candidates who wanted to jump off buildings. Not me. I'd be there at the final count, chewing glass.

When I kept banging on doors even after hearing those polling numbers, I had achieved full fucking manhood. Politics was over after this, and I would choose some other dumbass career. The kids running around with the clipboards, the committee people, the union volunteers, all the people who watched me grow up and loved me and cheered me on like Seabiscuit would not see my dismay. They would see a happy warrior, so help me God.

If Salvatore hit me with the addiction smear, it would be in the last week. He would unleash a scandal like Pandora's box with no time to explain. In the fog of war, he'd escape judgment. I braced myself but would accept whatever came. I had been accused of insurance fraud and many other bad things. Nonetheless, the danger snapped the pessimism like a twig. I was viable and had a puncher's chance.

Snyder took over the role of preparing me for editorial boards. I finally got endorsed by both newspapers, much to Oxman's chagrin. Elected officials like Senator Shirley Kitchen and Councilwoman Blondell Reynolds Brown jumped into the race and attracted Black voters and bragged I was endorsed by both rags. Councilman Frank DiCicco persuaded Italians to give the Irish kid a chance. Lace curtain lawyers, accountants, and staffers abandoned their cushy offices to walk blue-collar streets.

Bill DeWeese, the house minority leader, sat alone at the Palm Bar, facing the dining room in a seersucker suit and white bucks. His crew cut spared a strip of hair in the front that doubled as pompadour and comb over. Rubbing his jaw like a professor, he spoke first. "I just wanted to have a look at you." He hadn't even introduced himself. "I've nothing to give you and want nothing from you today."

He had heard about my "strenuous and epic entreaties" and thought a "congregative convocation was propitious." I didn't understand what he was saying. But that was his reputation. He was generally incomprehensible but had advanced prodigiously up the ladder in Harrisburg. "I heard you might win." He drank an Arnold Palmer and asked if I wanted anything. "I'm not going anywhere. I love this game. Maybe we can help each other sometime." He wanted to be Speaker of the Pennsylvania House of Representatives. I was glad I had chosen to run for the state senate. DeWeese was one of those quirky, interesting people who just showed up on my path. I wouldn't bet on him to get to the speakership, but he showed me there was a lot I didn't know. I would see him often in many challenging and delightful situations as we walked the tightrope of Pennsylvania politics.

Only two unions endorsed me despite Salvatore's dismal labor voting record. They liked his juice and followed the lead of Jonny Doc. But Joe Dougherty, the leader of Local 401 of the Ironworkers, was impressed when Mike McGeehan vouched for me. Joe Dougherty resented Johnny Doc's dictatorial style and arrogance. Joe became a reliable ally, and we would utilize his union hall for rallies. It would take eight years of relentless backbiting for Doc to turn Joe against me. My other union was Local 1823, Carpenters Floor Layers, and with the leadership of young John McGrath, we were a juggernaut.

\* \* \*

Fumo had not gone to the point of no return until one of the last polls. We were trailing by twelve points. He shrugged at Snyder. "I guess you were right. Maybe we should pull out?" All the resources had resulted in a double-digit deficit.

Snyder's eyes bulged. "Are you fucking crazy? We've come up thirty-five points! We could win this thing!" Snyder became a cheerleader and denied ever doubting. We were charging for the tape but still needed help. Vince wanted a big rally to stir up enthusiasm for one last key figure—Chairman Bob Brady.

Bob Brady was the barrel-chested chairman of the most effective Democratic party in America. Bob had paid his dues to become chairman. The right-hand man of Pete Camille had become sergeant of arms of city council, a plum that enabled him to make friends with ward leaders. He waited his turn and then held on for decades as chairman. Nobody played the angles better or watched his own back better. Bob urged unity but knew how to divide when it was in his interest. He had Johnny Doc breathing down his throat and ward leaders asking for jobs. Brady became the consummate chalk player. And just before our rally, his chalk was firmly on Labor's choice, Salvatore.

If Fumo was Machiavelli, Brady was Talleyrand. His warm relationship with Salvatore, the only Philadelphian in the majority caucus, made perfect sense. Fumo didn't condemn Brady or fly into a rage. He'd walked in his shoes. All he wanted to do was make Bob pause. If he could do that for just one second, it could mean the razor-thin difference, if he could be made to utter, even grudgingly, "Stack's got a shot," all the better.

On that bright November morning, Senator Fumo's driver thought there was another event. A line of cars and trucks waited to get into the parking lot of Local 401, extending down the block. When he pulled to the front entrance, mostly men and some women wore blue and yellow Stack T-shirts, work boots, and sneakers. Children held their parents' hands like they were going to the circus. Young men and women hurried like it was a Metallica concert. Iron beams supported the outer roof like Roman columns. When they walked into the hall and saw hundreds of hard hats drinking coffee and kibitzing, Fumo recalled, "I nearly shit!" He wanted a show of force, and this was beyond his wildest imagination. He crossed his fingers. Now Brady needed to show up.

Brady was a busy guy and might make an excuse. But he didn't want to offend Fumo, who wasn't dead yet. He didn't care about my feelings. I was a distracting sideshow, a beneficiary of Fumo's ill-advised quest to get revenge on Salvatore.

I wasn't as surprised as Fumo at the sellout crowd. The campaign had been a roller coaster of miracles and debacles. Anything was believable. Fumo despised morning and it was 10 A.M. on Saturday. Brady entered the hall looking grumpy and ready to leave as soon as possible. Fumo greeted me excitedly and pointed at the growing crowd. Brady thought about his labor support when he looked into that audience. His white and silver Saint Laurent sweatshirt, a South Philly tuxedo, and pristine ivory sneakers displayed his elegant working-class side. I felt like I had the flu, pale and sweating but unflustered.

When I had Vince to myself, I asked, "Why does Brady dislike me?"

He chuckled. "Hank's his buddy and you're an inconvenience."

I was being naive and worried about my own feelings too much.

"You shouldn't care. The important thing is he's here to see this spectacle."

The speeches began and the roof came off. By the time Brady introduced me, the crowd thought I was the second coming. I fired them up like we were the Eagles going against the stinking Dallas Cowboys. Those men, women, and children ran out in fury to drop campaign material all over Northeast Philadelphia. Bob could feel his breakfast. Now he was nauseous and uncertain. With crimson cheeks and a sweaty brow, he departed the hall a changed man.

"Every star has aligned," Vince gushed. "If we don't win, it wasn't possible." Getting Brady there was crucial. "We had to get him on the fence. Maybe he's not so sure about Salvatore now." When I argued that Brady was our chair anyway, he looked at me like I was mentally ill.

Howard Cain informed Fumo that the recent poll showed we were just outside the margin of error of 4 ½ to 5 points. "I knew it!" Ken Snyder bragged. "Thank God we stayed in this race."

Salvatore's Hoodies ramped up the aggression, tore down posters, and collected lawn signs despite several truces. Cindy Mariela ran our field operation out of my parents' basement, which she had named "the compound." Cindy was in her early sixties and had Mediterranean skin and brown hair. She looked Sicilian but was Syrian. She kept this a secret from the other children in South Philadelphia during her troubled youth. As a teenager, she found camaraderie as a ward volunteer in the days of mob and party blending. She knew all the politicians and all the tricks. Unlike the amateurs, when she phoned someone in Salvatore's camp, they took her call. Both sides were losing money by stacking candidates' signs into trash heaps. "You stop and we'll stop." They did—for fifteen minutes—but it was like negotiating with the Soviets. The vandalism and theft indicated we were getting too close for comfort.

We staggered to the first Monday in November. On election eve, Cindy sent me home early. "You've worked harder than any candidate I've known. Get a good night's sleep because tomorrow you'll need all your energy for the victory lap."

Jim McGinley's brother John was a Catholic priest who said a lot of masses at McGinley and Stack events. We knew him well, and it was a family affair to have him in our living room as the indigo sky gave way to orange. The lights were on at 1247 Southampton Road. A handful of friends gathered in the room where I'd done my first interview with the *Inquirer*'s Bill Miller in 1988. Cindy loved the compound but usually worked out of the basement, where our campaign movements could be concealed.

"Let us pray." Father John asked for the best candidate to win. "And we all know it's Michael."

John Del Ricci sported a butterfly Band-Aid over his eyebrow and a fresh shiner. "What happened?" I asked him after communion.

He shrugged. "Some of the Hoodies tore down everything we put up, even at polling places." He grinned proudly. "We warned them not to do it again." They hadn't listened. "Now they won't be physically able to do it again."

The ward leaders and precinct captains held walkie talkies and wore backpacks with campaign materials inside. As I drove around the district with Johnny Del Ricci, the familiar voices crackled with anxiety. Johnny's bravado faded quickly as he responded to our troops who were under siege. Gene McAleer breathed heavily. "Alpha One, roger. We need bigger guys." The Painters and District 21 had aligned with Doc's Hoodies and were menacing Stack poll workers.

These intimidation tactics weren't new to the city but were to my district. Gene was built like Arnold Schwarzenegger so I didn't know where we would find anybody bigger. I took a deep breath, meditated, then began freaking out. "Calgon, get me the hell out of here!"

Victory lap? I asked Johnny Del Ricci to drop me off at home and go help Gene fight the barbarians. All that big talk about me chewing glass and standing up like a man was a gross exaggeration. I took off my suit, sat at the kitchen table with a yellow legal pad, and began writing a concession speech.

I was refreshed enough to put my suit back on and join Frank DiCicco at Decatur School later that night. The red brick structure in Parkwood had been the Little Big Horn of my previous elections. The endless blocks of row homes and mazes of cul-de-sacs were heavily Italian and Republican. Senator Fumo surprised me by sending a personal letter to Italian voters that proclaimed, "The best senator for Italian-Americans will be Michael Stack." A little gentleman with a thick accent held up the letter at his front door. "If Senator Fumo wants you, that's a gooda nuffa for me."

Vince tried to get America's mayor, Ed Rendell, to endorse me, but he refused. "I like Hank." But Fumo wasn't afraid of Rendell. Voters were impressed by a letter from Ed, a photo of his grinning face and bushy eyebrows gushing about my qualifications. Vince challenged, "Let's see that mother deny it!"

We squeezed every hand as if proposing matrimony. I knew Frank DiCicco for fifteen minutes, but he introduced me as his dear friend. At other polling places, workers became my aunt or cousin or sister or brother. Everybody claimed me. Those Parkwood Republicans smiled like warm molasses. I'll never forget their kindness. When the metal doors of that gymnasium clanked shut,

Frank and I embraced. I went to the compound and sat on the bed in my boy-hood room with Tonya next to me, undaunted and slightly amused. Mom and my sister Eileen announced they were departing for Local 401 for the count. Mom was oddly calm and happy, in a joyous spiritual trance, disturbingly opti-mistic like that night Dad got smoked for district attorney. "I really think God wants you to win," she said without the usual equivocation, "it's God's plan for you." She specialized in God's plan for me as a Mother Teresa with a black belt in codependent.

I was nervous when they left, but not petrified. I imagined that union hall filling up as it had a few days earlier. This was like nothing I'd ever experienced in politics. In a blink, I'd gone from Dad pushing me on a bike and catching my fastballs, to this audacious quest for power. I thought I could lose but knew I'd given my all. If there was a new chapter after this, I was grateful to have gone on the ride and had so many friends help me. Deep calmness came.

I admit now that I hoped all the commotion of my childhood learning problems and the shame that followed my addiction would be swept away mag-ically in one fell swoop, the title of senator like rain washing the slate clean. I didn't always know that was a substantial motivation, but the years have enlightened me.

I hadn't stopped pacing for months but now endured an hour of quiet, maddening stillness. I walked into the bathroom, turned out the lights, and tried to pray. We tried to find coverage of the race on TV. Ironically, Ken Snyder appeared as an analyst on a show with local legend Larry Kane, and Kane called our race "one to watch." Snyder stared into the camera as though into my soul, warning I had a slight lead "but it's very, very early." Did this tool want me to lose? I had a lead—a damn lead!

It was a crazy dream. This thing might happen.

Snyder transformed from detractor to thinking he was my creator. After the *Philadelphia Inquirer* and *Daily News* endorsed me, I encountered Neil Oxman at the copying machine in the law office. I think I said good morning before he stormed up to me in a frightening huff. "Don't think for one second Snyder got you endorsed by both papers! That was me, understand? That idiot didn't do shit." He stormed off and slammed doors. Victory had a thousand mothers and defeat was an orphan. It was a rare treat to get adopted by an abusive mother like Neil.

We got the first ominous call just before ten o'clock. "It looks like we've got this," Cindy Mariela uttered hesitatingly. "Come over to the hall. Fumo's on the way." Other calls clicked and went to voicemail.

I felt dizzy when I said to Tonya, "Let's go."

She grabbed her coat. "Do we have it?"

My phone buzzed.

"Stay where you are," Cindy said, "just to be safe." Some bad returns had come in and the lead was shrinking.

I checked a voicemail from David Kushner, Rabbi Isaacson's assistant who monitored the Russian Jewish polling areas. He read off the results from three polling places inside Temple Beth Solomon. My margin of five-to-one was unprecedented. "You got this, bud. It's like nothing we've ever seen."

Then the third maddening Cindy call. "Looks like you're going to be a senator. We're up by a thousand, and I don't think he can catch us."

We were sitting in the parking lot of Local 401 when she called again. Fumo had turned around and gone back to South Philly. Now he was on his way back. I ran my finger up and down my vibrating lips. Ten minutes later, she was convinced it was safe to enter the hall. During all this mayhem, we got confused and accidentally entered through the rear entrance and wandered through the crowd that was waiting for me to appear on stage. People hugged us and tugged at our clothes like we were the Beatles until we reached the stage and Cindy pulled us up the stairs and through the curtains. She whisked me to my father, who was studying returns, appropriately, in a smoky back room in front of a computer.

Dad's crimson cheeks betrayed apprehension. He still couldn't believe it. He had to see the last tally before he could banish the bone-crushing juggernaut of the past. But Cindy introduced him to the reality. "Mr. Stack, allow me to present Senator Stack." The nausea and fatigue were simultaneously euphoric and sickening. All the repressed sadness from devastating losses poured out like a waterfall. Twelve years of labor led to a marvelous victory. Dad was ecstatic, but our relationship had been dramatically reconfigured.

In every election, supporters and well-wishers fill stages. Ours was a beautiful, overcrowded riot with people falling off the sides. As balloons rose and confetti fell, bodies pushed against each other in the maddening crowd. The dim lighting in the union hall cast a dreamy glow. Everyone owned a piece of the victory and had a story to tell. McGeehan and Fumo raised my arms like a heavyweight champ. My eyes were slits from endless grinning and lack of sleep. Fumo wore a "STACK FOR SENATE" cap, freshly swiped from my little nephew's head, and a flight jacket out of *Top Gun*. "It's okay Joe-Joe. That guy paid for it," I consoled.

Fumo's giddiness bordered on instability, an insane happiness that made him hug strangers and dance erratically. Darth Vader had transformed into a crazy Han Solo, and we celebrated like the Death Star had just exploded. The final tally grew to a margin of five thousand votes, and the man who had frightened powerful people and leveraged the president of the United States was my comrade-in-arms and sugar daddy. We were bound together in glory, but how well did I know him?

"Tonight, we have fun, pal," the Prince of Darkness said. "Then we go to work. I've got some more tricks to show you." That giddy glimmer in his eye turned dark.

Hours flew by like minutes as we connected with hundreds of people, from family friends who knew me when I was a kid to new acquaintances. Winners picked up new friends fast, but our loyalists were from decades back. These gleaming faces reminisced about the old races, which made this one so special. I knew in my heart that I would not have made it without the continued support of all those people at the core: my father, my mother, and Pat and Jim McGinley. If I had them, I could run for anything.

After the big celebration, I was an emotional basket case. My suitcase of old baggage burst open. I thought I'd be transformed into this new senator with no grudges, trauma, or fear, but waves of anxiety swept in. To make matters worse, in taking out a powerful senator with influential friends, I had incurred the wrath of a roster of new enemies. My journey to becoming an intelligent, visionary leader in Harrisburg required me to travel the streets of brotherly blood.

The next day, a group of us lounged on sofas amid boxes and piles of posters in the compound basement. None of us had slept much, and the presidential election between George W. Bush and Al Gore remained unsettled. A voice from the side door asked, "Anyone home?" Bob Henon, Local 98's political director, strolled cautiously into the room. Three beefy Hoodies carried trays of hoagies behind him.

I said, "Come on in, Bob, we won't bite."

Henon had black and gray hair and a dry wit. He was in his early forties and would later become a city councilman and convicted felon. But let's not jump too far ahead. "John sends his congratulations," he said.

I paused. The sting came back. Doc had lied and brutalized but wanted to extend a laurel. Cindy nudged my elbow. I accepted the peace offering. "Please tell John thank you." I put aside my rawness and felt hopeful for two seconds. The door slammed shut. Cindy was prophetic. "It's not over. They don't take losing well. We're going to have problems with them."

Ken Snyder wanted to walk me around the media like his show pony. "I've scheduled a press conference for noon outside your law office. Now act like a senator." Guys like him who never ran for office would give me advice like that all the time. "Only talk about policy and legislation. Don't talk about the campaign." His wardrobe suggestion was a sweater and jeans so that I'd appear relatable. Snyder hugged me like a brother—if he were Cain and I were Abel. Three TV networks covered it. I hadn't been able to get them together once during the campaign. The *Philadelphia Inquirer* used a photo that conveyed a cocky, youngish newcomer. I was sleepy and a little bitter but forced a confident grin. They would use that picture for years, particularly when I was in hot water.

It started to simmer only ten days later. Rumors swirled that Salvatore wanted to contest the election and was badgering Republican leaders. He had also urged Montgomery County District Attorney Bruce Castor, a publicity hound, to investigate me for insurance fraud. Castor was so ambitious; he might assemble a grand jury. Dad and I immediately ran to see legendary criminal attorney John Rogers Carroll.

Carroll's eyes twinkled through his bifocals as his fingers formed a triangle under his chin. Irascible, cynical, and frank at seventy-five, he didn't care that we were only working with rumors. Rumors became a reality without caution. I hadn't even been sworn in yet, but expensive white-collar attorneys would give me this advice for years. After he listened to the facts scrupulously, he was convinced there was nothing to worry about. It was like Brady's couch again. Two wise old men talking about me like I was in a frame.

"If he doesn't say anything." Rogers took a sip of his coffee. "But they always think they need to explain. Worse, they think they can explain." Years earlier, Carroll told me about his years of destructive drinking at Dad's behest. "That's what gets you in trouble." I followed the advice and kept my mouth shut.

Nothing came of Salvatore's desperate efforts.

# CHAPTER FOUR

# ENTER THE POOR WINNER

Bob Mellow invited me to the leadership luncheon a month before I was sworn in. Lunch was catered in that lovely conference room where I had been vilified and adored as I chatted with Allegheny Senator Jack Wagner. Wagner's easy smile and perfect sprayed hair seemed inconsistent with his Marine Corps background. The Vietnam veteran didn't notice I had just come out of the bush as he took a generous swig of his tasty beverage. I immediately lasered in on the tall brown bottle with the unmistakable golden label. Hank's Root Beer. The old senator had made a fortune, leveraging concessions at the airport and supermarkets.

"What's that doing here, Senator?" I asked indignantly.

Mellow caught my eye, then slammed his hand on the conference room table. "Get that root beer the fuck out of here!"

Wagner was shocked. "Are you kidding me?" He forced a chuckle.

I wasn't smiling. "That guy trashed me and tried to send me to jail."

Wagner was pale. "But you won the election! What do you care?"

I took a deep breath. "I'm from Philadelphia, Senator. I care!"

He shook his head partly from embarrassment, partly from dismay. "Boy, you Philly guys are poor winners."

I joined the other twenty senators in the Democratic caucus known as "the ladies auxiliary." Senator Vince Hughes was a big booster in my race, and at a fundraiser in my dad's office, he promised the excited crowd a majority. Fumo stood against the wall, arms folded, head shaking slowly in the negative. Hughes asked Fumo his opinion. "I just want to pick up one." We also had a new senator from Monroe County, Sean Logan, who succeeded a Democrat. He tried to hide his youth by growing a Tom Selleck mustache. We became fast friends and stayed at the same hotel on Carlisle Pike along with Jay Costa, Jerry LaValle, and Wayne Fontana.

Logan turned out to be a merciless practical joker, and I was an early victim. While gassing up at the Sunoco, I left the car running. Logan's driver sped up to the pump and Sean jumped out. Panic ensued when I saw my car was gone. As I ran around the lot, Logan appeared from the back. "Did you lose your car, Senator?" He flung the keys. "You Philly boys are too trusting. You should learn to lock your doors."

During a floor debate, he falsely told Fumo that I was about to vote against his bill. Fumo's eyes bulged, and as he broke into a sprint, Logan chuckled and grabbed at Vince's jacket like it was the leash of a playful pitbull. "That mother f . . . !" Vince yelled before Logan reined him in.

Vince's Darth Vader reputation betrayed his legislative brilliance. He was visionary and saw five steps ahead of senators and governors. But he was both savvy and humble enough to hire the most talented staff who foiled even the most cunning foes. While some senators leveraged satchels of cash, Fumo gained power. His mental agility and oratorical skills were reminiscent of my father in the courtroom. He harnessed facts quickly and pummeled opponents decisively. But his need to boast of Mensa membership revealed insecurity. Nonetheless, Republicans quaked when he strutted to the floor for a debate. Conversely, we got steamrolled when he was gone.

Mitch Rubin became a millionaire with Fumo's assistance and followed him around like a basset hound. Fumo made him a Pennsylvania Turnpike commissioner, and the short, bald guy with the caterpillar mustache became richer and more convinced of his own greatness. At my swearing-in, he grabbed my elbow. "Don't let him think he owns you. Be your own man or he'll take you for granted." Fumo knew I wasn't like the others. He spent years keeping me out of the state senate. When he needed me to win, he knew I could save his life. I wasn't some stooge. My parents were lawyers and public servants, educated and respected. He admired my intelligence and background, and often joked about our colleagues' lack of it—another sign of insecurity.

I hated him for years, as if he were the quarterback of the Dallas Cowboys. Now I was one of his star receivers. I took Rubin's advice to heart because things always changed. Fumo was not only talented but treacherous and selfish, a spoiled rich kid with a chip on his shoulder. I needed him to secure economic development funds and advance in the caucus. I loved him for what he had done and for what he could do for me. He had been my enemy. Now he was my blood brother. But relationships are like money, fungible. In politics, they come and go. They were like the one with Frank DiCicco, the one where we became "dear friends" five minutes after meeting.

* * *

Our world was turned upside down on September 11, 2001, when the United States was attacked. I was giving a speech to the fifth-grade class at Fitzpatrick

School when a teacher burst in, looking confused. A plane had flown into the World Trade Center. She thought it might be an amateur flying a small plane. She gave the news without seeming alarmed, and I finished my speech and walked out to that perfect blue sky as reports came in. I dismissed my staff and waited for instructions, but from whom? I realized I had an actual responsibility to protect our citizens. The strutting, posing, and playing were over. It was all very real.

Within days, Governor Tom Ridge addressed a joint session and announced that he would join President Bush as Homeland Security Secretary. Trivial battles of local politics evaporated as the very survival of our country teetered on the precipice. Senators occupied the front rows in the spectacular state house chamber, where Ridge explained our challenge. His square jaw and tall, athletic figure projected the quintessential brave American leader. He would no longer quibble with state budgets and school vouchers but monitor terror and invasions. I had escorted him to the budget address months earlier as a plum from Senator Mellow. Then he seemed mediocre and partisan, now like a superhero.

Lieutenant Governor Mark Schweiker succeeded Ridge, and Pennsylvania State Senate Pro Tempore Bob Jubelirer became lieutenant governor. Shweiker, a former Bucks County commissioner, was always deferential and polite when he presided over the state senate. He never played partisan favorites by making me wait. He was down-to-earth and likable, and showed amazing poise while succeeding to governor.

The country was at war and our state had been struck. I wanted to join the military, but Fumo advised that I was crazy. "You can serve by getting reelected." We had worked too hard for me "to go play Soldier Boy." In these dark times, he was portrayed in the media as an even darker figure. He predicted rightly that enormous amounts of funding would flow from the federal government to fight terrorism. He said, "Mark my words, they'll use it to investigate us."

He was right on both counts.

Former Speaker of the US House Tip O'Neill said all politics were local. I opened the district office in Parkwood, the heart of the beast, where I'd been trounced multiple times. I won by a whisker in 2000 and wanted to build on my success. I hired Cindy Mariela as chief of staff and Joe Stewart as chief counsel. As was the Philadelphia tradition, I tapped ward leaders or their assignees, but they would need to work. In a strip mall roughly fifty feet from the Decatur School, our mothership ran like a machine. Soon neighbors poured in and got their problems solved. My staff became proficient at constituent service encouraging lines reminiscent of those of Congressman Barrett. My directive was that the answer to any constituent request was yes. From passport renewal to electric bills, the word got out—if you had a problem, "Go to Stack's office." A committee woman once asked my father to get a family of ducks out of her yard. He was glad to call animal control, which happened to be a city agency. I followed his lead.

Pundit Chris Matthews wrote that if you weren't worried about your next opponent, you weren't a successful politician. I'd beaten a legend, but many thought it was a fluke. They jabbed about all that help from Fumo and claimed we stole the election using illegal Russian votes. Our campaign had been surgical in pounding Salvatore on the issues, but he was still popular after the loss. My freshness was getting stale already. That was the backdrop for the "Where's Waldo" story in the *Northeast Times*.

During the campaign, I was omnipresent. Now I was like Waldo! Where was I? I happened to be in Harrisburg, voting on legislation or working with other senators in the caucus. The journalist who wrote the story could easily have verified the facts. Nonetheless, the story set off a little firestorm and created drama on my staff. Fumo chuckled, "They always just make it up." I was outraged that the *Northeast Times* would completely distort reality. In retrospect, it was routine media jabbing, and I should've had thicker skin. But as my mom often proclaimed, I was too sensitive. Being trapped in Harrisburg listening to speeches from other Democrats was hell. Then session went into late hours.

Waldo was my first bad story as a senator, and I became a little more cynical. The media were not my friend. I always thought I could reach out with my effervescent personality and explain things. Vince said that was giving them a chance to "fuck you even more."

Waldo propelled me into fear-induced workaholism. After I stormed around the district making speeches at countless community centers, sports banquets, and block parties, Johnny Del Ricci gushed to minions, "He's an animal!" That was the highest compliment to a Philadelphia politician. The only politician who ever did it better was Ed Rendell, and it was close. But I liked being a maniac because it was our brand. One didn't embrace constituents out of love but from a rage that stemmed from deep insecurity. I was blessed with other skills, but none of them added up to a hill of beans if I wasn't ready to roll my sleeves and shake every damn hand in the room.

John Dougherty's star kept rising, and trades followed as if in a trance. He was better than Jimmy Hoffa because he never got above spreading rumors like a high school girl. My labor voting record was a hundred percent, yet suspicion spread. Philadelphia's parochial labor leaders heard amorphous rumblings about my perfidy. Dougherty and his gang reportedly met at the hall and outlined regular whispering strategies. Simultaneously, Doc tried to win me over by trashing Fumo. In babbling, incomprehensible conversations at the Philadelphia Sporting Club, Doc claimed, "You think he's helping you, but he's hurting you." He often stood naked after being in the steam room. I stared into my locker as he ranted, "You're with the wrong guy," or, "his days are numbered." It was very uncomfortable. I didn't run away because I wanted to hear what he was thinking. Then I regretted it. I never saw him exercise, but he was always sweaty.

I may have been a poor winner, but Big John was a terrible loser. Doc and Fumo continued their rivalry, but the chalk slid toward Dougherty. He represented the future, some would say. But what could he do ninety miles up the turnpike? Philadelphia had battles in Harrisburg. Fumo was the only Democrat who controlled the process. We relied on him to harness votes and leverage our best budget deals. Dougherty could never pull a budget together or organize voting blocks. He didn't have the intelligence or temperament and lacked the humility to acknowledge Fumo's supremacy. He was jealous and preferred to kill him.

All action revolved around the budget deadline of June 30. Any important legislative initiative got wrapped up in the process. Only a handful of legislators had any say in the budget. Most legislators lived in blissful ignorance, waiting to get told how to vote. The process was clandestine and difficult to read. The governor often seemed clueless, no matter who it was. I was approached several times by Rendell's assistant, Charlie Breslin, during his administration for information. We belong to the Philadelphia Sporting Club, and Charlie chatted with me about different legislative initiatives, but he was always probing. Often, he walked back to Governor Rendell, who was toweling off, and whispered in his ear. My relationship with Fumo provided the inside knowledge of legislative contents and timing. In 2006, Rendell needed gaming to pass to fund his budget. He didn't even know if the bill would move. Republicans wanted the revenue but had moral qualms. They overcame them to get cash without taxes from the budget but didn't want to vote for new taxes. It was the age-old story; everyone had their hand out. That's how legislation moved. Fumo always had the information on when and how, and he gathered it like Pac-Man.

Fumo's friends wanted state development funds, grant money, and contracts, and he could get or stop it. His annual Truman Dinner raised a million in one night at the Society Hill Sheraton, where Republicans joined the black-tie crowd of Fumocrats. At that fabulous party, everybody was a Fumocrat. People drank to excess and partied like it was the 1980s. I'd been awed by our Jefferson Jackson dinner in travels with my father, but this was a whole different stratosphere. Fumo's donors paid five and ten thousand dollars but knew that was a drop in the bucket. He made people rich who spotted opportunity and had the savviness to ask for his help. Developers got the investment to build apartment buildings. Technology companies received tax-free zones.

Fumo's close associates were South Philadelphian grinders with eighth-grade educations—not Mensa material. They surrounded him at his table, trumping senators as we sat nearby, astonished by the extravagance of seafood towers, Cuban cigars, Champagne, and Bananas Foster. Even if I had come aboard at a time when his stature was descending, he looked like the king of the world. The mayor, congresspeople, and celebrities like Peter Nero, the world-famous Philly Pops Maestro, kissed the ring. Fumo loved statuesque blonds, and his latest lady, Dottie, was six feet and breathtaking in a black strapless gown. She had been his personal masseuse, so he didn't have far to go for a date. Vince thanked the crowd for their "investment in exciting newcomers like Mike Stack." No wonder Johnny Doc was jealous.

The Republicans had an insurmountable majority in the senate, but it was sacred ground for all. Bob Jubelirer worshiped our traditions and mystique to the point of tears. He became emotional while praising bipartisanship, and tears streamed down his cheeks. He cried on cue when he wanted something. As an actor, I recognized that value. And I never saw two greater thespians than Fumo and Jubelirer, particularly as they debated. It was like a Hollywood swordfight between Flynn and Rathbone until the cameras faded out, and then they danced like Astaire and Rogers. Bob needed funding for the shining city on the hill, Penn State University, and put his arm across Fumo's shoulder to get it. The man who ran the commonwealth from roughly twenty blocks in South Philadelphia reasoned like Socrates with the Altoona Penn State trustee who didn't really hate taxes, just voting for them. Fumo didn't take me for granted because he couldn't. But he occasionally cajoled me to vote the wrong way, like the bill to shield Crown Cork and Seal from asbestos litigation.

* * *

One day, Fumo stormed into my office and tossed a memorandum onto my desk. It was authored by his counsel, Christopher Craig, and explained how shielding Crown, a can manufacturer in my district, would be a travesty to injured workers. Crown was a major employer and one of the few remaining manufacturers in Philadelphia. I turned a few pages of the memo and discovered an attached brief from the Philadelphia Trial Lawyers that Craig paraphrased. I supported the trial lawyers "except against my neighbors." He smiled. "No problem. I didn't know." I appreciated that Fumo could be reasonable and understood how important Crown and its two hundred jobs were. Nonetheless he voted against the legislation but didn't go nuts on the floor or twist arms.

I became a heavy-hitting senator during the process. The bill needed to work its way through the lower chamber first, where steely, pugnacious majority leader John Perzel could push hardest. Perzel had been the head waiter at Pavio's, a restaurant frequented by Boss Billy Meehan, who took him under his wing. In a short time, Perzel went from house member to majority leader and eventually to Speaker. His tenaciousness flipped the house to Republican, and he became the most powerful Republican from the most-hated city. State Representative George Kenney led the floor fight. But Perzel couldn't help him against the opposition. The trial lawyer's strategy to convolute and confuse the narrative worked perfectly to defeat the bill.

The real purpose of the bill was to limit Crown's exposure in litigation because of their acquisition of asbestos company Mundet. Crown never manufactured asbestos, and the bill limited liability to claims before Mundet's acquisition. It wasn't as confusing as it sounded in the house. Crown was not depriving injured workers of anything. They hadn't manufactured asbestos, only cans, and hadn't caused injuries related to it.

I got to know my colleagues better by visiting them in their offices and talking to them on the floor. I thought the bill would pass in the house and then require passage in the senate. Jay Costa, the dark-haired scion of a political family from Allegheny County, promised to help. He also promised the trial lawyers. After the bill was defeated by a substantial margin, he and several other senators reported I had their vote. Of course, they thought they'd never have to prove it.

Crown went back to the drawing board, and I got the unique opportunity to work with my father on the new bill. He had been their lawyer years before I got elected. Senate council advised there was no conflict in joining forces. I was also familiar with the skilled lobbyist that would help. The Wodjak firm persuaded Democrats, and Greenlee and Associates pushed the Republicans. We simplified the narrative for the second battle that started in the senate, and things went well. Crown's position, that it was responsible from the time it took ownership for new claims, sounded reasonable. My neighbors, employees with kids in college, descended upon the capitol. Personal visits from real people always made a big impression on me, and I knew it would work with my colleagues. Soon both sides wanted to help.

The bill made its way through the committee rapidly. I reminded Senator Costa of his commitment. "I thought that thing was dead," he complained.

"It's alive again and it's going to pass."

Jay chuckled like I was kidding myself.

I used my Irish blarney on my Italian friend. Why couldn't he be more like his brother, Representative Paul Costa, who protected jobs and families? Paul voted for the bill in the state house the first time.

"Be like pro-business Costa," I teased.

About the same time, I offered a resolution that promoted families having dinner together regularly. Jay's mother saw me on the Pennsylvania Cable

Network and urged, "Jazeel, you need to help Senator Stack save families." I had him cornered.

Senator Tommy Tomlinson was my Republican partner in the state senate. Many Crown employees resided in his adjacent Bucks County district. Tomlinson had a fabulous head of silver hair and the warm disposition of a funeral director. People had been dying to meet him for years, and it helped him become a state senator. We coordinated impassioned speeches on the floor while Crown employees waved from the Gallery.

Dad made the trip to Harrisburg to pitch the bill in our caucus room. He had been in politics his whole life but never had that kind of access. He revered public officials, but I knew what knuckleheads my colleagues were. Nonetheless, it was an honor to open doors for my old man, who had opened so many for me. And on vote day, it wasn't even close. We carried it, 41–8. Fumo and Tina Tartaglione were shocked at how badly we whipped them.

My reputation for tenacity and effectiveness grew exponentially. It was educational to watch all the fence sitters collapse once it was clear the bill would pass.

Johnny Doc used that occasion to incite the trial lawyers against me. They were his allies for several reasons, not the least being the number of injured union members needing representation. I had been an advocate for accident victims as an attorney, but Doc relentlessly exploited any rift. I could never make any remark or vote in obscurity. Anything I did that could be taken out of context or as an insult was whispered or yelled down the lane. Nobody bothered to check my voting record.

I grudgingly watched Fumo for years on the stage at our big Democratic dinners as he received thunderous applause. Chairman Brady praised him for "always bringing home the bacon." The strangeness that this enigmatic genius was now a close friend hadn't worn off. Our offices on the second floor of the east wing made us capitol dorm buddies, only our digs had mahogany walls, chandeliers, and polished brass. Nonetheless, I could visit Vince by walking twenty-five feet and seeing his gatekeeper, Sue Swift, a stone-faced brunette who blocked his office door. When I cheerfully appeared, she leered like grim death from behind her wooden wall. It wasn't just Fumo she was protecting. When the feds raided, they stumbled onto her secret embezzlement from senate accounts.

It was awkward visiting Fumo in his spectacular office with its giant computer screen in front of his face, but it got easier. He had a gleeful laugh when planning to stick it some arrogant lobbyist or giant soul-sucking corporation. He abhorred bullies after being roughed up as a kid in hard scapple South Philly. His adulterous father was convicted of fraud and gave his bank to Fumo.

At times, he hated his father but resented his maltreatment. He carried the ambivalence of shame and pride. The family was disgraced, his mother was betrayed, yet Fumo became wealthy. Kids teased and assaulted the spoiled only child, and he developed an underdog's mentality. Predictably, he saw PECO and Verizon as bullies who ate the little guy's lunch. Those who were bullied often became bullies. Vince spent every day looking for people or organizations to punch. I didn't mind helping.

\* \* \*

Senator Bob Mellow got elected in Scranton when he was twenty-seven years old. He looked even younger than that, so when a lobbyist barged into his office and demanded "to see the senator," Mellow put a box down and asked, "What's it about?"

The insolent man huffed, "It's none of your business, young man. I'll tell it to the senator."

Mellow didn't care that the guy had made a mistake. He should've been respectful to whoever he was talking to.

Mellow was from gritty Scranton and didn't like pretension. He, too, thought he was an underdog. Like Fumo, he came to power young. They were competitive and at times catty and immature toward each other. But Mellow backed me in my losing races and vied for my affection, while Vince had been for my opponent. The leaders were nothing in a legislative body without their members. Mellow wanted to hold onto his post of minority leader. Vince cherished his own since he controlled the purse. Both made sure I had all the staff and office space I wanted. At times, they were spiteful and disparaging, like an old married couple who had been together too long. They embraced in public and bickered in private. Mellow's vast, spectacular office suite sandwiched my quaint little office against Fumo's mahogany command center. I was nestled in there with two other senators, Vince Hughes and Sean Logan, like puppies between the big dogs. They could summon us on a whim or appear unannounced like jealous spouses.

I worked hard and hosted fundraisers in Harrisburg and Philadelphia. Congressman Ozzie Myers was recorded on the federal wiretap saying, "Money talks and bullshit walks." He had a point. Many Fumocrats relied on Vince to raise their money. Dougherty's minions did the same. But I wanted to be independent. Raising my own campaign cash was important, yet I liked Vince's style. He adored La Veranda, and we both considered it lucky. I had to defend myself against what was certain to be a tough reelection. I wanted people to know I had a tough big brother. La Veranda belonged to both of us.

# CHAPTER FIVE

# SCANDAL COMES WITH THE JOB

My father continued to run the ward and recruit other candidates to challenge Republicans. It still wasn't easy, and we ended up with some oddballs, one of which was a former postman named John Farley. He aimed to challenge Brian O'Neill for city council, even though he lacked sophistication and initiative. A fiasco ensued when he was unable to secure enough signatures to get on the ballot. The appearance of supplemental "kitchen table petitions" led to my father's indictment on election fraud. The tedious months leading up to it culminated in a sad, sublime turning of the screw. My dear friend Jim McGinley and long-term committeewoman Arlene Petroff joined him on a televised "perp walk." Turning this into such a media spectacle was an attempt to drag me into scandal. Our local partisan rag, the *Northeast Times*, flashed sensational headlines about my sinister maneuvers, demanding "What did the senator know and when did he know it?" like it was Watergate.

I was mortified to watch my father's slog from a lifetime of distinguished service through public embarrassment. He was almost disbarred after fifty years of practice and faced jail time. He was a tough man but took a physical toll from the pressure. I visited him at the compound to check in and seek counsel. He sat at his place next to the phone at the head of the long kitchen table, the powerful Northeast Ward leader, with a notepad and pot of tea. "We are not going to focus on negative things from such a despicable person," he emphasized. That such a great man could be made to suffer over a contrived scandal was heartbreaking. We tried to be charitable but soon vilified the despicable, unaccountable, lying, unemployed mailman and imagined him on the rack. Dad's skin was gray and his hands shook, but he smiled optimistically. His best performance was yet to come.

He performed magnificently at his indictment. Dressed in the same jeff cap and Irish sweater as the day he disposed of my Buick, he stopped to talk to a reporter. "I've written a novel, *Five Keys to the Orient*. It's a thriller and will be available in stores soon." The reporter was stunned, hoping to embarrass him. We were watching from a television at the shore. I didn't know whether to cry or cheer. "You tell 'em, Pop!" Tonya yelled at the screen.

Fumo worked behind the scenes to limit the damage and seek a plea deal. I was torn. I wanted the scandal to go away, but I didn't want Dad to plead to criminal charges. Instigators got in my ear and called my father selfish for jeopardizing my career by not pleading. He would not have faced that kind of heat had I not been a senator. But I generally kept my mouth shut and stayed busy. The charges remained like a cancer in slow remission, but the scandal lost steam. As my election approached, I stood tall and ready for a fight. Instead of becoming Daniel Webster, I was more like Jake LaMotta.

There were rumors that Salvatore would run again or some other big-name Republican. But my hard work impressed the chalk players. I faced Sam Mirarchi, a young assistant attorney general who bragged that big money was on the way.

Mirarchi had a full head of dark hair and a charming demeanor. Sicilian grandmothers pinched his cheeks at the Saint Leo's Italian festival in Mike McGeehan's neighborhood. I would have left him alone, but McGeehan demanded I get over there "to ruin little Sammy's day." Two Irish lads charmed the crowd, hugged every grandmom, and kissed every bambino. Sam had a pile of handouts nobody wanted anymore. When our eyes met, I could see his tear ducts filling, ready to overflow into a river of anguish. That was why I drove down Roosevelt Boulevard on that beautiful fall day.

My relationship with my dad had changed dramatically. He was the coach who helped me to the big leagues. But Fumo now guided me through the corridors of power. I sought Dad's advice, but he often deferred to Fumo. A subtle, uncomfortable vibe, possibly jealousy, permeated our communication. Perhaps he thought I brought on the heat and caused his indictment. He admired elected officials like they were movie stars, and it had to be annoying to hear "say hello to the senator for me." He told clients that he controlled me, that he had the senator in his pocket. Disputes with state agencies got resolved more easily. I couldn't track who he was talking to or what he was saying. It wasn't his duty to tell me, but misunderstandings often resulted in federal investigations. Of course, I wanted to help my dad, but I was more cognizant that elected officials were targets.

As a Philadelphia politician, I feared the feds. Fumo claimed they were trying to get us. I admired law enforcement and prosecutors and had interviewed for the job of assistant US attorney. But in Philadelphia, politicians were always going to jail for corruption. The sea was stocked full of crooked fish, and a friend dropped this line regularly, "but the shiny ones get caught." The same friend furthered cautioned "the higher you get, the more dangerous it becomes." He predicted they were in that very restaurant enjoying lobster bisque while perusing for new targets.

My father went into politics because he wanted to help people. I'd watched him do it my whole life. He represented people in court for free and made calls to get people out of trouble. But he was a rascal and a wrangler who took risks. He was both honest and cagey, if that's possible. You always got the impression that he was withholding something for your own good, or his.

He grew up in a crazy household with a drinking congressman father and a scornful mother, yelling in brogue or torturing with shrieking silence. His brother, Jimmy, had cerebral palsy and hydrocephalus that brought shame to Irish people back in the day. Dad spent a lot of time out of the house and recruited buddies as buffers at home. I didn't know much about him until we started campaigning together. But we never talked about what it would be like if we achieved the impossible dream.

He was an industrious attorney, but his best game was real estate. He had the foresight to see that waterfront property on the industrialized Delaware River would someday be valuable. Dad formed a corporation called Beach Street with other partners, which would blow up in controversy without warning. For tax purposes, he divided the shares among his children, and as one of five kids, I had a 4% stake. The company owned real estate from the time I was a teenager. Without my knowledge, the partners began discussions with a casino about buying the land. Then an obscure amendment was attached to a bill that allowed Beach Street to purchase riparian rights from the state. The customary price was one dollar because riparian rights were the underwater portion of land that was valueless unless developed above ground. The state had sold riparian rights for one dollar for centuries.

* * *

My almost fatal heart attack started early in my second term while standing on the senate floor. I didn't know about the amendment until CJ Hafner, our chief counsel, approached me during a recess.

"What's this Beach Street amendment about?" he asked.

I didn't have any idea. In retrospect, I should have demanded the bill be tabled. Instead, the gavel banged, and the roll call began.

I got nervous and asked the whip, Senator Mike O'Pake, what to do.

He advised abstaining from the vote. "You're fine, if you just don't vote."

He was half right and, in politics, that spelled completely wrong. I'd frozen. That's what I did when I was confused. I thought I should know the answer, and like a dumb pupil, it was my fault. Yes, it was my dyslexia. I had been faking knowing the answers even when I was clueless since first grade. This trauma repeated itself over and over. I wasn't just mad at myself but deeply, inexplicably ashamed. The furor that ensued would set it on fire.

A few days later, a front-page story identified me as voting on a bill to give my family a casino and rake in millions. They used the familiar photograph of me in the sweater from the 2000 election. I looked so satisfied, like I was going to lick my lips. This public controversy was far more intense than Dad's indictment for voter fraud. CJ Hafner paced around my office, blaming me for being evasive. A media specialist accompanied him to help put out the fire, but the frumpy dude was overmatched.

That was the start of needing extra consultants and lawyers to steer me through public controversy. I needed special tutors as a little kid struggling in school, but this was big boy trouble. I always envisioned that I would have press conferences with a free exchange of ideas with the media. That was pure fantasy. They were piranhas that wanted to feast on my carcass and had to be avoided for my very survival. John Rogers Carol advised keeping my mouth shut. I'd done it with my dad's controversy. I needed all the discipline in the world to do it now because they were chasing me around with microphones.

Fumo surmised I was in mortal peril and dispatched Ken Snyder to save me. We hunkered down and dissected the facts as sweat dripped down my temples. Characteristically, Snyder thought I was cooked initially, but after listening to my version, he felt better. The first big negative story came from a reporter named Chris Brennan.

Snyder shook his head contemptuously. "I am certain that when that idiot Brennan called, he thought you would be announcing your resignation."

I hate to mention Chris Brennan, the *Daily News* and *Inquirer* political reporter who raked me over the coals, often at Dougherty's prompting. He wrote so many stories about me. My pulse quickened whenever he called. I never heard from him when I accomplished something great. But the excitement of dodging danger felt natural and stimulating, even if excruciating, like a deep tissue massage from an angry Swedish drag queen.

Senator O'Pake could have helped by calling a recess when the bill started moving. I could've got myself organized, disclosed ownership of the land, and then asked for a ruling from the chair about whether to vote on the bill. I could've abstained or voted in peace. I should never have worried about stopping the process to ask for help. But I simply didn't know what to do. Nonetheless, I was angry with my dad for letting me get blindsided. When I confronted him, he seemed mystified. His partners assured him it was necessary to move quietly to avoid controversy. They were horrendously wrong.

After the initial explosion, the facts came out that my family didn't own a casino. But that damned photograph of me in the sweater was everywhere. The truth trickled out that I had disclosed in my annual ethics report the 4% share in Beach Street, even though it wasn't required. I could never get into the papers or on TV for my good acts, but with Beach Street, I ran from hordes of reporters.

After the coronary symptoms subsided, the exhilaration was like a drug. I hadn't looked for it, but controversies found me like a magnet. The shadowy casino silhouettes, whoever they were, vaporized, and any interest in buying our land sailed down the river over cheaply purchased riparian rights.

I felt like I had been framed. I wasn't really like Fumo and Dad, maneuvering secretly. But staffers and lobbyists started thinking I was. They were cynical about Philadelphia senators and thought I had constructed a cover story about Beach Street. Maybe I was dodging the feds, like Fumo.

All I ever wanted was election to the senate. I didn't care about money. But I was starting to look like a master criminal. Fumo liked money and how it made him look and feel. He had inherited a bank from his father and made $1 million a year as an attorney at Dilworth Paxson. Perks of his chairmanship paid for dinners, cars, and yachts.

Fumo followed in the footsteps of South Philadelphia legends who lined their own pockets and went to prison. They competed to show who could be most audacious. But Fumo always thought he was the smartest. In the 1970s, he was convicted of hiring ghost employees while serving as the head of the Civil Service Commission. On the day of his sentencing, the judge tossed out the conviction. Fumo had packed for prison but was free to go. After that, he felt he was being hounded by the feds and that he needed to stay one step ahead. Whether he had an in with the judge or not, Fumo always thought he could beat them.

I was mortified when he was asked why he wasn't clever enough to get a casino share. I didn't want to hear another word about Beach Street as long as I lived. Then I strolled into the appropriations luncheon while he told a story. No one could figure out how to get ownership in a casino without going to jail. Once again, he was talking about Buddy Cianfrani and all his slick deals. "Until now!" He pounded a fist on the conference table and pointed at me. "Only this fucking guy!" The other senators roared in laughter as the color fell from my cheeks. More and more, as a public figure, I just wanted to run and hide.

Fumo spent a lot of time trying to punch people in the face. He leveraged giant corporations, like Comcast and Verizon, to pay him off so he wouldn't regulate and tax them. They couldn't give him satchels of cash like Buddy, but they could pretend to donate to the public good. Fumo founded the nonprofit Citizens Alliance which could technically accept their contributions. Millions of dollars went into the 501(c)(3) to clean streets, paint murals, and fund neighborhood projects. Those funds also paid for vacuum cleaners and vehicles the senator used for personal business. He thought it was legal, but it failed the sniff test. For a man who believed the feds were always watching him, this was blind ignorance. Suddenly, there were rumors the feds were investigating once more, and the loudest, like a dog whistle, was Johnny Doc.

Doc accosted me at the Sporting Club while standing naked for the countless time. Fumo had always sworn Doc was a confidential federal informant, so maybe Doc wanted me to see he wasn't wearing a wire. I didn't see any wires, but I was trying not to look. Rumors were lethal and considered bad form, but this Two Streeter never got the memo. But the technical waiver could be granted if he wasn't the origin. Doc would always attribute the rumor to someone else. He'd say he heard from Ronnie Donatucci that Fumo was being investigated. Or he heard the feds were searching Fumo's office. It was considered cowardly to talk like that, but somehow, he cajoled, intimidated, and inspired labor leaders and politicians to follow him.

Rumors about Fumo and the feds weren't new. He always thought he was being watched and took countermeasures. He loved technology and wanted all emails and texts to be encrypted. I could never master the codes and thought whispering in each other's ears was easier. I missed many communications because I couldn't access the decryption system. Once, he stormed into my office, demanding an answer.

"Vince, I couldn't remember the new code. It never works."

He calmed down. "But it only took fifteen seconds to get off your ass and walk over." He couldn't help himself.

He was charged with multiple federal crimes, like trying to conceal email or destroy hard drives because he thought it was legal. He was paranoid but reckless and poorly advised. Thinking a technical legality was useful defied logic.

There was no question that Fumo was a target. Powerful politicians always were, but he put his chin out. His style was belligerent and verbose, inviting scrutiny and danger. Two of his staffers wiped clean thousands of messages using spyware worthy of the CIA. Vince claimed his attorney, Richard Sprague, advised anything not subpoenaed could be destroyed. But there was no legal opinion written in Sprague's hand.

Fumo loved Sprague until turning violently, irrevocably against him. And it was a two-way street. Sprague's fame came from winning a libel suit against the *Philadelphia Inquirer*. Vince hated the rag, so they were fast friends, and

Sprague, a father figure. The paper had pursued a decades-long vendetta against Fumo for blocking the sale of their North Broad Street white elephant. Fumo's friends usually had a connection to enemies, like Snyder with Mayor Street and me with Salvatore. Fumo was shocked when Sprague turned on him, and he became more vulnerable to the federal litigation onslaught. Not only would Sprague abandon his friend at the courthouse, but he also testified against him. Many other friends became unavailable for his entreaties. That he was dismayed was uncharacteristic for such a cynical politician. It was revelatory of his failure to grasp the mortal danger.

I should've known Fumo wasn't perfect a year before his emergent dark times. He was susceptible to reckless errors just like the rest of the humans. The flurry of senate activity gradually died down on a spring day in 2005. As I read through legislative summaries at my desk, a staffer leaned down and whispered, "Senator Fumo would like to see you in the caucus room." I didn't know why the kid whispered until I got to the mahogany enclave. Fumo and Senator Mellow were just inside the door.

"We'd like to give you a raise," Mellow said.

Fumo smiled. "We'd like raises too." They snickered like they had a secret. They explained how they would increase the base pay of legislators from 16% to 34%, depending on the position. They had Governor Ed Rendell's commitment to sign the bill in exchange for passing slot machine legislation. The groundwork had already been done, and the Republicans were on board. They didn't ask me for anything but wanted to see my reaction. I shrugged. They were the smart guys, and they seemed confident.

I changed my mind after thinking about it for a while, remembering that I had hammered Salvatore in the 1988 race for voting himself a pay raise. "I'm not sure about this," I remarked to Sean Logan, who was sitting at his desk on the floor.

He chuckled. "It could be a shit show."

What an understatement.

* * *

The vote took place at 2 A.M. on July 7, without public review or commentary, and Governor Ed Rendell signed the bill into law. Outrage over the pay raise began immediately and took several victims. Justice Russell Nigro became the first Pennsylvania Supreme Court Justice to be denied retention. He had no real involvement other than being a member of the court that would also review the pay raise. Chief Justice Ralph Cappy helped draft the bill, and Supreme Court opinions upheld the pay raise. Nigro had been a Fumocrat, and he blamed

Fumo for his defeat, claiming a Machiavellian conspiracy. But it demonstrated that the public was inflamed and would hold everyone accountable.

On November 16, 2005, Governor Rendell signed the repeal and criticized the legislature. Nonetheless, a total of seventeen legislators were defeated in the 2006 primary elections, including senate President Pro Tempore Bob Jubelirer and senate Majority Leader Chip Brightbill. They were the first top-ranking Pennsylvania legislative leaders to lose the primary election since 1964.

The debacle demonstrated to me that our leaders were not flawless. Brightbill and Jubelirer ran the senate with amused contempt. They had an eight-member majority, which was like a monopoly. We had to fight just for the chance at public debate. They acted like they were doing us a big favor by letting us make speeches against the bills they were jamming through the legislature.

I made a speech attacking the Republicans every chance I got. They didn't feel threatened because they would win the vote. My old man urged me to be heard wherever I went. I did it as a long-shot candidate and as a senator. "Let them know you're in the room, and they'll have to deal with you, one way or another," he said. I didn't care if it was *a fait accompli*, I'd be making noise. I made speeches during petitions and remonstrances, a segment allotted to senators to speak after all the bills were voted. Newt Gingrich used the technique in Congress with the "Contract with America." I tried to start my own populous movement.

Although I'd won reelection comfortably in 2004, Dad's prosecution continued. The attorney general wanted to subpoena my testimony. The headline "Stack Called Before Grand Jury" would hurt. My lawyer wouldn't give them the negative campaign commercial but compromised on an interview.

Bob Scandone was built like a bear and skilled like a streetwise F. Lee Bailey. He was Fumo's nominee for the federal bench in the dispute with President Clinton. He wouldn't have been available to represent me if the president had honored his deal with the prince: "You get your guy when I get my guy." But the tall, bulky lawyer was ready when prosecutor Pat Blessington provoked me to throw my old man under the bus.

Blessington twirled his silver handlebar mustache like Snidely Whiplash and asked if I'd seen my dad commit a crime.

"Nope! He's not answering that." Scandone leaned in on Blessington. "How would you feel if you were asked to say bad things against your father?"

The attorney general was silent.

"You wouldn't like it, would you? You wouldn't answer, would you?"

Blessington's face turned red, and his mustache drooped with the infliction of stultifying shame.

Several months later, a judge dismissed the case for failure to timely prosecute. They were scratching their heads, figuring out how to be mean, and forgot to go to court. The judge was a standup lady. If she weren't, the prosecutor would've been alerted that the statute was about to run by a clerk.

We were overjoyed that Dad wouldn't be going to jail or be disbarred, but the damage had been done. His rosy cheeks were pale, and he got tired easier. Years of anxiety tarnished his golden years and reputation. But he didn't quit or let the bastards keep him down. He kept writing books and painting. He sat at the head of the kitchen table with his cell phone and teapot and held court or offered painting lessons to grandkids.

His main passion was politics, but my old man did much more, including acting and comedy in high school and college. They did skits like *Saturday Night Live*, and he imitated voices and hilarious conversations. He was "the czar" of intramurals and could invent games in a split second. He learned to paint and gave away framed masterpieces. He was the master of ceremonies for mystery games where we figured out the murderer. Then he wrote one book after another about politics and espionage while observing the real characters, playing kingmaker. Had he not been doomed by the disease of politics, he could've been a professional writer of novels, plays, and movie scripts. He loved the game of politics to a fault. For all the excitement and fun, the poison and trauma probably deluded it. We were constantly weighing it on a scale, and it teetered in our favor. He was still in the game as ward leader, but it seemed to me there were better things in life. And not just for him.

My siblings were agitated that my prominence had brought the heat on Dad. Essentially, it was all my fault. I got gaslighted for being successful. He was our hero and always came through for us. He would return from the campaign trail when we were kids with a bag full of toys. Then he came to the rescue when we were young adults. He showed up in Paris when my sister Eileen was homesick during an international internship. After his surprise detour from a trip to Ireland, he took her to dinner, reassured her that everything would be all right, and flew out. Whenever I was in a jam at school or with the law, he strutted in wearing a dark suit or made the call to cut me loose. I got extra attention first because of my dyslexia, then because of my addiction, and finally because of my political career. My parents put years of effort into endless campaigns. I had a starring role in our family narrative. We were Irish and prone to jealousy. I didn't always understand why my sisters and brother may have felt animosity. But the heat from politics was heading for scintillating.

# CHAPTER SIX

# I GOT TO HANG OUT WITH HEROES

One of the greatest honors I had in early public service was to fight for cops and firefighters. Mary Kohler was an EMT with Hepatitis C who couldn't get a meeting with Mayor Street. She sat on her sleeping bag outside his office, disturbed that the city would not cover treatment for the bloodborne disease. She was on day three of her vigil when I brought her a cup of coffee. Mary smiled and gladly took the coffee to warm her hands—her body couldn't handle the caffeine. We crafted a friendship, and I made a commitment to try to pass a law that would cover Hepatitis C. In less than a year, the forty-year-old brunette waved from the gallery as the state senate passed an amendment to the Worker's Compensation law, finally providing payment for the disease that affected so many emergency responders.

We had more police officers die in 2007 than I care to talk about. Most of them were my neighbors. I visited the family of Officer Chuck Cassidy ten days after he surprised an armed bandit in Dunkin' Donuts on North Broad Street. His wife, Judy Cassidy, was generous in allowing me the honor of spending time with her family. Her two daughters and son were brokenhearted young adults. Yet Katie, Colby, and John shared the joy of having a kind father who wanted them to travel and learn. He worked overtime to ensure they could go on family vacations without him. The one condition was that they had to tell him what they learned. We sat on the sofa of the Morrell Park home, and they glowed in gratitude, eyes gleaming, as they praised his memory. My awkwardness dissipated with their warmth. I was a senator, but they made me feel a part of the family. Other officers' families made the same sacrifice. We were all part of the same family. I was blessed to get to know these brave officers and their loving families. If that's all I got to do in public service, it would've been enough.

\* \* \*

I thought the job was all about passing bills and improving people's lives, but it was about avoiding destruction. We had maneuvered through two substantial scandals in a short amount of time. Grandfather Stack cautioned against getting down in the game because you got kicked. Dad talked about him to a reporter in 1988 for the first time. My ears perked up like I was related to Elvis. Then we owned his New Deal heroic legacy. That was the last warm and cuddly story I ever got in public service. But my publicity was better than Fumo's.

Fumo's case was escalating in size and accelerating in speed. Stories in the *Inquirer* were filled with illegal leaks from the secret grand jury. Sensational stories exploded across the front page about Fumo using money from Citizens Alliance to pay private investigators to follow his girlfriend. A parade of trusted friends testified against him. His extravagant spending and use of a taxpayer-funded yacht, the *Philadelphia Spirit*, inflamed readers. The 501(c)(3) served as the senator's virtual piggy bank. The stories weren't close to accurate, but Pandora's box had opened. Nonetheless, he irrationally bolstered that the feds couldn't find any evidence of bribery. The pressure was creating a crack.

Fumo's stormy sea had created still waters for me. I looked strong in my district and had no scandals brewing. The *Inquirer* had been hyperventilating with stories about Fumo but seemed to take a break. I was minding my own business on a slow news day when I saw an article about an old piece of waterfront property and a company named Beach Street. The photograph of me in that stupid sweater appeared once more, along with the lie that I was getting a casino. Out of thin air, like it never happened before, the story set off another firestorm. The following week, the *Inquirer* reported that the feds were probing me. The sensational words flowed stunningly from pumpkin-headed reporter Chris Brennan. I was starting to smell a Whitey Bulger—or John Dougherty.

Fumo ranted that John Dougherty enjoyed a regular cup of tea with the United States attorney to urge investigations of rivals. I thought Vince was paranoid at first. About a month before the Beach Street story reemerged for the second time, Chairman Brady told me Doc "wants to pour hot tea on your face." Brady wasn't laughing. He was concerned because "you know that guy's crazy."

Bob called to find out if something happened. I couldn't think of anything. Maybe Doc dreamed something. "You better call him. I don't want anything to happen to you." I got three follow-up calls from others who heard the same rumor.

I got Dougherty on the phone after searching for the right number. He changed numbers like the weather and used burner phones. "I apologize if I did anything wrong," I offered.

He had heard that I had said "things about him." He didn't want to talk about it anymore, even though we hadn't talked about it at all. "Everything is good now, Senator."

One didn't need a PhD to diagnose a psychopath. But he controlled a powerful union, and the establishment was more than willing to look the other way or follow lockstep.

"You're OK with me, Senator." His tone calmed like a whistling kettle that's been turned off. I was almost embarrassed to inquire as to his Earl Grey desire. It just seemed a little dainty. Why not hot coffee? It would probably scald more. But there was no coincidence that the Beach Street story appeared a little while later. The man never physically challenged me, but he used the media like a sledgehammer.

Brady's analysis was better than Freud. "He hates Vince but wants to be Vince. He hates you because you're with Vince. He hates me but wants to be me. He's just nuts."

And Doc couldn't stop himself. It was all fun and games until someone would lose an eye or a career.

The ominous hand of the federal government was on my shoulder, but mysteriously so. I didn't receive any letters or phone calls indicating the feds were investigating. I wasn't like those defendants on *Dateline* who called the cops and asked what it was about. They always ended up in handcuffs. Nonetheless, I learned later that my brother, three sisters, mother, and father had been called before a federal grand jury. An agent asked, "What can you give us on your brother?" They could've talked about how I'm a poor sport in basketball sometimes and that I drank the last beer on numerous occasions. Yet they were forbidden to talk to me or acknowledge the probe. Christmas and Thanksgiving became weird.

Although Fumo was under siege, he immediately came to my assistance and hired Mark Sheppard, an expert white-collar criminal attorney. Mark practiced with Dick Sprague, who would soon turn on Fumo. I knew Mark personally and liked him, but he could be as bleak as winter rain. He was tall but slouched and had thick glasses and a sad expression. Nonetheless, he was hopeful that any federal investigation would go nowhere but wouldn't guarantee it. I got depressed visiting his dusty Rittenhouse Square office. He knew FBI agents and federal prosecutors intimately because he saw them so often. His dreary disposition emanated from seeing talented clients go to prison. His reassuring manner toward me was deluded by cautious cynicism. He wanted to find out what they were looking for so he could evaluate any danger. "Somebody is rattling their cage and feeding them information."

I asked, "Dougherty?"

Sheppard smiled and, after a pause, said, "Maybe."

Why wasn't I allowed to just be a senator? I was on my feet for every big budget vote and fought for the little guy. I'd visited schools and talked to kids about education. I helped my constituents by hosting expos that were more crowded than Eagles games. I stood up for firefighters and police officers. And after our country was attacked, I tried to join the military. My chief of staff, Cindy Mariela, admired my patriotism. She promised to help me, but she lied.

"Let's do it after the next election," she said. "Better still, the one after that one." She intentionally misplaced the paperwork countless times. Maybe Iraq or Afghanistan would be safer than Harrisburg or Philadelphia.

The Patriot Act sped through Congress like a runaway train, giving immense power to the FBI. Fumo claimed it was being used to put him in jail. As my second reelection approached, I had built a strong war chest and active legislative profile. I'd helped mold legislation in many areas through committee work and amendments. I didn't want to be a backbencher. I wanted to be bold like Fumo but more courteous, kind, and forgiving. Fumo's chief weapon was fear. Mine was likeability, a far less effective tool. But even that quality attracted venom. Fumo attracted federal heat because he was a brass-knuckle fighter. I was potentially guilty by association. I was hanging with the wrong people, like in high school. But he was fun to hang out with.

At his federal trial, Fumo claimed he was painfully shy. He didn't have the best personality in the world, but he was smart and witty and liked to laugh. One had to know him to like him. Although he could sometimes be scary, I discovered him to be warm and caring. Only close friends were invited to the annual holiday party at the spectacular five-story mansion on Green Street. He traveled in a fast circle with rich and influential friends who seemed to worship him. We spent hours eating, drinking, and singing Christmas carols with the prince and all his celebrity honchos. Steve Marcus was a hotel tycoon and father figure who wrote the check for the Truman Dinner and never missed the holiday festivities. Richard Sprague brought wealthy clients and brokered secret business deals on the leather sofa under the mistletoe. Peter Nero conducted the Philly Pops orchestra and played a mean Steinway next to a roaring fire. There were all kinds of women and interesting characters. But Fumo traveled the globe with the old men on private jets and yachts, staying in castles and villas in Europe and Asia for the rest of the holidays.

Fumo's decades-long adoration of Sprague vaporized like morning dew when he officially denied advising Fumo to destroy emails. Sprague had now joined with the feds. The betrayal was incendiary and devastating to Fumo's defense. He had always relied on Sprague's lionhearted brilliance to match federal power. Instead, he'd need to find a substitute, and there was no one like Sprague. Both great men acted as greedy children. The relationship became a petty, public squabble when Fumo refused to pay Sprague's exorbitant legal bills. Fumo presumed that since he made Sprague wealthy through sweetheart deals and lucrative referrals, this one should've been on the arm. He was wrong. Fumo had also advanced Sprague's position for a casino license and the subsequent ability to print money. Sprague probably feared for his own bacon, knowing his role in Fumo's shadowy dealings over the years. Who knows if Sprague would've stayed loyal if Fumo paid the bill. But he shouldn't have cared about cash. He counseled, "Money is fungible. It comes and goes and means nothing." He was emphatic. "Never put it ahead of family or friendship."

He simply couldn't follow his own advice.

With Sprague gone, Fumo needed a new story. What would explain all this federal scrutiny? The story would have to be a barn burner. Time was running out. He scratched his head and remembered recent Philadelphia history. A politician had been saved with the spinning of a cynical yarn. Maybe it could work again.

\* \* \*

In the 2003 mayoral election, John Street trailed Republican challenger Sam Katz by nine points. With twenty-seven days left, an FBI bug was discovered in the mayor's office. The FBI admitted that Street was under investigation. What first seemed like a death knell for Street and a certain victory for Katz turned upside down. The bug was exploited by Democrats as institutional racial prejudice and a referendum on the locally unpopular Republican-controlled federal government. As a result, Street won reelection by 16 points.

Tigre Hill directed a 2006 feature-length documentary called *The Shame of a City*. The film was named after Lincoln Steffens's 1904 book, *Shame of the Cities*, which sought to expose the wrongdoing of public officials in cities across the United States. It won best film at the Philadelphia Film Festival of Independents and was referenced in five successive issues of *Philadelphia Magazine*. Commentator Michael Smerconish called it "a true Philly horror film." Viewers were also introduced to the early emergence of Johnny Doc's Hoodies, who terrorized Katz and his supporters as they tried to campaign in the Italian market. Countless elected leaders rushed to Street's aid, calling the federal probe corrupt and a witch-hunt against effective Democrats.

Yes, it was happening again.

* * *

Fumo wasn't Black, but he was an effective Democrat. Fumo ran to the senate floor, trying to harness that sentiment by insisting President George W. Bush and his cronies were going after a powerful Democratic senator who got things done. Bush hated our beautiful city and the special way strings were pulled. But Fumo forgot the rest of the story. The reformers would use Street as a cautionary tale.

Philadelphia was a schizophrenic city that embraced corruption and thirsted for reform. In 2007, reform-minded Michael Nutter hosted sold-out screenings of *Shame of the City* to raise money and attack two of his opponents, Bob Brady and Chaka Fatah, both Street supporters portrayed negatively in Hill's movie. Nutter went from last to first in a blink and became mayor.

Fumo couldn't walk away from the budget process. He was still in some kind of strange denial that the heat would dissipate. For a while, so were the rest of us. But Fumo's vulnerability became crystal clear, and the backbiting began. Anthony Williams demanded to play a bigger role in the budget process since he represented so many Black people who were excluded. "We all respect Vince and know he'll be fine," he said. "But the budget has been too secretive for too long."

Anthony was a clever fellow and understood his audience. No one ever spoke directly, but in code. He was saying that Fumo was toast, and it was time for someone new. Fumo may have contemplated succession for the first time. "You need to jump in and take him on," he later said to me. He'd never needed help before. He wanted me to stop being so nice "so these guys can see you're serious."

The subpoenas kept coming, and the chugging indictment train would be arriving soon. Nonetheless, Fumo watched my back and made sure Mark Sheppard was focused on my case. Sheppard spent hours muttering in maddening vagueness. I was probably fine. Indeed, I was most certainly fine, nothing to worry about. Then suspicion whipped across his face, complete with squinting eyes and furled brows. "Unless there's something you're not telling me." Every time I left his office, I was convinced I'd probably end up in jail.

The budget never passed on time. We were like horses in the corral waiting to be fed or let loose. We were in session until the late hours throughout June. Final passage usually came after an all-night session in early July, after all the inside leveraging had been done and the boredom and monotony were no longer sustainable.

Fumo caught me by surprise. I was on the plaza overlooking State Street at dusk on a sweltering evening. He nearly gave me a coronary as I loaded boxes into my car for a quick getaway. The pink and orange sky was magnificent as I contemplated a different future.

"I think you're going to be alright," he said decidedly.

I'd never seen him outside the capitol. He was usually behind an oversized computer screen at his Resolute desk or swashbuckling on the senate floor. But he appeared from behind the manicured bushes, no encrypted text.

"Are you sure?"

He smiled warmly and started toward the marble steps. "Let's just say I like your case a lot better than mine." Then he stopped smiling. "If I had your case, I wouldn't be worried."

That's when I knew I'd be there the following summer and he would not.

In winter 2008, the senator who had been my worst enemy and best friend stood on the senate floor with his staff lined up in two rows behind him. News accounts predicted an impending indictment. I still believed Fumo might work a miracle, but it wasn't to be. He blamed the Bush administration one more time, then announced that "tomorrow I will be indicted." He thanked his staff for being the source of his success and said he would soon resign. It was unclear whether he would resign as appropriations chair or from the senate. Either way a mad scramble would ensue.

# CHAPTER SEVEN

# THE TRUE STORY OF HOW JOHN DOUGHERTY WENT NUTS

The blood was in the water. Hands rang and hearts fluttered. A path to power may have opened. Everyone wanted to know when Fumo would resign. John Dougherty made it clear he was running for Fumo's seat upon his official resignation. It seemed absurd that the labor boss would covet becoming a freshman senator in the middle of the pack. Maybe he wanted the title, but he had bigger plans than being just one of twenty. First, he would try to be careful.

Doc masqueraded as a statesman by refusing to announce his candidacy until Fumo resigned. Nonetheless, Fumo poked him in the eye by announcing he wasn't resigning—just not running again. His dramatic floor remarks were misunderstood. "I only said I was stepping aside as chairman of the appropriations." He planned to focus on his federal trial instead of reelection. But Fumo needed a successor in a hurry. His archenemy might skate by because Fumo hadn't planned. His delusion that he would prevail over the feds once more jeopardized us all. The ice water had finally hit him in the face. Now he understood Rome was burning. He didn't have many options and time was running out. Who would jump into a race with a 10,000-pound gorilla named Dougherty standing there? What unlikely idiot would have the public profile and the bad judgment?

I worried he'd consider a deal with his bitter enemy. Bob Brady would certainly broker it. That was his special art, and he made countless ones to secure peace with others. Brady wanted to maneuver Doc away from his own back. I didn't want to see a Munich-type deal where peace would later bring destruction. Whoever ran needed their head examined, and Fumo went out and found the most unlikely candidate to step into his shoes. That candidate needed Prozac and, to Fumo's most loyal backers, so did he. "I need you to help me sell this guy to the caucus," Fumo said. He planned to introduce his abecedarian at a plush dinner at his Green Street mansion.

The western senators loved catered affairs in the giant city. Fumo was ready to wine and dine once more. As much as they razzed Philadelphians, they were impressed by the City of Brotherly Love, with its skyscrapers and gigantic ironclad bridges and world-class museums. We gathered amid the sparkling chandeliers, Persian rugs, and crystal. Elegant staff and gorgeous girls served expensive wines. Chateaubriand made its way around the immense mahogany table where fifteen senators anticipated the remarkable. The affair was festive but surrealistic. The non-reality hadn't really hit that our legendary leader was transitioning to new battles and probably prison. He could've given Cicero or Pompeii a run for their money. There would never be another Fumo, but we expected something bold. When the doorbell rang, the suspense elevated. The room was silent, and I knew the next moment would define our narrow world for years to come.

Senator Shirley Kitchen battled weight and blood pressure problems for years. She had become one of my most unlikely and reliable friends. She represented the poorest, most violent part of North Philadelphia and scuffled habitually with the mayor and neighborhood rivals. Shirley also tussled with the media. "We don't hide," she boasted.

An *Inquirer* photographer waited in the bushes outside her home, trying to snap her at home on a session day. The picture captured an angry woman with the flu. The media played their little games and Shirley played hers, standing strong before The Man. She was rock solid and usually calm unless somebody tried to hoodwink her. We had conversations by rolling our eyes, shaking our heads, and muttering. We understood our language. I counted on her to tell the truth, and she counted on me to be a partner. When Larry Farnese entered the room of Fumo's towering brownstone, shaking in his boots, we looked past him for the big shot. His ill-fitting dark suit failed to cover a saturated shirt. Beads of sweat dripped from his forehead, and a prodigious nose dominated his jowly face. Fumo threw his arm across Farnese's back and pushed him toward the table like a piece of rare meat. "This is our candidate," he announced to the sound of crickets. Fumo's unconvincing smile collapsed into a nervous frown as he maneuvered Farnese around the room in under two minutes, then out the front door as if he never arrived. Farnese thanked the senator profusely over his shoulder but was cut off by the slamming door.

What the hell was Fumo thinking? Farnese had run for office before against State Representative Babette Joseph. The former hippie was in her late sixties with curly black hair and sandals, and she'd roughed up Larry two years before after dispatching a pack of Jewish grandmothers to heckle him at his Rittenhouse Square Park announcement. He got distracted and stuttered and didn't have a good answer on how to help seniors. He lost the race by only one hundred votes and had filed for a rematch when Fumo found him. Larry's grandfather had the famous name as president of the Board of Education, but for unexplained reasons, Larry and his parents hated him. None of this mattered because Farnese wasn't ready for prime time, and I couldn't explain it away. But I could feel Shirley's look like a blazing sun enflaming my cheeks.

"This is going to be the next Fumo?" she muttered incredulously. "You got to be kidding, Stacky."

I took a breath and whispered, "He'll do until someone better comes along."

I thought Fumo was meticulous, but I was wrong. This was a sloppy act of desperation to stop Dougherty.

Shirley's eyes protruded like she'd seen a clumsy ghost, and her faint words drifted like a troubled stream into my ears: "Trifling, trifling, trifling."

"This is the guy Fumo has picked," I stated. "And we will deliver him."

She waited to hear my punchline. "If you say so, Stacky."

I should have been more frightened of Dougherty—everyone else was. The small chalk immediately bet the house on him. He got busy threatening and cajoling. I didn't know Larry, but I followed orders.

My dad had no doubts. "Vince helped you, so you help him." Dad recounted tales of treachery in the Democratic Party; this was nothing new. "Sometimes you go down with the ship. Always be loyal to your friends." That was his code and I hoped it would be mine. Larry was a tough sell, but I would do my best. I honestly thought Dougherty would understand. Although he was fidgety and borderline psychotic, he showed hints of diplomacy.

In the previous year, he backed insurance executive Tom Knox for mayor against Bob Brady and others. Ironically, Dougherty had served as the party's treasurer and stood behind Brady at countless events, smiling affectionately. But Doc now had a boot on his throat; Knox had an 11-point lead with only weeks to go. John appeared giddy and magnanimous when he strolled into our backyard at the shore. He owned a house near us in North Wildwood, and on that crisp fall day, he swept in like the salty breezes on our faces. "Senator, I'm here to see the bosses, your dad and the judge." His confidence gave him uncharacteristic charm. "I know you're helping Bob. It's OK." He wanted us to know, "you have a place with Knox and me. But Brady is all done."

After the sloppy hugs and his departure, I asked my dad, "Do you think he's right?"

He pursed his lips and looked out at the choppy waves in the inlet. "Maybe."

Dan Hilferty was the handsome, opportunistic CEO of Blue Cross who finally agreed to host a fundraiser for me. High above the skyscrapers, the breakfast at the Pyramid Club was well attended. I was surprised by the number of Doc allies who suddenly wanted to support me. I surmised that Hilferty was beholden to Local 98 because they were cherished customers. During his introduction, Hilferty seemed uncharacteristically cautious with his praise. Doc accolades feared being misinterpreted. Johnny tore into them with hearsay upon hearsay accusations such as "Jimmy Pie heard Tommy James say you said I was a crook," or words to that anxiety-inducing effect. But the usually effusive businessman was only being polite.

Doc's right-hand man was pumped up. Bobby Henon was Local 98's political director and a future city councilman who wanted to be my best friend. Henon's mother attended my senior expos and raved about me. Bobby's big, full head of brown hair was neatly cut and made him look younger. His sharp, sarcastic wit contributed to a stocky charm. He and consultant Larry Ceisler yanked me aside like they needed the nuclear codes. Larry liked me because the 58th Ward delivered his ex-wife to the bench, relieving him of alimony. Each draped an arm over my shoulders like warm smallpox blankets. I needed to be smart and support Doc.

They waved envelopes praising my prestige. I never accepted campaign contributions personally. "Give it to Dan." They were disappointed because they were used to making things look like a bribe.

I was committed to Farnese because Fumo had helped me, and I was loyal. "I like John," I said. "He's Irish Catholic and we have a lot of same friends."

They didn't pick up the irony.

"I won't do anything to hurt Doc."

They just stared.

"I promise, I'm just giving Farnese money."

They looked at each other for guidance. "That sounds all right. That's fair."

We shook hands and embraced as Ceisler waved the envelopes at Hilferty, who was watching.

A week later, Joe Dougherty, my old friend from the ironworkers union, ranted venomously to his members about my stealing money from Local 401 to give to Farnese. I had become a betraying sack of excrement. Ironically, Joe had been one of my few labor backers in 2000. Now he wouldn't take my calls or speak to my agents. Nobody could poison people better than Johnny Doc.

Larry Farnese was reminiscent of *Curb Your Enthusiasm*'s Larry David character. He rarely inspired confidence. The more I spoke to him and witnessed his nervousness and ineptitude, the more worried I became.

Doc swept into the race like a tsunami, quickly gathering key endorsements, including most labor, and raising mountains of cash. Fumo miscalculated that

Brady would endorse Farnese because he abhorred Doc. Brady harangued Farnese for falsely claiming his support and took a robust disliking to the upstart. Since Farnese was the darling of liberals, it was obvious Doc would get their support. Typical Philadelphia hypocrisy dictated that duplicitous interest groups should partner with the brass knuckle labor boss who was the likely win.

The third candidate was avowed bisexual Ann Decker, who was married to a man. Farnese had been a champion of LGBTQ causes, but Decker shockingly coordinated with Dougherty. The gay groups ran for the fence and suddenly Doc outed his own daughter to pull them off. But he used the gay issue most advantageously when he threatened to out an opponent of Henon's. The Doc gang took no prisoners. It was all collapsing. Farnese was in danger of losing all the liberal support. He had to win all of Center City to offset Dougherty's South Philly base. From my distant encampment in Northeast Philadelphia, it looked like a disaster. I didn't see how he could win.

With every mishap and embarrassment, where Farnese was the brunt of jokes, he relentlessly marched into the face of laughter and contempt through metal and glass doors at countless community centers, rolling up his sleeves. They loved debates in Center City, and the media coverage was unprecedented. Farnese's naivety and determination prevented him from seeing his life in peril. He was a lawyer trying a case against a criminal. It was that simple. Oxygen poured from the room when he called Dougherty a thug at a crowded charter school on Spring Garden Street. It was getting late in the race. Out onto the train tracks he went. The murderous stares of Doc and the brawny Hoodies ubiquitously upon him. The halls were packed with hoodlums who echoed boos and hisses every time Farnese called Dougherty a thug and a criminal. Doc's cheeks crackled like bacon, fists clenched beneath the table as he waited to claim victory and fix Farnese forever.

Fumo saw the race as a carbon copy of my 2000 triumph. Ken Snyder adopted Howard Cain's brilliant methodology using tracking polls. Dougherty's negatives were ridiculously high. Although he had a big following, the public knew he was bad news. But they had to be brought out, so the only question was money. Ken Snyder was conniving and self-interested, the quintessential hired gun. But he had panache and creativity in the production of campaign commercials, and the one he constructed for Farnese was brilliant and hilarious. It portrayed a cartoon Doc picking daffodils as a man's voice, imitating a child, mockingly recited his brushes with racketeering and extortion charges. The narration made viewers laugh and brought forth steam from his ears.

Intimidation had brought him to the big time, so he turned his attention to the capital. My state senate buddies were from nice places like Allegheny and Monroe Counties. They didn't know Doc or Philadelphia but soon received threats from labor groups. "You Philly people do it different," Sean Logan said. "You take no prisoners. You're scary. I'm glad I don't live there." And it was escalating.

Representative Bill Keller was a Fumocrat who jumped to the Doc team. On the way into the Jefferson-Jackson Dinner, he passed me. "You made the wrong choice, and you're going to be sorry."

I stopped. "Are you talking to me, Bill?"

He kept walking backward toward the parking lot. "I'm just saying be careful."

I'd never seen this before in a Philly rumble. Threats were usually implicit. But Dougherty incited elected officials to act like mafia hitmen.

Fumo hounded me for more money. I contributed close to $100,000 from my campaign fund even though I had my own election to worry about. Each check I wrote resulted in more false vitriol that I was stealing union funds to give to Farnese. I raised money from a broad base of supporters, and many were receiving threatening phone calls. Farnese trailed badly and seemed consistently inept. He was a lawyer who delivered pizzas because he couldn't get a job after law school. He had been ridiculed by coaches and teachers and discounted time and again. Eventually, these were the things that won my admiration. He just kept coming.

Fumo reassured me that Farnese was surging even though it didn't look like it. He painted a doomsday portrait if Dougherty won. Doc would use the same terror tactics in Harrisburg and take over our caucus and maybe the whole senate. The labor boss's perfect storm would fill Fumo's power vacuum and rain hell down upon us.

Larry's message hit home downtown with the good government types but was ignored in the pragmatic, tribal row homes of South Broad Street. As the campaign came to an edgy close, I watched the news coverage with trepidation. Cameras were set up at Dougherty's anticipated victory party at the famous Galdo's restaurant. The red carpet sausage party featured Dougherty embracing bulky union men and opportunistic officials like Senator Tony Williams as cameras flashed and spotlights swirled. It was too late for second-guessing, but I was worried about the immediate future. "It's going to be razor thin," Fumo said, "but I think we have it." He remembered Salvatore's 12-point lead with ten days left in 2000, which convinced Salvatore it was over. Dougherty must have done the same because he appeared doubtless. News accounts hardly mentioned Farnese, and when they did, they mispronounced his name. But the beefy grins fell away with the early returns. Larry trailed at first but steadily surged. By 9:30 P.M., it was clear Farnese had the upset and my phone erupted.

Barbara Deeley attended the morning mass in 2000 when we beat Salvatore. She had hung out in Dougherty's world and reported what was being said. They were coming for me. My financial help was credited with beating Doc. It was an exaggeration. But she took credit. "My senator always does what he thinks is right," she told them, "and he always wins." If they didn't like it, they could file a protest like Salvatore wanted to. They were the worst losers. They could never congratulate you for a well-fought campaign. Doc's people told Deeley they were going to make sure I lost in two years. "Better make it four. He won his primary tonight." They would now pay closer attention to my election cycle and ambitions.

They hated me for winning in 2000, but this was much worse. Dougherty would never forgive me. Nonetheless, the texts poured in: "Congratulations, boss," and, "Move over, Fumo. There's a new sheriff in town." I knew it was trouble. Tonya started calling Dougherty "The Crazy Man" that night after hearing about the threats. We laughed but should've cried.

So why was this the race that sent Dougherty into the lunatic stratosphere of no return? His unquenchable desire for power could not be satisfied while the prince dominated the city. But he never had the guts to take him on directly, like at the OK Corral. Doc won all the proxy wars and successfully got Fumo so jammed up with the FBI that he had to go. He could never shake his jealousy of Fumo or Brady. They had titles like senator, chairman, and congressman. With no one in the running, he wouldn't have to go *mano a mano*. He would walk in as a senator and cast a giant shadow that would obliterate the memory of the South Philly Robin Hood. Inexplicably a putz named Larry stumbled into his path. There was no way Farnese could win. But he did so, hurling horrible insults and telling hurtful truth like no one dared. Had it been somebody big and strong, like a city councilman or a dynamic woman, Doc might've retained his sanity. But he looked down his nose and saw Farnese, and the psychotic break became permanent.

# CHAPTER EIGHT

# FARNESE BECOMES MY INTERN

I was like Babe the pig, always looking to make friends in the city. That was easier said than done. But I couldn't win John Dougherty over. We analyzed why Doc never tried to put a full-court press on me to become a partner and decided it couldn't be done. Bob Brady said, "He's jealous of you too, like he is of me and Vince." Tonya was convinced that Doc was evil and despised anyone successful in Philly politics who wasn't his creation. She was more black-and-white and had given up all hope of conciliation. She thought we needed to escape the city. However, Dad had taught me to convert yesterday's enemy to tomorrow's friend, and I couldn't shake his pragmatic wisdom that coursed through my genes. Doc claimed to admire my parents and my public service tradition. He even visited my father in the hospital at my request near the end of his life. Days later, he was spreading terrible rumors that I was being investigated for corruption. I was determined to answer a higher calling to serve and work around Doc's hateful antics, but it wasn't easy.

Farnese needed immediate coaching. He was tone and style deaf. He wore pink ties to Harrisburg and drew sneers from the conservative western senators. To his credit, he was outspoken on gay rights but to an audience focused on guns and taxes. But things would change. He stepped into Fumo's gigantic shadow and couldn't find a flashlight at first. *Politics PA* said he was like my new intern. The learning curve was steep, and the caucus was starting to quake. I needed a soldier and operative to maneuver and fight in a world of fearful, duplicitous, ambitious little children. Our caucus wasn't named "the ladies auxiliary" for nothing, and we would fight like mean teenage girls.

Fumo was delighted to humiliate Doc, but his badly planned succession sparked a sweeping fire that burned for years. Farnese desperately wanted to make peace as Fumo prepared to face a jury of country folks who knew Philadelphia's venality. His efforts were rebuffed with extreme prejudice.

Dougherty's mother passed away shortly after the campaign, and Farnese was partially blamed. He went to pay his respects and was nearly assaulted. Brian Stevenson, a brawny, ginger-haired enforcer, stood in Farnese's path to the church steps. "You are not welcome here." Farnese just wanted Doc to know that he cared. "John knows you're here. He wants you gone." Doc was the poorest loser. Even Barzini attended Don Corleone's funeral, and he's the one who tried to assassinate him.

With Fumo's impending indictment, we were stuck in another budget stalemate. Governor Rendell sought to expand gaming to table games to balance the budget, but the usual conflicts about spending and taxes stalled things. While everyone stood around, waiting for something to happen, a man in uniform entered my office. Master Sergeant Jacoby had visited my Parkwood office regularly, usually carrying a packet of forms for me to sign. But he made a special visit to Harrisburg.

Matt Franchak had taken over as my chief of staff and usually did what was asked. He knew I had been trying to enlist in the military for years. He appeared on the senate floor looking concerned. "Can I talk to you over here, Senator?"

Farnese yelled, "Oh, brother!" because Franchak never left his giant pile of manila folders unless there was trouble. Was there a new criminal investigation? We slowly walked to the sizeable green leather chairs near the front senate entrance.

Franchak gripped a file like it had nuclear codes. "Jacoby thinks he can get you into the officer's basic course, but you need to make up your mind right now."

I took a breath because it was a major commitment. I was over forty, and for me to get an age waiver, time was ticking.

"Master Sergeant Jacoby says it's now or never," Franchak urged as he opened the folder, and my quivering hand accepted the pen.

Two days later, adjutant general Jessica Wright swore me in as a United States Army second lieutenant. She said, "You'll do great, sir."

Two days after that, I was on my way to Fort Lee, Virginia, for basic training. I was the second-oldest in the class, and when I encountered First Sergeant Suttles, a hardened, sarcastic redhead, at 5 A.M., I was concerned. She sternly directed me to cut my hair even shorter, and I almost fainted. About fifty of us stood at attention in our army physical training gear of gym shorts and T-shirts with the bold inscription "ARMY," waiting nervously to run. When Chief Macintosh, a muscled, dark-skinned Iraq veteran, strolled around shaking his head in disgust, I knew I'd made a big mistake.

I regained my poise after a week of training, happy to be away from the mundanity of Harrisburg. The legislature had reached new heights of drudgery to make basic training exciting and new. I spoke with my dad on the phone, and after we talked about my decision, he brought up another major topic. "I'm not getting any younger and my health isn't that great." I had dreaded this day. "I'd like you to take over as ward leader." I had hoped my career as a senator might take me away from ward politics, but not in Philadelphia. Once you were in, you were never out.

"Haven't I been a good son?"

He chuckled and we agreed to try to make the transition telephonically at a special ward meeting in the next few days.

After running and drilling all day, I returned to my room and got on the speakerphone. I don't think I was violating any army regulations by carrying on 58th Ward business from Fort Lee, Virginia. I hadn't asked for permission. I don't think there was ever a politician from Philadelphia who tried to execute such a delicate procedure while experiencing in-depth training. Different committee people were audible and amusing as they clambered and congregated in the basement of our family home. Everybody knew what the meeting was about, and things moved seamlessly until the formal motion.

"I object." It was Jimmy Lewis, the bitter and obstructive Dougherty-aligned member. We could never figure out Jimmy's animosity because my dad had helped him get numerous promotions with the Board of Education. I felt like accusing him of being unpatriotic. Didn't he know how hard this was?

I didn't need to because Lady Liberty was in the house. Pat McGinley's distinctive voice charged, "Oh, Jimmy! What's your problem?" She was always doing that for me. She had worked tirelessly to get me elected and was prouder than my parents. "Mr. Stack and the senator have always been kind to you. You have no reason to cause trouble."

Lewis argued that the party rules required ten days' notice and didn't allow for a telephonic election—technically correct. We were sure Jimmy was a scholastic type who stayed up late at night studying the rules. More likely his backers put him up to it. In practice, the ward rules were usually pragmatic. If he wanted, he could file a protest, but the committee people elected me unanimously with only his abstention. My dad's forty-six-year reign as powerful Northeast Ward leader came to an end, but his legacy would continue.

I was lucky to have that special lady in my corner. Pat McGinley stepped into the line of fire from the time I was a kid. She was the only woman I knew, other than my wife, who gave you the truth right between the eyes, jumping in front of a car to save you. She had five children and treated me like one of them. Three months after that succession, she died unexpectedly of pulmonary disease, and my heart melted.

The last phase of military training was the most dreaded at Fort Benning, "Mother of Infantry." We scaled ropes and ran maneuvers in the woods. We blew things up and rounded out into muddy, grimy soldiers. Before that, our professors and trainers had been special forces officers and Blackhawk helicopter pilots who had become lawyers. They were stars in the army on fast tracks. Our latest commanding officer seemed like a step down from the high-level commanders we'd had at Fort Lee and Charlottesville. Nobody liked the silver-haired captain who ridiculed us. But when I begged for leave to attend Pat McGinley's funeral, he became like Ike.

He looked into my eyes. "To receive leave, this lady must've been like your mother. I assume that to be true. That's what I'm putting on the form, that she was a surrogate mother." Truer words were never uttered, and I grasped them for the first time. As I boarded the jet at Atlanta International Airport, I knew I was on a very special mission.

I swept into Saint Christopher's Church just in time. My crew cut jarred the family—it was a big surprise that I had joined the Army. Once again, it seemed like everything I did was a secret.

As we waited for mass to start, a family crisis was brewing. My nephew was struggling with severe opioid addiction and had recently overdosed. I revealed my own struggles and implored him to get help. I think I might've helped, and I couldn't have if I wasn't there. My brother-in-law Mark quipped, "Why did I not know any of this about you?"

\* \* \*

One of the greatest experiences of my life was joining the military, but it took me back to my learning trauma. Every time I thought I was free of the problem, it reared its ugly head. Once again, I would need to humbly explain myself to an authority figure and ask for understanding and guidance. I went to the commandant to explain my dyslexia, and the possible need for special accomodations. I thought I would have to gather medical documentation and walk back through all that shame to prove my case. "You are an officer in the United States Army. You are to be commended for overcoming that challenge so far in your life." He was a great guy. "You are on your honor. You don't require any documentation." The relief I felt was unbelievable. I had forgotten the accomplishment of graduating Villanova Law School. I always had to work twice as hard just to do as well as my classmates. I liked the challenge of putting myself into stressful situations but took my eye off the academic piece. The amount of anxiety I expended was exhausting. I always thought I could exert my will, but dyslexia doesn't yield to will. Time and again I forgot the black hole havoc it wreaked unless I slowed down my thinking.

I checked in with the instructor of the ethics course before taking my first exam. I suggested I might need a separate room or extra time, but he was reassuring. The West Pointer was slender like Obama, with steely arms like Atlas. He was another compassionate Army leader who gave me the thumbs up after I scored one hundred. "You'll be able to handle Army testing. If you don't do well, we just test you again." They put us in situations to succeed. Still, I had little freakouts after losing documents on the computer. My head spun as the screen jumbled and letters became Chinese. Five-minute tasks took two hours, and I concealed the anxiety with my usual smile.

In the early days at the legal center on University of Virginia's campus, I didn't tell any of my classmates I was a senator, but word got out. Classmates commended my low profile and thought it was humility. But I didn't want anyone to know the gentleman from Pennsylvania might wash out. After a while, I started to excel and felt comfortable being called senator as though it were a nickname. The JAGs were gossipy, and word got out that I had it together.

I showed up ready to run, and the Army made me faster. I became one of the elite runners and a top physical fitness performer. If you were good at PT, the brass ignored your other defects. I wanted that advantage. Halfway through training, Run Group One charged up O Hill, the excruciating steep incline that incinerated our quads. Helicopter pilot James Crumbler had been a dominant force and usually won the running contests. We raced each other every day, embracing the agony for bragging rights. As we broke into a sprint, I pulled ahead and heard the desperate pitter-patter of a runner falling behind.

Crumbler gasped for air at the peak. "Stack. I can't believe how fast you got. I used to smoke you!" He was right. They say you can't teach speed. They're wrong.

At Fort Lee and UVA, the bald lieutenant colonel who led our run group was tough as nails. "In Run Group One, if you ain't first, you're last." He was a Phillies fan, so we talked about them during the runs. We had all gotten faster over the fourteen-week course and were in the last week of training before Fort Benning. Runs were picturesque and educational as we passed Jefferson's library and the Roman columns and rolling hills of Charlottesville. During this last week, the colonel took a different route through a rear entrance, past administrative offices and classrooms, and into a compact dining area. We just followed and weren't quite sure what was happening. Then we discovered the surprise as officers waited to pull out seats at tables and serve us pancakes, eggs, and sausage. The commanders who had ordered us around became our servants. That kind of class was remarkable, and what a lesson on leadership. They understood they were nothing without their team.

# CHAPTER NINE

# BACK FROM THE ARMY TO JOIN THE WAR

In addition to having powerful enemies, Farnese lacked the confidence of other politicians. Somehow, he deserved the disrespect. Indeed, he expected it. He knew he would be undervalued and insulted in most situations, but to his credit, he went through the door every time. My job was to keep pushing him, and I was often the one handing him orders. Many times, those orders came from Fumo. Farnese had been bullied in grade school and at Malvern Prep but managed to play varsity baseball. He went to Villanova and Temple Law. I liked his grit. I had been disrespected and counted out and kept coming back also. If Fumo could stay out of prison, we might have a shot at controlling the capitol and city. I felt more powerful with Farnese as a reliable ally and Fumo calling plays from the sideline, and I was hopeful I could emerge as a top dog.

Fumo ruined the plan by getting convicted of all 117 counts. All the bravado he prevailed over the federal government was nonsense. The desperate maneuver of testifying on his own behalf proved disastrous. Public service had robbed him of his family. His relationship with his children and their mother was in tatters. He was a lonely, broken man who tried to play the game of power most effectively. After all, Pennsylvania wasn't the Roman Empire with robes and eloquent speeches, but a place where brass knuckles ruled and blood flowed. He admitted to playing tough while standing up for the little guy, but the jury wasn't listening. His battles with addiction and mental illness and heartbreak were revealing but not extenuating. Even the nicest politician would've been fresh meat before a federal jury, but Fumo wore a black hat.

The wit and warmth I experienced with him didn't project. The feds asked for a twenty-year sentence. The pundits thought they might get it. Fumo was incredulous. "They never showed I took a cent." He was ridiculously proud of that. His cousin, Senator Buddy Cianfrani, had been convicted of bribery because he was greedy and stupid. It was like a contest between the two, even though Buddy was dead. Fumo was hoping for house arrest, and he was deluded.

But the judge gave him a break of four years, six months, in Ashland Federal Prison Camp. The prosecutors were livid. They had destroyed their nemesis, and it wasn't enough. They would keep a careful eye on their obsession, even as he went behind bars.

The cameras flashed and the reporters cackled as Fumo scowled and blinked, pale and exhausted, as he walked through the prison doors in leg irons and handcuffs. He wasn't Hannibal Lecter, but they made him look like him.

Before he went away, Fumo attempted the overthrow of Senator Bob Mellow. He recruited me to lead the overthrow with Senator Sean Logan. But the boys from the west thought I was too nice for such a serious task. After that, he partnered with Tony Williams as his heir-apparent for appropriations chair. Fumo called him "treacherous but unintelligent," but Tony was a Doc ally, so who was the stupid one? Now that Farnese was my protégé, I had my own vote and his.

The western senators had been my crew and were usually on the same page until Fumo pushed me for leader or appropriations chairman. Suddenly I became a threat. Senator Jim Ferlo, a short, hot-tempered limousine liberal with an absurd mustache, disparaged my easy-going way and fashionable dress. They wanted someone tougher and more serious, not the senate's best-dressed. Ferlo would find a way to oppose every move I made. I introduced Farnese over wings and football at the hotel sports bar, and he didn't quite fit in. He was more Lebec Fin than Buffalo Wild. Sean Logan's nickname, *Finuche*, or fool, telegraphed that maybe we should find new digs.

I was named the best-dressed senator along with Senator Jake Corman in 2001. I got needled regularly, and competitors said I only cared about fashion. But women and gay men liked it. It was the first thing brought up when I got introduced. I rolled my eyes, but it helped me stand out. I was a legislative workhorse who proposed groundbreaking bills, not just another pretty face. My stylish attire became a source of mean-girl acrimony and spiteful vitriol throughout my career. But they couldn't stop me from wearing the electric blue suit.

We Democrats rarely won against the Republicans. We salvaged respect on the rare occasions we could. With Fumo gone, we weren't even that. We were usually excluded from the budget negotiations and hid that fact as a shameful secret. Our only role was to vote against the draconian Republican budgets that came with Governor Tom Corbett. We waited impotently as the budget dragged into summer as the Republican senate negotiated with the Republican house and the governor. It was soul-sucking, and I began to question what I was doing with my life.

I served during the terms of governors Ridge, Schweiker, Rendell, and Corbett and found them all decent and hard-working. Expedient Rendell relied on

Fumo until he was vulnerable, and then he found others. He often made deals with the Republicans without notifying us. We were insulted but inarguably irrelevant.

Governors waited anxiously for the majority to hand them a budget they could sign. Our role as Democratic senators was to rail against horrible Republican budgets or cheer Rendell's, but it was inauthentic because we hadn't played a role. If we could secure budget priorities for the poor or underserved, even scraps, we'd vote for it. My desperation at not playing a more impactful role in serving the people of Pennsylvania increased as I watched the paint dry on the senate walls.

The Philadelphia caucus was always divided between selfishness and envy. Any semblance of unity came from Fumo's ability to negotiate goodies such as grants, capital budget dollars, and appointments to boards. The power vacuum remained open, but Tony Williams, Vince Hughes, and Allegheny County's Jay Costa tried to fill it. I was ready, too, but waited for an opportunity.

Fumo was emphatic. "Costa is a pussy and would be a disaster." Fumo had never advocated for Tony Williams, but believed Vince Hughes was weak and unacceptable mainly because "the Black lady senators hate him because of his wife." Hughes's wife, Sheryl Lee Ralph, starred in *Dreamgirls* on Broadway and later the Emmy-winning series *Abbott Elementary*. I liked Senator Hughes because he helped me get elected and was affable. Sheryl Lee was charming, lovely, and charismatic, and her talent for flattery was uncanny. She loved Mellow and was so effusive that he blushed. She once praised him from the stage of a Broadway show as I sat next to him. That was when we were a big, happy family attending the Pennsylvania Society together. Nonetheless, the jealousy was palpable, and there was racial animosity from the African American members. We were a privileged group but did not act like it. Magnanimity was trumped by pettiness.

Tony Lepore was Bob Mellow's gregarious chief of staff. His hefty, seemingly jolly demeanor concealed a calculating mind. He held senators' hands and became their therapist. Thus, he knew all the secrets. Hughes enjoyed a closeness with Lepore that was surpassed only by Mellow. In another existential moment on the balcony of the east wing, Hughes startled me. "I want you with me, Stacky." He used my nickname when he wanted something. "I got something figured out with Costa. Lepore's going to come see you." He was like a secret agent, but smooth and silky. I waited.

Farnese's office on the fourth floor was where a freshman without influence was logically stored. He spent days sweating, pacing, and torturing his staff. The slights and slaps were endless. He was in the impossible role as Fumo's successor and couldn't get traction. Yet the prince's last gesture was to attend Farnese's maiden fundraiser at the Waterfall Room.

The glittering Schuylkill River looked clean as Vince's remaining investors filled the room and coffers. But a surprise guest blocked the doorway with his prodigious size. Tony Williams smiled warmly and embraced me like a long-lost brother. "Thank you so much. I really appreciate your support."

I was clueless. "What support?"

He snickered. "Oh, Vince didn't talk to you? My bad."

Fumo was standing by the staircase, sipping a frosty martini. He could see my spider senses tingling. "I know. I know." He held up his hands, trying to block me. He was a little drunk. "I know he's terrible, but he's our best shot." Fumo wanted the angry Black guy who had tried to cut his throat for years to become appropriations chair. I wanted that martini. "It's so we can fuck Mellow."

I shrugged.

"And because Costa is a pussy."

After Farnese's initially bumbling speech finished eloquently, I grabbed his arm. His crisp white shirt turned gray with sweat when I whispered the news. "You got to be kidding me! What the fuck!"

Farnese was an only child and always would be. He was immediately thrown into uncertainty in the caucus politics. The last thing he needed was to make enemies, and it was the first thing that would happen. There were no friends, just allies.

Bob Mellow requested a meeting with me at the newly renovated Allentown rest stop on the turnpike "so we can enjoy a big cinnamon bun and not be disturbed." It would be friendly and clandestine. I expected Mellow to have a fake beard and sunglasses. But the jovial Tony Lepore strolled in with Mellow like they were Hope and Crosby. Lepore's leather briefcase was inconsistent with his holiday sweater and mom jeans. Maybe he'd pull out a contract and fountain pen. Mellow teased Lepore for his insufferable fawning over legendary Pittsburgh Penguin Mario Lemieux when he was seeking a casino license. His squeaky, almost inaudible "Mr. Lemieux . . . Oh, Mr. Lemieux" cracked me up.

Now it was time to talk about my big future. Mellow believed Costa had earned the right to succeed Fumo and would be more grateful than Williams. Hughes was on their team. They wanted me to become vice chair of appropriations, a new creation. Mellow gushed that this would be amazing, giving me a budget and additional staff. I deluded myself that it was real. Frankly, I trusted Hughes more than Williams at that time. Costa was a friend, and I was convinced that the days of Fumo-like power were gone forever.

When I saw Farnese the following Monday, he asked, "So what are we doing?"

I said, "We're going to back Costa."

When I told him about vice chair, he blurted, "What the hell is that?"

Tony Williams never reached out after the first encounter at Farnese's fundraiser, so I didn't get a chance to negotiate an alternative strategy. My decision would've been different had I known him better. The reorganization vote took place in November 2008 under the bright lights of our elegant caucus room. Mellow announced he wanted Vince Hughes to be the caucus secretary, and Costa, appropriations chair. There were no rumblings. Then he announced my appointment to the newly created position, and hisses echoed off the wall. Tina Tartaglione wanted the job for herself because she had seniority. It was a typical moment in our caucus, fighting over things that meant nothing. Tony Williams was flabbergasted and announced he was withdrawing as a candidate for appropriations chair because of treacherous mechanisms.

"I can see what's going on here," he blurted, "and it's not right." He should have stayed in.

My dad always advised, "Make them vote against you. Don't let them off the hook." That way, you get a look at who your enemies are.

Tony's dad, Hardy Williams, was a silver fox who ran for mayor. He was charismatic and cunning and maneuvered his son into his senate seat on the last day for petition-filing years before. Tony was intimately acquainted with clandestine moves, so his outrage was misdirected. He'd been outplayed, pure and simple. Our slate won, and Farnese acquired the new, dedicated enemies of Tony Williams, Shirley Kitchen, Leanna Washington, and Tartaglione. I could mend fences with my winning personality, but for Larry, it would be far more difficult. He would be forced to grovel and apologize incessantly.

Why did the west win the chair? Philadelphia was the economic epicenter of the entire state, yet we couldn't agree on our own candidate for appropriations chair. There was a vacuum with Fumo gone, and several wanted to fill it. Costa performed better than Fumo thought he would, but there was only one Fumo. Mellow seized control of the appropriations budget because he wasn't afraid of Costa. I didn't get my own budget, but the title seemed to impress Harrisburg hands and aggravate my Philadelphia colleagues. We were crabs in a crab trap. No one was allowed to get ahead.

I had a little extra campaign money and wanted to promote my new clout. A prominent billboard on I-95 near Academy Road hosted my giant smiling face with the caption, "Congratulations to New Vice Chairman of Appropriations; Senator Mike Stack, Philadelphia's next 'Go to Guy!'" I admit it was gratuitous, but my constituents loved it. The other crabs hated it. They ran to Mellow to take it down, like spiteful school children.

Impressions were reality. I got a new nickname: GTG. My stock went up, at least in the zero-sum game of the ladies auxiliary. My friend from the electrician's union probably seethed. Trash-talking meant something mortally important to him.

Fumo wouldn't host elegant parties anymore, but he did throw one last shindig reminiscent of mobster legend. He hosted a red carpet bon voyage party in South Philadelphia before going off to the elegant confines of federal prison. The South Philly tradition of celebrating going to the clink was absurd and alive. Politicians and captains of industry attended to bid adieu to the prince of the city.

David Cohen, who helped build Comcast into a global cable giant, patted my arm. "You've been a good friend to Vince," he said.

"He helped me and I'm loyal." We clinked glasses.

"You've gone further for him than would be expected. You're a standup guy," he replied. Cohen was a big fundraiser for Joe Biden and became ambassador to Canada.

Fumo beamed on a stage, holding hands with a lovely brunette boutique owner. He thanked everyone for their friendship and announced their engagement. He seemed delighted and disconnected from reality. Tonya and I watched in amazement as Fumo joked about his cousin, Buddy, who was unable to consummate the gift of three prostitutes on the eve of his incarceration. "I can't do anything," the senator said. "I'm going to fucking prison." Fumo chuckled, and the crowd laughed.

I still needed his guidance and began exchanging letters with him in prison as though he were Hannibal Lecter. Fumo's brain grasped the game as the stakes grew higher, but I also missed his companionship. He had been my battle buddy. The last three years were filled with turmoil over his indictment, trial, and succession. Before he was found guilty, his one-time friend Mark Sheppard advised, "Stay away from Vince. He's desperate and dangerous." Sheppard was working on my case. "He's under incredible pressure and there's no telling what he would do." I inferred that Fumo would wear a wire to entrap me to save himself.

He wasn't well. He blinked incessantly and repeated himself. In those last days, he was always sweating and manic. Could Fumo be dangerous to me? That's how Sheppard saw him once he stopped paying the bills. Even if he did try to get me on a wiretap, it would have been the fruitless act of a desperate man.

In those last days, Fumo stormed around the senate floor, trying to remain relevant. I saw him in the hallways by himself, carrying manila folders about the gaming bill. On one occasion, he grabbed my shoulder and spun me around. We were going to a meeting with Governor Rendell. He hadn't been invited, but I had been, along with several other Philadelphia senators. We hustled down the long, dim corridor to the governor's office, and Fumo stormed in.

Rendell looked terrified as an outraged Fumo decried his exclusion. Rendell nervously placated him. "Now Vince, it's not important whether you were invited or not, just that you're here now."

Fumo threatened to choke Rendell's chief of staff, who quaked nervously in his size eight shoes. The house Democratic appropriations chair Dwight Evans entered, and Fumo threw a chair at him and yelled, "I'll fucking kill you."

Evans was tall and hefty with a shaved head. "Bring it on, old man," he challenged.

Somehow that meeting ended with everyone shaking hands, but Fumo was clearly unhinged. Two nights later, he passed out on the senate floor with a heart attack. Anthony Williams and I helped put him on the gurney reminiscent of the one that carried Senator Lynch, and escorted him to the ambulance.

* * *

Ashland Penitentiary seemed to improve Fumo's health. It wasn't exactly Club Fed, but not Attica. His letters were warm and witty. He lost twenty pounds, and his blood pressure was perfect. He was reading for hours every day and sleeping for the first time in years. I worried he might soon be doing yoga and chanting.

Fumo's early letters described his routine and excoriated the feds for railroading him. The system had been rigged against him because he was so effective. They had never gotten him for bribery. He never took a cent, unlike his cousin who collected satchels of cash. He was burned but not beaten. I updated him on the different members of the caucus and their maneuvers as if it were the family newsletter. Animosity toward Mellow grew with Costa's ascension to appropriations chair. "Now that asshole can control everything. He never dared to interfere with me."

Rumors circulated that Mellow might retire, so the next leadership election would be mayhem. Costa thought I was breathing down his back and wouldn't allow much vice chair action at appropriations. Mellow welched on the promise of my own budget. Yet Vince Hughes and Costa were like Batman and Robin, glad the Riddler was gone. I felt unappreciated.

The legislative battles evolved around the passage of the gaming bills. The Republicans controlled the process and stockpiled contributions from casino interests while Costa and Mellow seemed beyond their depth. We passed a law to make it illegal for the casinos to contribute to politicians, but there were countless loopholes. The same went for our policy of transparent government, which became all the rage after the pay raise debacle. Everything was supposed to be out in the open, yet no one knew what was going on except the savvy insiders.

Fumo had a trainer who was supposed to whip him into shape, but he paid him to leave him alone. All the extra rest and reading had given him more time to think. And when he had more time to think, he came up with more people to hate.

Steve Wodjak was a mega-lobbyist whose family had secured an interest in the Sugar House Casino just down the street from La Veranda. In the 1970s, Wodjak represented the Parkwood area of Northeast Philadelphia as a state representative and appropriations chair. He got indicted and left office. Soon after, he founded Wodjak and Associates, a premier consulting firm, and got rich.

Richard Sprague followed Fumo's guidance to casino ownership and was ready to get paid. These cronies forgot who made them. But another one didn't belong to Fumo. Louis DeNaples was a Scranton businessman who'd been the target of federal authorities for decades. He was an intimate of Bob Mellow's who would win a casino license and be indicted for it. Then the indictment was quashed, and the case thrown out.

I learned that if Fumo wasn't hating, he wasn't living. The intricacies of his legislative sabotage were tedious. I shared his advice and asked Matt Franchak and others for hypotheticals of how to screw his foils. The casinos had multiple lobbyists working on different aspects of legislation. Different amendments, and amendments to amendments, were being dropped into bills during multiple committee meetings happening simultaneously. My head was spinning. Then I got a letter from Fumo, indicating, in a gleeful tone, that Mellow was now under federal investigation. His fellow convicts trafficked in courthouse gossip, and one of his guys had talked to another guy who had heard about Mellow.

As a minority senator who wasn't Fumo, the only way to become a player in the legislative process was through amendments. Even though it seemed futile, Fumo emphasized that big shots listened nervously when legislators made speeches and offered amendments. I would announce I was standing up for the little guy, but I was trying to stick it to the big guy. The casino moguls were hiding in the shadows, holding their breaths. It didn't matter how slim the chance of passing something was. They got paranoid and believed you had the wrench to break the machine. One such wrench was reform through transparency. That's the last thing casinos wanted. So when I rose, they couldn't shut me down without a sniper on the balcony. The sleeping media might wake up and smell a story.

The Democrats felt alarmed. They wanted to get through the process of expanding gaming quickly and without pain. I wasn't getting headlines but got noticed as a clever senator. The two reform senators who had upset Jubelirer and Brightbill came to Harrisburg to clean up the corruption. "Citizen Mike" Fulmer and John Eichelberger were easily convinced to support my open government amendments. Senator Dominic Pileggi, the majority leader, asked me politely to "leave my senators alone. You're going get them in trouble."

Who, me?

Fumo's grudge against Mellow got more intense. He urged "taking him on in caucus so they can see you're tough." I had been through numerous bruising campaigns and knew how tough I was. But the absurd eighth-grade-level machismo continued. The western guys said I was too nice, but they meant too threatening. Fumo wanted me to show them. I didn't want to fight Mellow, but Fumo urged, "If you want to be leader, you will."

The early exchange of letters with the senator was heartwarming—I got a chance to talk to my old friend without distractions—but I started to feel manipulated. Was Fumo just making up this federal scrutiny story? Was he using me to get revenge on Mellow? I dragged my feet until the next letter. "Time is of the essence. You must attack before he's indicted. This is imminent. If you wait, you'll look opportunistic and will fail."

I didn't want to waste my life sitting in a caucus room waiting for others to make decisions. The senate wasn't everything I'd hoped it would be. We were an institutional minority. Either I would help bring dramatic change, or I'd do something else. Most of our members had hit the lottery in winning their seats. This was the best job they would ever have, and they didn't want to rock the boat or cause any controversy that would put that in jeopardy.

I had the skills to be the leader. But the guys I'd been friendly with for years were threatened or underestimated me. Fumo said they were all weak and only respected bravado. He'd been the only one with balls. My collaborative style wouldn't work. I needed to be rhetorically violent. I got myself psyched up.

For purposes of this next part, I'd like to explain how legislative battles worked in Harrisburg. In my first weeks as a freshman, I carried a binder filled with copies of bills and amendments. Most of the other senators carried nothing or a manila folder or newspaper. Soon I figured out it wasn't the content of the legislation but the gusto of the battle. Most senators didn't even understand what they were voting on. Even when I learned to fight, like in this upcoming battle with Senator Mellow, I didn't understand the intricacies of the legislation. I don't think it's important for the reader to understand the bill, only that it sparked drama. I was no different than many senators who relied on my staff. When I brought Matt Franchak to the floor, it was to explain to me and to others what I was doing from a legislative standpoint. But the real purpose of my amendments was to demonstrate to the other Democratic senators that I was tough and a strong leader. It was showmanship no different than WWF cage matches. There were so many hidden deals in the nooks and crannies of the thousands of pages in the gaming bills. Many secret millionaires were about to be made. All I was doing was creating an illusion that I could stop it, that I could somehow pull back the curtain. The amendments were simple tools to challenge Bob Mellow for power and show the other senators. I was a formidable leader. The typed words were superfluous compared to the belligerent intent.

I took a breath and threw water on my face, knowing it was showtime. Franchak drafted the reform amendments and followed me into Mellow's elegant suite. We slid into the same emerald leather chairs from eight years before. I had come to see Mellow before my first swearing-in and remembered all the times he had worn a "STACK FOR SENATE" T-shirt and how he balled out Jack Wagner for drinking Hank's root beer. I didn't believe I was trying to set Mellow up. I was dancing with Fumo's evil tactics but was going to try to execute in the least harmful way. Mellow was initially receptive to my reform measures. He wanted to finesse me. He said, "The Republicans will never go for it." Nonetheless, he would offer them in the state government committee. That evening, they would move most of the gaming bills through Senator Jake Corman's committee. I made it clear that if they failed, I wanted to offer them on the floor. That way, I could ring the bell, letting everyone know reform was coming. Then, if they tried to shut me down, I might look like a hero in front of the cameras.

I shared my suspicion about Fumo's motives with Franchak, but he thought I could trust him. "Vince brought you to the dance, and I don't think he wants to hurt you." He followed me out to the bright lights of the chamber, carrying the amendments. The floor was crowded with activity, and the multitude of voices created a muffled thunder. The last rays of sun cut through the heavy iridescent curtains and stained-glass windows. The chamber was always like a cathedral. The murals by Violet Oakley depicting scenes from Pennsylvania history were captivating. For years I had been satisfied just watching the action in such palatial settings. But things were about to change. Maybe it was a risk. Once I made up my mind, put fear and sympathy aside, I knew I would execute. I was going to do some amazing acting.

Mellow stood outside the committee room just off the floor, looking pleased. He was kindly, like the best coach I ever had. "You have some amendments?" He waited for them like piles of cash, rubbing his hands. Everybody loved Franchak, and Mellow was no exception, because he was a Boy Scout in a den of thieves. But he had come a long way toward deviousness that combined brilliantly with his radiating decency. We had to be rough sometimes, and he earned a badge in savviness.

He handed over the folders like a scalpel. I pointed to each amendment number on the folders and calmly explained their intent. Bob knew they were poison pills.

"Thank you so much, Bob."

He slapped my back and smiled.

"Oh, Bob," I added. "If they go down, I need to offer them on the floor."

He forced a grin.

The gavel struck, Jake Corman winked, and all the insiders and lobbyists, hot women in tight skirts and men in bad suits, stood at attention around the table, shoulder to shoulder. The most attractive lady lobbyists had been hired out of Central Casting to throw meaningful glances at rural senators who'd never seen talent like that.

I received two or three votes on my amendments. Most of the Democrats voted against me. We watched Mellow as he shook his head in forced disappointment. "Tough one," he said.

I thanked him again and told him my intention.

His grin fell. "I offered your amendments. They failed. Now you want to disrespect me by offering them on the floor?"

I needed him hot. "I want to do what's right. We need transparency for the people," I said, and he almost gagged. There was nothing more absurd to a career politician than that. His only person was Louis DeNaples.

"Here's your fucking amendments!" He threw them from a few feet away, and they landed perfectly on my chest.

I clenched them, trying to get the folders to open and the papers to fall for dramatic effect. They flew into the air. I flailed, pretending to want to catch them, but they fluttered violently to the floor, causing palpable gasps to echo throughout the chamber. Senators and staff froze. I felt my cheeks redden. My performance was superb. Even Franchak was transfixed.

Now I needed a battle royale with Mellow, something out of the WWF, chairs flying in a caucus room in front of our quaking colleagues. That wasn't easy because they would dart off like frightened kittens. They often needed to be dragged into the room. Surprisingly everyone was there and in their seat, ready for a show. The only thing missing was popcorn.

Mellow called the meeting to order and knew he had a problem.

I spoke first. "I'd like to talk about what just happened in the hearing room." My sharp tone silenced the room.

"Let's have the staff step out, please," Bob said. That elevated the tension. There were microphones around every senator in this suddenly overcrowded room. Mellow recognized me ahead of the agenda.

"We'll never be in the majority so long as we act weak." I telegraphed that word for Senator Boscola, who often described Mellow with it. "I offered real reform, and you, Bob, literally threw it in my face, embarrassing me in front of the Republicans."

Mellow should've said, "That didn't happen" in a calm demeanor. Instead, he got defensive and angry. No one knew anything about my amendments until we were in a brouhaha. Mellow was adamant that my amendments "could threaten passage" of the gaming bill.

What was wrong with that? The members wanted reform too. Why weren't they informed by Mellow? Then I acted angrier. "Your humiliation of me was a humiliation of this caucus." I threw in some profanity and so did Mellow, and all eyes bulged. They had never seen me this hot or high-minded. I had been through tough campaigns and muscled through law school. I overcame betrayal and disappointment. But my colleagues didn't know me at all. Now they were getting a good look.

My boisterous performance against Mellow shocked them. Some were frightened, but Andy Dinniman, a Chester County swing vote, was mesmerized. "That was amazing!" he gushed afterward. "I never saw that side of you. That's what we need."

Shirley Kitchen whispered, "What has gotten into you? Remind me to never get you mad, Stacky."

Jim Ferlo glared hatefully. That was the moment I lost him forever.

I had no possibility of passing the amendments and knew it. I just wanted a chance to make a speech on the floor to solidify my new crusader image. The majority was so confident they had the votes to pass the bill that they told Mellow they liked me and had no problem with me wasting my breath.

Late that night, CJ Hafner approached my desk. "Senator Mellow says you can offer your amendments and he'll try to help." At around 11 P.M., I made a speech demanding the sunlight of transparency: Our citizens had a right to know who was influencing gambling in Pennsylvania. The media had gone home. I didn't get any headlines. I lost the battle, but the performance was magnificent. I had hurt Bob Mellow's feelings, but it had to be done. I showed the caucus that I was a leader and meant business.

Fumo gushed over my performance. I couldn't wait to read his review. I hadn't enjoyed exchanging mail this much since my high school sweetheart. "I was on the edge of my seat," he wrote. "My heart was pounding out of my chest, and I couldn't wait to see what happened." The fight was just on time because his source assured him that Mellow would be indicted within the next week. I wanted Fumo's approval, but he wrote, "Although the twists and turns were breathtaking, I must say, the ending was disappointing." He wanted that bill derailed like only he could have. He devoted a page describing how he defeated one of his own bills to screw the people who had welched on a promise. Maybe someday, I'd be that powerful. I would have sunk the bill if I could.

Within a few weeks, it really happened. Mellow was indicted for fraud and embezzlement related to his office space in Scranton. The key federal witness was his estranged wife. It wasn't surprising. The first Mrs. Mellow tore down Bob to my wife at a dinner during our first year in the senate. It was only a matter of time until he resigned. The real war for succession would be on.

* * *

Vince Hughes had been a pal, and I presumed we would work together once Mellow left. But I couldn't decipher a garbled voice message in the winter of 2010. Hughes called me Stacky and faded out while saying something about Costa. I returned home from National Guard duty and was still in fatigues when Tony Williams called. He was clear. "Please call me back about your good friend Hughes. He's sticking a knife in your back."

My ears rang and I held my breath. My hands trembled as I dialed the number.

Williams scoffed, didn't even say hello. "Thought I'd tell you about your buddies." Tony chastised me for not communicating better with him, and then he told me that Hughes had made a deal with Costa: Costa would be leader and Hughes appropriations chair. They offered Williams caucus secretary, which he considered an insult. He asked whether they had spoken with me since I was their ally. They responded that I'd probably come along.

Williams felt I should be insulted to be dismissed so nonchalantly. That was how the relationships worked. It was never about who you liked but the opposite. He wanted to stick it to them but feared they had somehow locked up the rest of the caucus. He proposed we work together to form an "opposition team." It was only logical that either he or I run for leader. He didn't believe the two Philadelphians could win both appropriations and leader. I was surprised when he suggested me for the top job.

The alliance rose out of thin air and seemed illogical. Williams was boisterous, selfish, and conniving. Fumo had wedged us regularly for his convenience.

He always said, "If everyone is singing Kumbaya, we got a problem." He elaborated, "We want them all at each other's throats, then they need us."

I misunderstood Williams. He could be intimidating but was willing to forget the past. Our caucus was weak because the members did not have honest relationships with each other. Everybody snuck around and made deals with either Mellow or Fumo. I had been guilty of dealing with Costa in the same way. But once Williams poisoned the well about the presumptive duplicity of Hughes and Costa, revolt pushed folks toward us.

Williams was more intelligent than Fumo understood. He was respected among the members, especially Shirley Kitchen and Leanna Washington. Leanna had a rough childhood and was a survivor of spousal abuse, and Shirley was streetwise and could fend for herself anywhere. She represented the hood in North Philly and battled rivals like John Street and council president Darrell Clark and demanded respect.

Farnese was an only child who had lost his creator to federal prison. He had a famous name. His grandfather had been president of the school board and then disowned Farnese's father. Farnese bristled when well-wishers praised his relation. He was frightened about the dramatic change and cherished security, as only children would.

Williams was the son of a senator, the silver fox Hardy Williams, who had run for mayor of Philadelphia and wooed women voters with his sexy charisma. We connected in that we both walked in the giant shadows of our pops.

Farnese's strategic thinking was that if his big brother Stack bonded with sturdy friends, he'd keep Larry safe. He worked as my campaign manager and pushed me into unlikely relationships. When his texts weren't answered, he'd call. If I didn't answer, he would track me down and ask me to recite the number of solid votes I had for leader. "Go get some more votes," he'd say.

Our first gathering was a luncheon at the unlikely Leeds steakhouse near the Turnpike. We could avoid being seen by lobbyists and staffers. Williams stood at the head of the table and announced in front of eight other senators that he was supporting me for leader. "But he needs a lot of education and improvement." He scolded me publicly so all could see he was calling the shots. Then the senators took turns describing my shortcomings. Tony coached that "Mean Mike, the one who yelled at poor Bob Mellow, had to go." He said the members liked Nice Guy Mike better. My job was to listen to my critics and thank them for their disparagement. Williams urged me to stay out of disagreements in the caucus room and leave that to the team. "Just be magnanimous to everyone, all the time." My phone had to be on, and I needed to always be available to our team.

I strolled past the bar while the senators ate dessert and noticed one of my favorite lobbyists, AFSCME Local 21's Barry Bogart. His apple cheeks were crimson and his curious eyes twinkled. He didn't understand what I was doing off the beaten track while Costa and Hughes were back at the capitol "cutting off your balls."

My heart pounded. "You think so, Barry? Then why are there nine senators in the next room backing me for leader?"

He chuckled for a moment. "I knew you wouldn't let them get away with it. What can I do to help?" Seeing Barry at the bar with an icy martini and a gambler's disposition was a most fortuitous event. I needed allies fast.

My new senate team was fragile, and getting labor guys was crucial. Barry knew exactly what I would ask when he offered his assistance, and I didn't disappoint. He didn't expect that I'd ask for fifty grand, but he appreciated the audacity.

"I'm for you, but I'd like to not get killed, if that's OK. Do you have a committee that's not that obvious?" Vision PAC eventually took in close to a million dollars. "This is my place," Barry said.

It was smart to meet there.

"From now on, put it on my tab. We need a guy with guts like you." I'm not sure Barry even thought I could win, but that's what it's all about. Your friends are the ones who are with you when it's not a sure thing.

\* \* \*

Williams came up with a brilliant idea to improve our team by recruiting veteran Senator Michael O'Pake to be appropriations chair. O'Pake had been a rising star in the 1990s but narrowly lost for attorney general only because he also ran for his state senate seat in the same election. He was the senior member of the caucus and served as whip yet had been dismissed as irrelevant by Costa and Hughes. O'Pake came from Berks County and had a charming and ingratiating manner. He was in his late sixties and unmarried. Williams's direction was savant, yet I began to question his motivation. The disease of paranoia ran rampant. Why would he suddenly be so helpful? O'Pake had been through numerous leadership elections and advised that "they bring out the worst in people." The next months would be filled with insecurity. All of us were privileged to serve in the senate but had irrational fears that we would lose everything in a parochial twenty-person election.

The lobbyists hedged their bets, giving to both sides. I put thousands of miles on my car and picked up frequent flyer miles visiting senators in their districts. I wanted to see where they lived and walk around Main Street. I contributed to their campaigns and took them and their spouses to dinners and Broadway shows. O'Pake was excited and proclaimed it had never been done like this before. "Usually, people just snuck around and did backroom deals." Fumo read my reports and implored me to visit him in prison "so I can really show you how to do this." He didn't want to put his secrets down on paper for fear of "incurring more charges."

Once again, I was experiencing a dreamlike existence. The quixotic idea of being a senator had dramatically changed. Instead of Mr. Smith going to Washington, I was Mr. Stack going to visit prison. Instead of being inspired by Abraham Lincoln, the Great Emancipator, my muse was Vincent J. Fumo, The Terminator. But I was excited to drive the eight hours to Ashland, Kentucky, to see my mentor. The drive through the snowy mountains would give me time to think. My dad visited politicians in jail regularly. He always said that when people were down, they appreciated you the most. That's also why he always pushed me to go to funerals. "I know they're not fun, but we're doing it for them."

I told myself it was a badge of honor, but I really wanted access to Fumo's brain. His letters revealed a sharp mind and clever disposition. He knew what made senators tick and all their soft spots. He had beaten Craig Lewis for appropriations chair in 1984 by one vote. He surprised Lewis by getting one senator to flip and getting rid of another, Jim Lloyd, who lost to Salvatore. I recalled my dad's example in 1988—Lewis had been the senator who refused to thank his supporters.

Several missing pieces in my own political puzzle were filled.

"Make sure you bring a lot of dollar bills," Fumo emphasized. I imagined some kind of magic trick that illustrated a lesson. "I'm serious. DON'T FORGET THE DOLLAR BILLS!" I had twelve singles in my pocket after driving through two different snowstorms in West Virginia.

It was like being in a movie. I never envisioned having an imprisoned mentor. I wanted to get into the senate, make momentous speeches, and crusade for the people. Instead, I shuffled through security with a notebook and a pocket full of one-dollar bills. Vince was going to tell me what he didn't want to put in letters.

Ashland Federal Prison Camp hosted a large, barbed-wire-encased facility for violent criminals where I mistakenly went. Thirty yards away was a single-story, red brick structure that looked like a local library. The American flag hung limply on a metal pole. A sign at the entrance prohibited blue jeans or T-shirts. I wore a collared shirt and khakis and walked cautiously through the glass doors. The guard at the reception desk announced over the PA system that inmate Fumo should report to the community room. Metal tables and vending machines hosted visiting families, and there was a festive hum of conversation and activity.

Fumo exploded through the metal swinging doors like a shaggy Johnny Fontane charging to the stage. His emerald canvas jumpsuit appeared tailored, and his confident grin unforced. His salt-and-pepper hair hung long and neat. The gray beard made his usually clean-shaven face look older. Several African American inmates waved to him from tables, and he went over and met their kids and spouses and hugged and shook hands like a brother. Never had I seen him look more relaxed. He was in his element.

He hugged me like we were on the stage again in 2000. "Sorry I didn't come right out. I had to get the warden to take care of one of my guys." He was running things and trading appointments like the warden was Bill Clinton. "You got the dollars?" What lesson was he going to teach? Finally, the mystery would be solved. He led me over to the giant vending machines, scanning the room suspiciously. The painted circles around them were like three-point lines, which served as barriers to inmates. "I'm not allowed there. I need you to get over there and get me the wings." He rubbed his hands and licked his lips. "Been thinking about them all week." I retrieved the bowl of greasy fowl, and we went to a table. "Get your notebook out," he said.

The things senators wanted were personal. They wanted their kids to have jobs or be promoted. They wanted to be on boards that were influential in their own district. They wanted to be integral. "There's a list somewhere with all the appointments the minority leader makes. You need to get it and use it." But the key was to show the members that I cared. It was like trying to seduce a woman. The magic of picking up votes was showing politicians devotion. He failed that test in marriage because he gave it all at the office. Leverage came through love. Two senators had children employed by the State Liquor Control Board and one at the Pennsylvania Turnpike. When I later offered, "We're getting Jimmy promoted," I got a western senator's attention. Vince knew where the bodies were. The senators gladly accepted campaign contributions, but most yearned to be on the winning side.

I couldn't keep track of Fumo's love-hate relationship with Williams. He warned about his treachery. He thought he could flip Leanna and Shirley against me. Andy Dinniman had won a special election in a Republican area. The professor taught at West Chester University and reflected his affluent district on economics. Fumo didn't know him but thought he might cut a deal with Costa. Dinniman was a centrist who felt the caucus had gone too far left. He didn't have to be an academic to notice we were an institutional minority, and he was ready for someone to rock the boat. My performance against Mellow had mesmerized him, and he became one of my staunchest allies.

The race would come down to two senators from Northeast Pennsylvania. John Blake had surprised the establishment in a five-way race for Mellow's seat. I made a tactical error by banking on former Scranton mayor Joe Doherty. One familiar member of the establishment had been for Blake. Unbeknownst to me, Mellow held him in his back pocket. John Yudichak, an ornery and independent man, would fill the seat vacated by Ray Musto, who was indicted a week before retirement.

Musto was like a grandfather to me. His thick, curly white hair and jolly demeanor made him an attractive mentor. When we traveled to Israel with a Jewish Federation delegation, Ray counseled me to stop worrying about my future in politics. Age and his thirty-eight years in the senate taught him that "everything works itself out." But Ray should've worried more. While in Congress in 1980, he met with undercover FBI agents posing as representatives of a fictitious Middle Eastern sheik. Musto declined a bribe from the FBI and was never charged in that investigation. But in 2010, a federal grand jury indicted him for accepting more than $28,000 from an unnamed company in exchange for help in obtaining grants and funding. Ray's health delayed the trial, and he was eventually declared mentally unfit. He passed away before trial. The criminal case was dismissed posthumously on April 30, 2014, so maybe he was right, and it did work out.

I courted Blake and Yudichak with reckless abandon. They claimed they wanted dramatic change and boldness. They lied.

\* \* \*

The buzz in Harrisburg gave me a substantial chance of winning. I thought Blake and Yudichak gave us a ten-to-ten tie with a chance to get Rich Kasunic, a Fumo confidante from Somerset County, as my eleventh.

Progressive champion Daylin Leach from Montgomery County gossiped that I had only a handful of votes. The senator who supposedly rocked the vote with his progressive mayhem inexplicably supported company man Costa. Leach tweeted it was going to be a landslide, which was anathema to internecine conflict and frightened potential supporters. Leach was immature and unaccountable, like an overgrown child. He alienated most of the southeastern senators with his leftist egomania and disloyalty to our region. His alliance with Costa was injurious, but the loss of Philadelphian Tina Tartaglione was fatal. She was jealous of my ascent because of her greater seniority. Seniority meant nothing if Philadelphia wasn't preeminent. At one time she had been a friend and helped me get elected, but she suffered catastrophic injuries in a boating accident in 2005 and morphed into a version of her mean mother in a wheelchair. Marge poisoned her further by reminding Tina of her history with my dad. She conveniently forgot that he visited her regularly at Magee Rehabilitation Center after her mishap. But this was typical of Philadelphia Democrats. They would rather make an alliance with the west than have one of their own gain preeminence. It was why Liberty Town struggled to become the next great city year after year.

Days before the election, I hosted a dinner at the Capital Grille in Philadelphia, followed by orchestra seats at *Jersey Boys*. I arranged a backstage tour to meet some of the actors. Farnese was dumbstruck about the wonderful night and the resources it took. Ten senators and one state supreme court justice attended. We looked like sure winners.

The pressure was getting to Farnese, who was hanging on by a string. For him, it was life or death. He would be more vulnerable to Doc's vengeance without clout in the caucus. Yet Farnese continued to play a significant role in encouraging the relationship with Williams. He believed we were natural partners who would corroborate and help coalesce the team. But Doc's evil talent for spreading soul-shaking lies disrupted our foundation.

Rumors that Williams was secretly for Costa ran rampant. Doc was better than Stalin at creating homicidal paranoia. He was not above sending anonymous letters to the media, committee people, and elected officials. Doc pretended to like me during this time but detested Brady openly.

Our party chairman was a master operator who stood unchallenged for decades. He did this by spotting potential challengers and converting them into allies. He was a shrewd leader who knew how to make judges and please ward leaders. But the guy from Two Street preferred poison to pleasantries. He wanted to kill his enemies instead of converting them. So he was hateful and jealous. He despised Brady because he wanted to be him and couldn't. Soon we heard rumors that Brady was screwing us. We didn't even know Brady was following the leadership race. It was an insidious but predictable pattern. We were ready for the mental institution by the weekend before the election.

\* \* \*

My rotating system of calling senators had resulted in uncertainty. I listened to the tone of their voices and heard deception. When Williams mentioned he was watching NFL games and felt good about our race, the compulsion to look into his eyes was overwhelming.

"Why don't I come over?" I asked.

He paused, then said, "Alright."

Farnese answered my call after one ring.

"What are you doing today besides going crazy?" I asked.

"That's all. Just climbing the walls."

"Want to join me watching football with Williams?"

"Absolutely!" We knew we could sit together and know who was lying.

It was a positive thing that I visited Williams at home. He lived near Cobbs Creek Golf Course in a blue-collar suburb of Southwest Philadelphia. The neighborhood was probably 90% Black and eerily close to the Osage Avenue block that was burned to the ground in 1985. Williams donned a black velour sweatsuit, immaculate white sneakers, and a flashy Sixers ball cap. His cousin and aid Michael was thrilled to see us. I brought a pepperoni pizza and a two-liter of Pepsi, and we relaxed and took in three games. I almost forgot we were there to monitor the situation as part of a paranoid roller coaster ride.

My phone vibrated, and I walked out of the room to take a phone call from Brady. He was just checking in about the leadership election. "I'm not sure you can trust Williams, and I'd keep an eye on Farnese."

I was watching them from the laundry room. "Thank you, Bob, but I think they're alright."

Farnese became further distressed that Brady didn't trust him. "That guy never forgave me for taking Vince's place."

I said, "You didn't. Just his seat." Once again, Brady's wariness of Williams and Farnese must have been stoked by Doc's devious rumor mill.

* * *

The next Tuesday was the election. The nausea and anxiety of yet another election were upon me. I took the team to breakfast near the capitol. Leana Washington was so confident she demanded something good from the winners' spoils. "You figure it out, Mike, but it needs to be big." Dinniman had no doubts. The caucus wanted new energy and that was me.

When I returned to my office, John Yudichak was waiting in the reception area, pretending to read a magazine. We shook hands and he said, "I want to thank you for everything." Then he picked up a bucket of ice water and threw it on me. "I just told Jay Costa he has my vote." I contemplated putting him into a headlock and choking the life out of him. Instead, I walked him to the door of the suite. In the fog of disappointment, hearing the thump of my heart, I saw John Blake enter Costa's office and Tony Lepore grinning, his cinnamon-bun-chomping face radiating across the balcony. I could hear the faint, haunting melody.

That fat bastard was the singing lady.

The disgust I felt was reminiscent of that in other losses but more intimate. Many of the people who looked into my eyes so earnestly were lying. They took everything I had to offer and voted against me. I felt used and disrespected, but I made those bastards vote. I wouldn't back down like Williams two years earlier. We agreed the election could be by secret ballot, which I regretted. Tony showed me the piece of paper where he'd written my name for leader. I was disappointed that he believed I didn't trust him. I lost 12–8.

Although I felt physically ill, it was heartening to know I had the fortitude to go all the way. I had developed skills and character from years of service and learning, but the members were threatened by change. Costa offered continuity and predictability. He was a nice guy and wouldn't rock the boat against the Republicans. I emphasized that in my speech, and our relationship suffered for years. He and Hughes sought vengeance by demoting me to lesser committees and taking me off appropriations. Once again, I was all through. I hated losing, but I thought of that damn Abraham Lincoln again. I sought solace from my dad, but like others, he didn't grasp the depth of the perfidy, the soul-sucking anguish. My own people had rejected me. Jim Ferlo savaged my friendship with Fumo, even though that munchkin hung on his coattails. The prince's coaching remained a secret.

Fumo wrote encouragingly after the debacle: "You took Williams and those people as far as you could. I'm proud of you. Now get ready for the next fight. Winners never quit, and quitters never win."

I was now fully convinced that I was different from the rest of my colleagues. I aspired to something more important than just the gratitude of having a potential lifetime job with a big title. I watched Michael O'Pake grovel with Williams to hold onto his job as whip after I lost. He pleaded, "I can't go home after all these years without a leadership position. What would people say?" Williams gave in.

Many of my team begged Costa to forgive them. Andy Dinniman demanded to know of any would-be repercussions. He didn't want to lose his chairmanship on the education committee. Costa was forced to claim there wouldn't be any so he'd continue to look magnanimous. But that didn't include me.

Fumo showed more bravado from prison than all the sitting senators. We exchanged dozens of letters, and I learned more from him in that last year than ever. His teaching style was seductive. He could garner for me the arch of the covenant and untold power if I listened. He had taught high school biology and knew how to explain and entice. He could've done anything with his life. He would've been a great CEO, but he relished the combat and mind games of politics.

Fumo still had axes to grind but plotted while reading and resting more than ever. He had a physical trainer in prison. I imagined him on the bench press, pushing out sets while instructing his guys in the yard. They called him senator, and he negotiated with the warden so his buddies could get better accommodations. Favors were currency, and he knew how to spend. Fumo was a former banker who gave financial advice to inmates. He'd heard the tales of bunkmates, hedge fund kings, corporate raiders, and drug dealers and became ever more convinced that money was of little value. "It was fungible. It comes and goes and should never be your priority." But his perspective changed upon his release, when he cut his children out of their trust because he needed the money for a comeback. Fumo dangled his bag of tricks. Power was better than money and he would dazzle me. "Stick with me, pal," he said. "You won't believe what I'm going to show you."

Mike O'Pake was single and had amassed a significant fortune as a senator and lawyer. His charitable work for Saint Joe's University and numerous Catholic charities was well known. Any hospital in Pennsylvania would've been available for his heart surgery, but O'Pake wasn't alarmed and wanted to be loyal to the Berks County hospital that he had bolstered over the years. It was a fatal decision for him and me. Eight votes dropped to seven, and Williams and Washington weren't up for an even longer shot struggle. Costa was smart enough to pull them in with committee assignments and appointments. The old magic of the previous run wasn't there. They announced at our table at Leeds to count them out.

Standing in the parking lot next to the highway that led to the turnpike, Farnese asked, "Now what do we do?"

I said, "We go to the movies."

On session evenings, Larry bent my ear with incessant conversation throughout the entire movie at the Harrisburg Mall, but his alarm could only be reduced with my quarterbacking whatever plan he devised. He tortured me at every movie. He was my campaign manager and searched endlessly for opportunities. He felt our enemies were in the caucus room and a growing number were influenced by Johnny Doc, who gave them Eagles tickets and campaign cash.

Tony Williams had tried to heal the rift with Dougherty during our leadership run. We met at the glass-encased Marathon Grill at Nineteenth and Market Street in Philadelphia. The sun practically blinded me as Dougherty strutted in with Brian Stevenson, his bulky bodyguard who would later become a federal informant.

"You're gonna need to listen," Doc said. He went on a diatribe about all the disrespectful things I had done over the years. One incomprehensible verbal puzzle went something like this: "I know you said I was under federal investigation and about to be arrested. I heard that McGeehan said he heard you said it to Kenny Adams after that story in the *Inquirer*. He said his cousin Jimmy, who works for Bill Keller, heard you said it."

I shrugged with confusion. I hadn't said anything about him getting indicted or arrested, but I was sorry that that's what he heard. It was the typical conversation with this maniac.

At the end, Doc said, "You're okay with me, Mike, okay? We're okay."

I wasn't.

Williams remarked, "I don't know how you just sat there and took it. But good job."

# CHAPTER TEN

# JUST LEAVE ME ALONE TO
# FIGHT THE GOVERNOR

There wouldn't be a leadership race in 2012, but I had the opportunity to fight for the underdog against a much bigger adversary. The bell rang when newly elected Governor Tom Corbett decided to cut the adult basic health insurance program to balance the budget. Slashing this program was an insult to working women, who were the primary recipients of the low-cost insurance. But I was the only one who seemed to care. I thought the program was vital, and I made speeches every day and proposed several legislative fixes. I called Governor Corbett heartless and cruel during more than one hundred floor speeches. I wanted him to react and take me on. Much to his credit, he never crossed swords. He stayed above the fray as governors should. In fact, Corbett endorsed my idea to transfer funds from the legislative reserves to pay for the program. Referring to the reserve as a political slush fund was hyperbolic and enraging to the leaders of each caucus.

Although Senator Jay Costa promised no repercussions after the leadership battle, I was removed from the appropriations committee and assigned to weaker ones, like local government. During my demotion, Kermit Gosnell, an OB/GYN, was charged with murdering three infants who were born alive during late-term abortions. He also killed at least one female patient. Gosnell today is referred to as America's biggest serial killer because, according to testimony, the murder of live-born infants was a routine practice. An employee testified that she had seen Gosnell kill hundreds of infants. An assistant admitted that he had probably killed one hundred live-born babies himself because Gosnell told him it was a normal part of abortion practice "to ensure demise."

Gosnell lived in the Mantua neighborhood of Philadelphia and owned the Women's Medical Society Clinic, dubbed "the house of horrors" during his criminal trial. In a 2010 raid, authorities found the intact remains of forty-six victims stored in plastic bags. Not only was Gosnell performing illegal abortions and committing murder and rampant code violations, but he was also a prolific prescriber of numerous illegal substances, including OxyContin. How is such a maniac allowed to run free? Why did the Pennsylvania Department of Health and the Philadelphia Department of Licenses and Inspections not shut down this madman? That's what I wanted to know, so I walked across the senate floor to see John Eichelberger, the chairman of the most obscure and irrelevant committee in the chamber. The local government committee, home of freshmen backbenchers and an insurrectionist named Stack, was about to become relevant.

Eichelberger defeated powerful Senator Bob Jubelirer as part of the backlash of the disastrous pay raise fiasco. He happened to be pro-life but was minding his own business when I dragged him down to Philadelphia to convene a hearing that received more media coverage than he had gotten in his entire career. We subpoenaed witnesses from the city departments that failed humanity. My old buddy Senator Vincent Hughes was dispatched to spy on me and report back to Costa. Farnese proclaimed, "Stack has done it again! He took the lamest committee and set a ratings record." I know now it wasn't the committee or the title that made one important, but the person. They even made a movie about the tragedy, *Gosnell, the Trial of America's Biggest Serial Killer*, starring Dean Cain.

Philadelphia Mayor Michael Nutter decried, "We've had a monster living in our midst." Governor Tom Corbett was "appalled at the inaction on the part of the health department." District Attorney Seth Williams raved, "My comprehension of the English language can't adequately describe the barbaric nature of Doctor Gosnell." My work with Senator Eichelberger on the local government committee wasn't the only reason for the media feeding frenzy, but it was one of them.

I found a new freedom in speaking frankly against things that were wrong without fear of repercussion. I didn't worry about my position in the caucus or gaining notoriety. Fighting for working women and the poor rarely garnered headlines. Doing away with the program was still inhumane and outrageous, so I was surprised to have the floor to myself.

Corbett had the physical gifts of a governor, with his thick silver mane and steely blue eyes, but not the political acuity. In addition to cutting women's health insurance, he slashed Penn State's funding and the funding for public education across the state and in districts of powerful Republicans. His own party began to detest him, and his polling nose-dived. Yet he refused to change course as he sailed toward the waterfall.

\* \* \*

My dad loved planning the family treasure hunt at the shore during Easter weekend. He drew up clues that family members placed under seashells, tires, and old, rusted anchors. We ran around Stone Harbor in a frantic search for the basket of goodies from the Dollar Store. He was a camp counselor at Big Brothers as a teenager and knew how to organize activities. Then at Saint Joe's University, he was czar of intramurals. The man orchestrated the fun, but in 2011, his health issues were becoming chronic. A toe injury got infected as a complication of diabetes, and he was transported to Temple University Hospital. I was a trustee and got him the best medical attention. That ability alone made all the political trauma well worth it.

I videotaped the exciting finish of the hunt on my phone. A bunch of grandkids rummaged through the cardboard boxes of prizes like they were diamonds and pearls. He smiled after viewing the action from his hospital bed, and then began to sob. I'd only seen him cry twice: when one sister died on the operating table during open heart surgery, and when another sister, her husband, and baby died in a car accident. Usually, he was pleasantly stoic. He didn't want to be sick and miss that treasure hunt. I had never seen him so vulnerable, and I was frightened of losing him.

"Getting old is not for sissies," he said. It was just us in that hospital room. After a few moments of quiet except for the ringing and clanging of medical machines, he pushed his glasses closer to his eyes. "You should put your name out there for governor after your reelection to the senate." I didn't care about politics right then, but he always did. "People should think about you in that light." I just wanted him to get better but knew he wouldn't.

Dad told me more about his childhood in those last days. It had been a misadventure of bad supervision. He admitted to sneaking into the Palestra for a Big Five doubleheader when he was ten. From a nosebleed seat, he spotted a stylish young man near the court, holding a magnificent leather bomber jacket next to him. Dad crept down the wooden bleachers, row by row, until he reached the one behind the man and jacket. As the final whistle blew, he made his move, swept up the jacket, and tore across the court, leading a parade of angry pursuers.

He described it from his hospital bed with the relish of a movie director constructing an Oscar-winning scene, running down corridors, hiding in bathrooms, standing on toilet seats, knees knocking as angry voices echoed and doors banged. Panting and perspiring, he escaped to his Catherine Street home and placed his treasure on a hanger, nestled behind others, hidden in the dark of his closet. He barely slept, heart thumping, fear and excitement shooting through his mind. He couldn't find it the next day after school. What had become of the jacket? Was it a dream? He tiptoed into the kitchen, where his mother was drinking tea at the table. The floorboard squeaked, and in her usual brogue, she said, "It went to the charity," without turning around.

Why did I get to know him best near the end of the road? Every time I heard an ambulance while jogging, I feared this was it. The mysterious, big-city political boss reverted to being a mischievous little kid before my eyes. He didn't have a mean bone in his body. He loved that I was a senator even though he had never made it to elected office. He was an enigma of unfulfilled ambition.

At one time, being party chairman was in his sights, but Mayor Rizzo told him he was too young. Then the mayor recruited him to run for Congress but pulled his support at the last minute. The next time Dad vied for chairman, the Bambino said he was too old. Dad kept pushing me so I wouldn't grow too old to achieve political fame.

Time marched on but had its own clock. His was running out. His ambition meshed into mine. It had always been about winning that senate seat for the first time. Now he just wanted me to put my name out there for governor. No problem.

* * *

Tonya and I emerged from the elevator at the Waldorf Astoria and were immediately surrounded. Acquaintances suddenly thought they were friends. People who liked Tonya now adored her. I was transformed from a guy who couldn't win a caucus election to an exciting gubernatorial hopeful. Matt Franchak had simply whispered in the ear of a reporter and shared information with some known gossipers that I was "looking at governor," and the fire spread. The Pennsylvania Society was where all the investors and politicians convened to handicap the big races. Governor Corbett was bleeding, and Democrats were lining up to take him on. I just "put my name out there" and felt the earth shake.

We were an attractive couple. Tonya was youthful and pretty but also blunt and funny. I still had my hair, looked elegant and slender in a black tuxedo, and could make an effective speech. I was from Philadelphia, where most of the Democratic votes came from those who served in the military, a rarity for Democrats.

Other Democrats were ahead of me in the line. Allyson Schwartz, a well-known congresswoman and liberal stalwart, had been planning a race for years. Rob McCord, the state treasurer, was wild-eyed with ambition. Katie McGinty was effervescent and intelligent and had served in the Clinton administration and in Governor Rendell's cabinet. There were other candidates, including an unknown furniture salesman from Central Pennsylvania named Tom Wolf, and John Hanger, a former Environmental Protection Agency secretary.

My bold foray lasted a few uncomfortable months. A story appeared in the *Inquirer* on February 24, 2013, entitled "The Right Democrat?" The photograph of me was complimentary, which was rare. Tom Fitzgerald's story described how I had made the obligatory pilgrimage of all would-be statewide candidates to the Pennsylvania Farm Show in Harrisburg and didn't get much media attention. He wrote that I was betting voters of Pennsylvania were ready for a "machine politician from the city much of the state loves to hate." I was leader of the 58th Ward, "son of a beloved ward leader and grandson of a New Deal congressman."

I undercut the premise that Allyson Schwartz would be the first female governor because she was not strong on crime. "This state is not really a Democratic state," I said. "It's a conservative hybrid." Allyson was offended by the article because I said she was too liberal. But I had said she was an articulate and energetic leader. I'd been one of her few ward backers when she ran successfully for Congress. Fumo implored, "Get her into Congress and out of here." As a member of our caucus, Allyson got an inordinate amount of press coverage and knew how to take credit.

Soon Fitzgerald wasn't the only one saying that I might be the right candidate because of my moderate credentials. Jerry Pappert had prosecuted my dad during the kitchen table petition scandal as acting attorney general. As a panelist on *Inside Story*, the local ABC political talk show, he predicted I could win the primary. Then a Quinnipiac Poll gave me a two-point lead over Tom Corbett. Allyson Schwartz had a three-point lead, and Rob McCord was trailing by a point. I don't know how they did these polls, but most people didn't even know my name. I tried not to get swept away in the unreality of the poll.

The resources necessary to run for governor were outlandish, and I didn't know where the money would come from. Tonya asked about my stress level with the gubernatorial run. I hadn't planned it and didn't know what to do. She pointed at her eyes. "Look here," she said. "You're not running, just putting your name out there. Got it?"

The ride was thrilling for a while, and I got a kick out of saying I was running for governor. When the words came out, it felt like an acting role, and I was convincing. But deep down, I knew this wasn't the right time. As I considered my next move, Ken Snyder, Fumo's former communictions director, called from Chicago. He had disappeared from Philadelphia once Fumo was indicted, apparently concerned he would be subpoenaed. His rival consultant, Howard Cain, was indicted for tax evasion during the Fumo investigation.

Cain made a plea bargain and testified against his benefactor. As part of his guilty plea, he admitted that from 1991 through 2006, he filed no individual federal income tax returns, failed to report more than $1.6 million in personal income to the IRS, and paid none of more than $400,000 in taxes he owed. Cain was sentenced to ten months in federal prison. These were the people who advised us. It's amazing that all of us didn't go to prison.

Snyder must've thought it was safe to poke his head out. No one had seen or heard anything from him in years, but the smell of money had brought him back. "If you're going for governor, I'm in," he said. "But I don't see where the money's coming from." He had seen my campaign finance report that showed $600,000 in the bank. "But if you drop down and run for lieutenant governor, I think you'd win."

The consensus was building that Allyson Schwartz would emerge as the nominee. There had never been a ticket with two southeast candidates, but Snyder believed that such a ticket could win by boosting the number of votes from our region. I didn't know if I wanted to be lieutenant governor, but I was looking for something new. Since I had just been reelected to the senate, I could take a less risky shot than governor and hold onto my seat. It might be a unique learning experience.

I'd grown to like Allyson Schwartz. She was very liberal, but not like the progressives of today who border on radical, and I was perceived as moderate. Her former senate district was affluent and suburban, and mine was blue-collar with many cops and firefighters. But when the incumbent Congressman Joe Hoeffel vacated his seat, she impressed me with her savviness and diligence. She knew she had to be more moderate and asked if I could help her. She was a hard worker and an excellent candidate. She beat future state treasurer Joe Torsella in a close US Congressional race.

The tension that developed between the two of us during my gubernatorial exploration was further exploited by my old pal, Johnny Doc. His fingerprints were on my loss for leader. He had a close relationship with John Yudichak and may have swayed him against me. Dougherty seemed to follow me around, trying to anticipate my ambition and then foil it. He had never been a supporter of Allyson Schwartz until he thought I was running. She was a suburban liberal, and he was a brass-knuckle union leader. Dougherty had nothing in common with Allyson but immediately rushed to endorse her and provided large amounts of cash and Hoodies. At her party during a Democratic state committee convention in Harrisburg, it was like *Alice in Wonderland*. All the grizzled labor guys and slick opportunists wore Local 98 "Schwartz for Governor" sweatshirts. I tried to get one for my collection but was icily rebuffed.

Snyder continued to pitch the idea that a Schwartz-Stack ticket could win. He flew in from Chicago to meet me in a rented Center City office. He and his pollster were adamant. "Allyson Schwartz is going to win the nomination for governor, and then she is going to be elected the first female governor of Pennsylvania." My job as lieutenant governor would be easy. She might want me to be an attack dog or to just stand against the wall and look pretty. But I could get out of the state senate and have a new public service adventure. I could run statewide and win. Countless Philadelphians had failed statewide. It was a spectacular chance to set myself apart in a low-risk way. After all, no one cared about lieutenant governor.

Snyder had convinced me. But I wouldn't really join the ticket. Pennsylvania elected lieutenant governor separately and then merged them into one ticket for the fall general election. I would run my own campaign and put myself in a position to win, even before the likely governor was determined. My race was different than many others in the history of Pennsylvania. I was a bolder, savvier politician and didn't need a gubernatorial candidate to hand-pick me. I would get myself to the show and thus be independent.

Snyder's pollster did a superb job identifying surprisingly important issues. There were several pertinent issues that stood out and eluded all the other pollsters. Pennsylvania Democrats supported marriage equality, a ban on assault weapons, and women's health care rights. Even the LGBTQ communities in Philadelphia and Pittsburgh had not boldly demanded equal marriage rights. They were cautious, but I was already a cosponsor of a marriage equality bill. Even if Pennsylvania was a pro-gun state, most Democrats and all soccer moms wanted an assault weapons ban. I had always been supportive of women's health care. I was excited to be the star of our statewide commercial.

My campaign manager, Marty Marks, from Pittsburgh, said, "Get ready to be famous for two weeks and then completely forgotten." When it came time to produce a commercial, I was standing in shirt sleeves and khakis, my natural way of dressing, and talking directly to the camera. The background was plain except for some set lights. This was the first time I could speak the truth directly to the people of Pennsylvania. I had always fought for marriage equality, women's health, and an assault weapons ban, and now everyone would know it if I raised more money. Snyder cajoled me to keep calling for dollars so he could run more commercials and get more commissions.

Two of my opponents were from the west, including former congressman Mark Critz, who President Clinton had campaigned for four years earlier. State Representative Brandon Neuman was young and popular. Schuylkill County's Matt Smith and Dauphin County's Brad Koplinski had campaigned for over a year. Jay Paterno, the son of the famous Penn State football coach, was a serious threat until he failed to garner enough petition signatures.

Even though I thought I was the best candidate, I benefited from being the only one from Southeastern Pennsylvania. I had my home region all to myself as the other candidates cannibalized each other. I could win this race, but then would come the forced marriage with the gubernatorial nominee. Allyson was perfect, but would she make it?

An ice storm froze power lines that winter. Governor Corbett was doing his best to show leadership and get the power back on. It was one of his better moments. He answered his cell phone immediately.

"Governor, you've been doing an excellent job in dealing with this emergency," I said. "Please let me know how I can support your efforts."

Corbett was pleased with my encouragement. He never got irked about my floor speeches or critical press releases. A few minutes later, a clever political commercial depicting a friendly businessman driving a Jeep aired above the ticker tape of news. No candidate had enough money to run commercials at the beginning of the new year all the way through to election day. But Tom Wolf's commercials ran and ran, and we were all stuck inside. Wolf apparently had money to burn, and I knew McCord and Schwartz must have been going nuts. I was glad I had decided to run for lieutenant governor. The candidate with the most money for TV commercials would usually win. Nothing else mattered. Experience and credentials weren't required if one could sell fresh and new. And the furniture merchant was selling it.

McCord had gotten rich as a Wall Street investment banker and had a hyper energy that made him both attractive and unsettling. As state treasurer, he brought innovation and technology to the office and improved investment strategy. Yet he was obsessed with becoming governor.

Schwartz had been an excellent senator and congresswoman and a prolific fundraiser. Fumo was pleased that I supported her for Congress because it got her out of his hair in the senate. She elbowed her way to the head of all our press conferences and knew how to get headlines.

Both McCord and Schwartz were wild-eyed with ambition and had an enormous fundraising capacity. But they didn't have Wolf's money. Nobody did. He promised to spend $10 million of his own cash, and he was doing it. The financial pressure triggered mistakes. Allyson fired her fundraising chief because she couldn't compete with Wolf. McCord went nuts and abused the office. He complained that Wolf's spending was a campaign finance violation, and then he was later charged with extortion. His desperation led him to strong-arm contributors by threatening to pull business.

When I complimented Wolf on his campaign, he shrugged. "Well, the secret was I had $10 million. My opponents didn't." It was that simple. The statement struck me as cynical and didn't match up with the good-natured geek who drove a Jeep.

I captured almost 50% of the votes in a five-way race. I won by over 40 points. Wolf won by 11. Now we were a ticket. While he was lucky to have me with my relationships in the senate and my savviness, he didn't act like it. Gubernatorial candidates usually chose weaker, non-threatening running mates, but his team hadn't thought it through. My usual enemies, seen and unseen, hadn't been prescient enough to sabotage. No one had anticipated my drop to lieutenant governor. I arrived without the usual shrapnel, uninjured and ready to serve. I was received with dismay and frigidity. They never invited me to campaign events, which was strange and counterproductive. One of my campaign aides from the primary got a job on the Wolf campaign and reported that they would regularly run me down for being a machine politician with a close relationship to Bob Brady.

I encountered similar animosity in the Clinton campaign from people who never met me. Nonetheless, most Democrats thought Wolf-Stack was a great ticket. Tom Wolf was the inexperienced businessman with bold, new ideas, and I was the savvy senator from the big city who could help us win over the legislature. The Wolfies were contemptuous and suspicious, but I ignored their stupidity and immaturity.

Corbett never laid a glove on Wolf, who ran his Jeep commercial and another ad where his employees raved about what a great boss he was. I didn't appear in any of his commercials. I had only one debate with Lieutenant Governor Jim Cawley on a Harrisburg radio station. Jim was the perfect right-wing foil who guaranteed we'd raise taxes and destroy the economy. I scoffed and accused Corbett of gutting public education. We had a great rumble and raised our voices without yelling. There were hot sound bites, and I think I did well. Cawley and I shook hands and knew there were no hard feelings. He had class and was very supportive in the transition. He said his advisors underestimated me, but he told them, "I see this guy in the senate every day, and he's formidable."

Wolf didn't want my company on election night. I suggested we appear together after we won. "That will be just for family, Mike." He didn't even want me to attend the victory party. I thought maybe the guy was just quirky. Then I recalled the different campaign stops where he looked offended when I appeared. I'd have to fight to get introduced and his aide, Mary Isenhour, seemed aghast. These people were silly and weird. I tried to have thick skin and not take it personally, but I knew I was on their kill list. Back then, I was content to let Tom be the big star while I waited in the wings.

I liked Katie McGinty and introduced her to the senate committee that would vote on her nomination to Rendell's cabinet a few years before.

Conservative senator Mary Jo White roughed up McGinty for a liberal environmental record during the Clinton years. McGinty attended Saint Hubert's High School and Saint Joseph's University. Starting from a working-class background, she rocketed into the elite world of policy wonks who advised the president. Her long brown hair and freckled skin gave the appearance of youth, but her omnipresent grin telegraphed arrogance to the Republicans. I told the committee that we grew up in the same neighborhood in Northeast Philadelphia, and they stared coldly. But that's what senators did at nominating committees, tenderized the appointee so they understood who was boss. After her nomination was held up for six weeks, she was confirmed. Then she ran for governor but couldn't overcome better-funded candidates, including Wolf, and she finished in fourth place.

In the closing days of our campaign, she asked to meet. I had seen her just before introducing President Obama to a screaming crowd at Temple University. She asked if I had met the president in the "grin and grip room." I told her it had been surprisingly pleasant. Obama was far more down-to-earth than I expected and wanted to know how he could help us. He looked into my eyes and had unusually soft hands. Katie hadn't made the cut for the grip room but apparently had for the cabinet room.

We met at a saloon in Northwest Philly, and it was clear we were going to win. Yet McGinty was concerned we didn't have a plan for the billion-dollar budget shortfall. Josh Shapiro was advising Wolf, and she didn't believe the commissioner had a specific plan. Katie knew my senate connections could lead to a fiscal solution. Then she revealed why it was so important to her: "Homegirl is going to be chief of staff." Shapiro's solution may have been to hire an outside consultant because that's what the governor did. Katie wouldn't have to worry about having a budget proposal, just getting one passed.

We stayed in Philadelphia on election night and filled the sheet metal workers' hall with balloons and fans. I had a VIP party on the second floor, and it was everybody from the party on the first floor crowded into a smaller room.

There were always new revelations about the history of hate in our city. I could never understand the feuds. None of the politicians in Philadelphia agreed on anything other than common contempt for rivals. Daylin Leach, who had voted against me for leader, stood by my side on the victory stage. My dad always said, "Yesterday's enemies may be tomorrow's friends." Leach was an example.

My career transformed monumentally in a short amount of time. After Fumo's indictment, we moved mountains to get Larry Farnese elected and incurred the permanent wrath of John Dougherty. We'd failed in two leadership races and had been sent to Siberia by Costa and Hughes. But I'd been resilient and resourceful in utilizing irrelevant committees to impact public policy. I'd utilized the crusading zeal of Senators Eichelberger and Fulmer to gain support for a variety of good government amendments and expose a murderous monster. I'd lost my father, who had shown me the way, and explored running for governor. Now I would become the second-highest elected official in Pennsylvania.

Senator Andy Dinniman approached me on the senate floor with a mischievous smile. "We knew you'd come back but never like this!"

Brady phoned before we hit the stage. "I've never seen anything like it. You're shutting out everyone. You won 100% at many of these divisions!" Then he revealed that Ed Rendell had urged him to support Mark Critz in the primary. The former mayor was against the hometown candidate. Rendell inexplicably referred to my "shady family." Interestingly, Brady waited until I'd won to tell me.

I never understood Rendell's acrimony. We never had an unpleasant exchange. Maybe he resented the story from Neil Oxman about the ice cream scoop of butter, which I repeated too many times. I always liked Rendell, but obviously he didn't like me. Perhaps he blamed me for standing next to Fumo as he threatened to strangle him. It was all in a day's work—no offense intended—but Rendell was blessed that most people never held their grudge, even after he lied or welched. He bragged to Rob McCord, "With Mike Stack's hair, I would've been president." But Rob was humbler.

The Fumo who became a reassuring father figure while incarcerated gradually reverted to his Darth Vader ways. Disparaging remarks in his emails against the US attorney and FBI were intercepted and warranted resentencing. The feds sought ten more years for Fumo's appalling lack of remorse. He was transported across the country, back to the same federal courtroom he had left years before. Public Enemy Number One had not slipped in the rankings. They put him on an old Army plane that reeked of fuel and a rickety bus that injured his back. The resentencing was a sold-out event. Tonya and I witnessed the spectacle. We waited in line for the packed courtroom, where dozens of well-wishers were turned away.

Gasps of shock careened off the walls when Fumo appeared, looking like a wild man. His gray hair was long and unruly, his prodigious beard unkempt. The chains on his legs and arms clanked as his eyes bulged like a homeless maniac ranting about the end of days. Nonetheless, the judge cut him another break with only eleven more months. Later, Vince bragged that his Unabomber appearance was an act "to bust their balls."

Fumo came out of prison ready to get back in the game. He wasn't broken. He returned to his mansion with his kids' trust money. He would get it back to them when they needed it. The former senator was back in khakis and Oxford shirts and thoroughly against my running for lieutenant governor. The job had no power and no upside. If I had stayed in the senate, he could've made me leader. He forgot that we already tried that twice. Now I was a statewide winner.

Vince called to congratulate me the next day "for whatever it's worth." He offered, "You're going to have a problem with this guy." He watched Wolf's victory party on television and was struck. "I never saw a governor win and stand on stage alone. This guy is a narcissist." Vince thought he was dangerous. I thought Fumo was paranoid. He was just trying to wedge my new mentor. Maybe I could learn from Wolf, the successful businessman, while he tried to balance the budget. Boy, was I wrong.

I had dinner with Tom Wolf the night before we were sworn in. My two aids, Matt Franchak and Dylan McGarry, joined Katie McGinty and Mary Isenhour at our table. Tom picked up the check, and we were friendly but not warm. We were struck that Katie and Mary didn't seem to know each other or Wolf very well. I had a close relationship with most of my staff and usually followed their advice.

In our new role, we tried to do the same things as other lieutenant governors but added my special charisma. Wolf had no directives other than to help with the senate. I didn't invent the job, but I knew the most important thing was to be prepared if I ever needed to step in as governor. I knew that I had more experience in government than Wolf and perhaps any previous lieutenant governor. I was serious and focused but would not force myself upon the governor.

Two weeks before swearing in, Sergeant Nelson, who ran the governor's protective detail, visited my senate office and asked me to accept protection. I had watched lieutenant governors for years step into the black SUVs escorted around the capital with armed guards, and I thought it was ridiculous. I didn't want to do it. I liked my privacy and particularly I liked my wife's privacy. In the past, there had been controversy involving Jim Cawley's wife's job as a real estate broker. State police drove her to New York regularly, and negative publicity emerged. Sergeant Nelson later announced they would no longer take her to New York. It struck me that the state police were reacting to media criticism. This was worrisome, so I wanted to think about it for a while. But Sergeant Nelson was adamant that we should also live in the lieutenant governor's residence to make protecting us easier.

Senator Joe Scarnati succeeded to lieutenant governor when Catherine Baker Knoll died of cancer. He and I were elected in the same year, but his climb was faster. He became president pro tempore, the leading Republican senator. An adept politician with a keen sense of his surroundings, he encouraged me to proceed. "They have their own way of doing things. They're kind of a strange group." They were indispensable for traveling around the state, "but be careful."

How was I supposed to know who was a sociopath and who wasn't? It was my first time being lieutenant governor, so I obliged Sergeant Nelson and moved the family to Fort Indiantown Gap, the place where every lieutenant governor since 1968 has lived. The former governor's mansion was an unfurnished, four-bedroom house on a military installation. During my annual training with the National Guard, I couldn't wait to get off the post. Now, sadly, I could walk home from duty.

* * *

Just before the swearing-in, a reporter asked if I would hold onto my senate seat. I was headed to a do-nothing job, so I decided to start one last fire. "Maybe I'll hold onto both," I quipped. Chris Brennan wrote a hyperbolic story like his Beach Street serials. I would be getting two salaries and have two different office staffs. He knew it was fiction, but he didn't care. I hadn't yet caught onto the fact that Brennan usually asked questions based on prompts from Dougherty. The union boss had expanded his operation in Northeast Philadelphia and was itching to name my successor.

Fumo was pleasantly surprised at the new opportunity to create leverage. But governors were different than senators. And quirky borderline personalities often felt threatened. This was unique, not like wrestling for recognition with my legislative competitors, where the prize was your name in the last paragraph of unintelligible news stories. Now everything was radioactive. The higher you went, the greater the danger. Nonetheless, when Governor Wolf came to my office with Katie McGinty and asked me to resign my senate seat "so we can have a fresh start together," I was happy to oblige.

# CHAPTER ELEVEN

# PRESIDING OVER THE SENATE

I told you at the beginning that this was partly a true-crime story. You've accompanied me on this journey and met some of my enemies. But many others were in the weeds, rubbing their hands in anticipation, their hearts thumping as they peered through the scopes of high-powered rifles. Frankly I didn't grasp the danger. I didn't think the job was big enough to make me a threat. I was wrong.

I didn't know Sergeant Nelson—I'd only made his acquaintance two or three times. But within weeks of accepting protection, several troopers reported he didn't like me. Troopers like Greg Dietz, one of Tonya's favorites, was suspicious of Nelson. He and others would stir her up about Nelson's incompetence and venality, and how the detail was suffering. Naturally, she tried to help. All these perfect strangers became ubiquitous companions, attending Thanksgiving meals and birthdays and being with us in family crises, death, and heartbreak. Some would report back to Nelson every little quirk, real or imagined, and he'd stir up the people who were appalled at my presence on the ticket. They watched from the beginning and thought, "We've got to find a way to get rid of this guy."

Pennsylvania tradition dictates that the lieutenant governor be sworn in before the governor. My inauguration took place in the state senate where I had spent twelve years, and my colleagues were happy to see me kicked upstairs. I wasn't leaving the senate exactly. I would see my old pals every day as the president but wouldn't have to endure the monotony of the caucus room.

My friends who had knocked on doors with me since my early twenties crammed next to my dad's old comrades and committee people. Pat and Jim McGinley were in heaven with my pop, and I felt their presence beaming around the room. The packed Gallery was bubbling and vibrating with an incredible energy. After the near-death experience with the sword-wielding honor guard, I gathered myself and joined Mom, in her judicial robes, at the dais as Tonya held the Bible. Governor Wolf attended with Katie McGinty glued to his arm like he was the goose that laid the golden eggs. The honor guard from First City Troop looked magnificent in military blue with gold tassels. The ceremony was grand but not pretentious. It was a celebration of all those who had toiled with me over the years. I was so hopeful because I could preside over the senate without being in a fight for prominence. I could finally be a true public servant.

My speech recalled the advice of my father. After my losses, he advised writing thank-you letters to those who had disappointed. I would need them in four years. I launched a last barb at Senator Scott Wagner for his belligerent, divisive partisanship in bragging that he brought a baseball bat. He would smash anyone who disagreed. But most of us knew we needed to work together. "Throw your bat away!" I said. We later became friendly. The speech was twenty minutes long and well received, yet my father's friends were sad "that he wasn't here to see it."

I know he did.

The hard part was over, and that's how I imagined the next four years would be. We adjourned to a holding room at the East Rotunda with Tom and Francis Wolf before strolling cheerfully into the frosty January air. Justin, my stepson, joined us on the podium with former governors Tom Ridge, Mark Schweiker, and Ed Rendell. It was still dreamlike. My life had become a whirlwind of triumph and tribulation. I couldn't believe my luck and foresight. This was going to be an awesome job with mostly ceremonial responsibility. It was like the great escape—I had slipped under the barbed wire and into the woods. No one would want to pour hot tea in my face.

A brilliant blue sky broke through the clouds as Wolf began to speak—nervously, choppily—misreading several words on the teleprompter. But his theme was excellent, and his delivery improved. Government was broken, and he would fix it. His speech was about eleven minutes long and made me second-guess the length of mine.

Later, we danced the night away at the inaugural ball. Wolf continued to look at me like a hamburger he hadn't ordered. Nonetheless, someone must've gotten to him because Tonya and I were summoned to the stage to wave to the well-wishers as Wolf and I raised arms together in the first and last gesture of unity. Katie McGinty led the procession to the stage like a conga line, hooting and cheering like a tipsy cheerleader. At one time, Katie sought my help to connect with Wolf, and now she had built her own cheery connection. My new relationship with Wolf and his advisors wasn't acrimonious but amorphous. It was weird, but I wasn't alarmed. Nonetheless, Marty Marks observed that the governor's body language changed in my presence. I gave him the benefit of the doubt because he was new to politics.

Mom, my sisters, my brother, and my nieces and nephews and their dates occupied several tables near the stage. Everybody danced and celebrated, and we were joined by Senator Farnese and other state representatives and council members from Philadelphia. Many of the Philadelphia house members were delighted that our city finally had representation on the big ticket. They immediately asked for favors and special meetings that I had no idea how to grant but would certainly try. Not to be repetitious, but I just didn't see what could go wrong.

Farnese joined us at the lieutenant governor's residence, known as State House, claiming a small room on the second floor. He would be our houseguest for the next four years, whether we liked it or not. Dealing with his anxiety at the movies or in the caucus room was one thing. Now he would be in the living room by the fire, expressing his neurosis and feelings of being slighted all the time. He worked hard to dredge up new things for me to worry about. When Wolf didn't invite me to certain events, Farnese called it "disrespectful." If I wasn't agitated, he wasn't happy. That was his technique to keep me proactive in our fight for leadership. If I was calm, Farnese was alarmed. There was plenty of disrespect to go around, but I ignored it.

I offered Governor Wolf my loyalty and flexibility and expected nothing in return. This was a job I could do well, and I wanted the paranoia to stop. I knew that former governor Rendell didn't want me on the ticket. I was tired of trying to figure out why I wasn't his cup of tea. People trashed me behind the scenes, but I asked Governor Wolf to judge me independently. Rivalries in Philadelphia clouded honesty, and hateful gossip was circulated daily. I was hard-working and straightforward, and he would never have to worry about me. He nodded earnestly like the good-natured Jeep driver from the commercial, but he wasn't really listening. My offer to meet once a week to make sure we were on the same page was ignored.

Wolf's first budget proposed substantial tax increases and massive spending. He hired an outside firm to assemble a tax-and-spend budget that would fly in the face of conservative sentiments. Katie McGinty had been worried that there was no budget plan. Now that problem had been solved by people with no practical knowledge of Pennsylvania politics. Usually governors consulted legislative leaders and their budget secretary. Budgets were far different than numbers on balance sheets. The Republicans wouldn't go for the tax increases, and they ran the show. But it was an opportunity for me to demonstrate blind loyalty. When he asked me to give a speech to a group that would probably throw fruit, I agreed.

My delivery was terrific, but the Pennsylvania Chamber of Commerce audience jeered and laughed. Some of them shouted, "Come on, Mike, you can't believe this!" My sensible positions on economic issues garnered respect from the chamber, a rarity for Democrats. But I had them with many people on both sides of the aisle. It was a sign of weakness and insecurity that Wolf's advisers perceived as a threat. They were agitated and alarmed when I attempted to build bridges for the governor that they had not pre-authorized.

Nonetheless, Senator Costa wanted me involved in the process, and he implored Katie McGinty to bring me to budget negotiations. Anthony Costa, Jay's son, was now a member of my staff and another channel to influential Democrats, but she declined. But I didn't stomp around feeling persecuted or demanding to be in the loop. That was why I left the senate. I had plenty of duties to keep me busy. All my friends reached out and asked me to help. Anyone who couldn't get an appointment with Wolf met me instead.

\* \* \*

My rumble at the radio station with Jim Cawley led to friendship. He was the quintessential handsome, conservative zealot, with fabulous thick brown hair, a frozen-in-time pompadour, and a gleeful, ironic sense of impending doom. He wasn't born of the manor, though. He came from Bucks County, home of blue-collar, bootstrap Republicans. They had become successful through grittiness and hard work and attended underdog schools like Temple University and Saint Joe's. We were on different sides in the political game but understood sportsmanship. I was a Temple trustee, and Jim was a distinguished alumnus. We were from the same region and hated the same people and the Dallas Cowboys. We bled green and knew there were more important things than politics. He graciously hosted Tonya and me for lunch at State House before our term.

Communication in the governor-lieutenant governor relationship was crucial. Cawley missed some opportunities by failing to communicate with Governor Corbett clearly. One such missed opportunity was for him to serve as chairman of the Pennsylvania Emergency Management Agency. Statute dictated that the lieutenant governor serve on the board, but Corbett appointed a cabinet member chairman. Jim recommended that I meet with Wolf immediately and ask for his commitment. I had served on the military affairs and emergency management committees and understood the procedures. If disaster broke out, I wanted to be able to support the governor's efforts. Cawley advised me to cut out a niche to serve the administration without working side-by-side with the governor. Both Tonya and I appreciated him taking the time to explain what the job would be like. I liked his idea about the agency, and I also prioritized criminal justice reform.

Finally, he offered caution about the protective detail. His wife had been embarrassed in the media, but Cawley, like Joe Scarnati, thought it was indispensable. Cawley and his wife were relieved to be leaving the life. Tonya and I were excited to be coming in.

I convinced Governor Wolf to appoint me as chairman of the Emergency Management Agency Board, and over the next four years, I secured ratification of several disaster declarations. I cut out a role for myself independent of the governor. Presiding over the senate was tedious, challenging, and time-consuming, yet it was rewarding to serve with my old colleagues and help move bills and amendments through the legislature in a fair and balanced way. In the early stages of my term, I was busier than ever, serving as chair on numerous boards, including my own creation, the Lieutenant Governor's Veterans Task Force. Invitations to speak and visit came from all over the state, and I accepted most of them.

The folks from the Department of Community and Economic Development sought help in promoting international relations, and I loved celebrating different cultures and advancing international economic opportunities for the state. Any ethnic group that asked me to offer a resolution in the senate, I did. Now they were showing up again, and I was ready to host the consul generals from any country. I celebrated Mexican Independence Day in Philadelphia and spoke clumsy Spanish. I hosted forums for Turks and Israelis, led press conferences for Koreans and Kazakhstanis, and encouraged Indians and Pakistanis to invest here. The band kept playing as the DCED international office staffers regularly brought in representatives of countries I'd never heard of, and I assured them that Governor Wolf and Pennsylvania would help. I didn't have a lot of power, but I knew how to take a picture.

Wolf rarely asked me to represent him, but invitations poured in. I didn't ask permission from the front office. Gossip emerged that I was inordinately ambitious because I was so visible. I went all around the state to wherever I was invited. The protective detail made travel far easier, and they seemed to enjoy the activity. Naturally we liked some troopers better than others. Greg Dietz, Rob Brown, and Chris Cope were efficient and personable. I also enjoyed their company on long rides and wasn't afraid to make them laugh. They reported that my personality was more gregarious than Governor Wolf's. He could be stern or guarded. I was a politician and wanted them to like me.

The Philadelphia police protection team wanted to be involved when I visited my hometown. I knew so many cops from my neighborhood and felt comfortable with the leather-clad, boot-wearing Philly officers. The two details got along great, and we would link up in Philadelphia. Often standing right next to them was former state senator Bob Rovner, who couldn't wait to see me. He was always like a proud papa but also served as my advance man and introduced me to thousands of people as we walked through Philly. Rovner had helped me get elected in 2000 partly out of a grudge against Salvatore, who had kicked him off the Temple board. Then he became my biggest fan and constant companion. He handed out business cards everywhere, and people knew I was coming when they saw Rovner.

We particularly appreciated how the detail helped us represent Pennsylvania at inspiring events like the Pope's monumental visit and the exciting 2016 Democratic National Convention. The troopers spent so much time with me that, invariably, I considered them friends. I could've been a careful politician, wary of opening myself up, but I took a risk. They were dedicated and well trained and enabled me to perform public service better. Nonetheless, they could be suffocating and unreasonable. They insisted on protecting me when I went running or to the gym or movies. I exercised my prerogative to give them the slip like my predecessors had. Mark Schweiker broke loose to go to his favorite Sea Isle City watering hole. When his trooper barged in after a frantic search, Schweiker commented, "How'd you find me?" I wasn't above instigating a heart attack occasionally, but mostly I freely let them watch me.

I wasn't a backseat driver and didn't act like their boss. They worked for the state police, and I didn't tell them what to do. If they asked my permission to go around accidents or put on their emergency lights, I told them to make their own decisions. We treated the detail like family and would speak to them as such. I wasn't above telling a trooper from Penn State that he didn't know his way around Philadelphia. And plenty of them didn't know much about sports. It only got heated once with Trooper Dietz because of his extraordinary ignorance about music. He opined that the rock band Rush was overrated, and I retorted with prejudice. They attended Thanksgiving and Christmas at my mom's house and were a fabulous buffer from some relatives.

There was never a problem with the detail other than logistics and the occasional preference for certain officers. But here's a spoiler alert: I dropped a couple hints that trouble awaited from accepting protection. Scarnati and Cawley warned to be careful, and there was that strange Sergeant Nelson. I told you about the uncomfortable relationship with the boss and the misgivings of his staff. Well, it would all come home to roost. Governor Wolf would set off a controversy by intimating that the troopers were maltreated. He didn't name a single officer or describe a specific incident, but it caused our family incredible pain and placed my political career in peril. But before that, we were having a really great time together.

* * *

My old nemesis, Johnny Doc, was on fire to name my successor to the senate. I didn't know how much until I saw Councilman Henon at the Capital Grille in 2015. He embraced me like a long-lost brother while patting me down for wires. I had been a key endorsement and given him a lot of money in his election, mostly at Tonya's prompting. She wanted to get "the maniac off our backs." Doc and Henon appreciated the gesture for about three minutes. Suddenly, though, love was in the air.

"Senator, Governor, Mike . . ." He giggled like a schoolgirl. "Please come see your friends." He hooked my arm like we were going to the prom.

"Which friends?"

He reached for the door to a private dining room. "Your dear friends." And like Monty Hall, he revealed the grinning evil troika behind door number one.

Big John stood from the champagne-and-fillet-filled table next to Ryan Boyer, known as Black Doc, and Wayne Miller, the slender, slippery sprinkler union head. They were the captains of the Philadelphia building trades alliance and snapped to their feet, offering steak and wine like bouquets and chocolates.

Doc couldn't help but fall back into his tyrannical ways, "Give me any-one—ANYONE—but Sabatina."

In retrospect I should've given the decision a little more thought. But I was Irish and did the opposite. I thought this was just political competition and an old feud, not bloody mortal combat. As Bugs Bunny said, "What a moron!"

* * *

John Sabatina Jr. filled the remainder of my term. Since I was the ward leader with the most divisions and controlled the caucus, Sabatina was easily endorsed by the caucus. We held the meeting in the compound basement. Bob Brady attended, and my mother and Tonya put their ears to the door in the adjacent room. The transition had been surprisingly seamless, but the first election for the full term would be a death match against Dougherty accolade State Representative Kevin Boyle. His brother, Brendan, had worked on my staff and sought my guidance in his run for state representative. I was the first Democrat to beat an entrenched Republican, and Brendan and others were trying to follow my lead. Dad was a mentor to Brendan, and we helped him win on his second try after George Kenny retired. I met Kevin when he was a student at La Salle University when I addressed his political science class while campaigning in 2000.

We were all friends until the Two Streeter got involved. Then Brendan lunged for the congressional seat like his pants were on fire. Allyson Schwartz announced for governor. Doc thought I might want to go to Congress, so he lined up key building trades endorsements for Brendan. But I had no congressional ambitions, one man among four hundred. One among twenty or fifty was maddening enough.

Doc used the ancient Irish technique of setting the lads against each other and dispatched Chris Brennan to write of the Northeast Donnybrook between the Stacks and Boyles. Weeks before that, we dined in Harrisburg to celebrate the future. Dougherty recruited and funded the Boyles, setting them on fire with hate and utilizing his skills of ruining friendships with lies. The Boyles became obedient proxies. The brothers gladly spread Doc's hateful fiction. They didn't have the courtesy to slander third-hand—they simply said to anyone who would listen, "Stack's getting indicted."

My endorsement guaranteed my skin in the game. Dozens of community leaders sought my reassurance, and I steadied nerves and guaranteed victory. I tried to stay in Harrisburg and off the battlefield, but Sabatina Sr. implored Tonya for help. She had never been interested in politics until Sarah Del Ricci was defamed, terrorized, and defeated when Doc's Hoodies helped Republican Martina White. Tonya's fiery sense of justice ignited, and Sabatina Sr. utilized her as a conduit to me. She made calls and bolstered troops, and her presence signified full Stack commitment. She was shocked at Dougherty's ruthlessness in turning her trusted aid, my ward chair, against us. I installed him as ward leader in a badly executed plan to get free. Tonya had directed his action and swore he was loyal. But he immediately flipped the ward's endorsement to Kevin Boyle. All hell was breaking loose.

I stormed back from Harrisburg for an emergency ward meeting and extricated him on the grounds that my installment had violated city committee rules. I was reelected by a large margin on a Saturday morning and was lucky to get saved from a bad mistake. Every time I thought I was out, they kept pulling me back. Nonetheless, Sabatina Jr. squeaked out a victory by five hundred votes, and Tonya claimed a piece of it. She would gain a place for herself on Dougherty's list. For now, I looked like the King of Philadelphia, but in our city, the man who was king could soon be dead.

Fumo called my decision to help Sabatina a mistake. He proclaimed, "The kid will be ungrateful, and the father will be back with Dougherty before you know it." But that was because he didn't think we could win. I loved Fumo, but he treated me like one of his wayward kids. He didn't understand the alliance with Sabatina because he was in jail. It had come about through a perfect storm of vendetta.

I wanted to be high-minded and above the fray, but Marge Tartaglione was a special case. When Sabatina Sr. approached me in 2011 about joining forces to defeat her, I had just left my sick father in the hospital. I recalled his years of abuse from the beehive bully. Sabatina Sr. and I shook hands and agreed to be partners in bringing Marge down and getting other people elected. John Sabatina Jr. would have otherwise never have been my successor in the senate. When I told Dad, he was cautious. "Do you really think you can beat her? She's tough." He had been in and out with heart and diabetes complications, and I wanted to lift his spirits. "Maybe we can't, but I'm happy to try."

Marge Tartaglione had been the longest-serving election commissioner before that shocking defeat. Dad got so many letters and calls in the hospital bed that they were piling up. Cheery telegrams like, "The witch is dead" and "Karma's a bitch" hung from balloons. Old friends like Mel Greenberg, who lived in Florida, reached out to gloat. I got more credit than I deserved in Brennan's clout column but was delighted to do a mitzvah for my old man. I didn't want to be a political boss exacting revenge forever. For that moment, it was all right. Sabatina Sr. and I stayed friendly after that triumph, and "the kid" was made. What a real gift to get someone back for your old man.

\* \* \*

I loved presiding over the senate because I was free of all the gutter politics of the past. The dirty business of the city trenches was over. As lieutenant governor, I didn't need to scuffle for prominence. True public service came from being an objective arbiter in the brilliant process called democracy. I was no expert on parliamentary procedure, but I understood the legislative process. Senators wanted to move their bills or at least get heard. I understood their personalities because I'd been in their company on the senate floor or in the dining room and spent time talking to them. Decorum emanated from patience and respect. Senators got irate when they were frazzled or misunderstood. Inexperienced lieutenant governors misinterpreted that as belligerence, but I gave everyone a chance to be heard. The heated debates didn't escalate to acrimony and disrespect because I wouldn't allow it. To hold that big gavel in that spectacular chamber was a wonderful experience.

The senate secretary, Megan Consedine, was a lawyer and guided me through complicated procedures and debate rules. Soon I was an expert at the rules I'd never quite understood as a member. I made a lot of rulings and acquired a reputation for fairness. Democratic senators suspected Megan would trip me because she was Republican, but she was smart and patient and made me look sage. It was fun to recognize my colleagues and highlight some unique personality traits. Kim Ward, who later became the president pro tempore, loved karaoke and dancing. She was tickled to be introduced for a speech on the floor as "the Dancing Queen." If I didn't do it, she was crestfallen. Smart-aleck media commentators would say I conducted the senate like a nightclub singer.

My experience with presiding was not without excitement. I was pleased to cast two tie-breaking votes in 2015 and 2016. One defeated the anti-labor paycheck protection bill of my baseball-bat-wielding friend, Scott Wagner. Governor Wolf even broke his silence to thank me. I asked if he needed anything else and he said, "no, that's good," and I heard a click.

# CHAPTER TWELVE

# USING HOPE AS A LAW
# ENFORCEMENT TOOL

Emily Dickinson wrote that hope was the thing with feathers that perched in the soul. "Pathway to Pardons" was the transformative and premier policy accomplishment of my term, and hope was a big part of it. Through the pardons process, people can get a clean slate and a second chance at a productive life. Teddy Roosevelt used his bully pulpit to get things done. He was one of my favorite Republicans. I did the same with my office. Even though I had no actual legislative power, I could convene meaningful meetings. In my role as chairman of the Board of Pardons, it was clear that the criminal justice system had been biased and punitive. A pardon could be the silver bullet that killed the punitive past. All the legislative initiatives took too long and left the citizen with a record. That black mark prevented progress. Pardons hadn't been utilized enough. The process was confusing and required way too much paperwork. It also took too long—five years through the arduous process. My goal was to streamline and simplify. I asked Governor Wolf for more staff and technology and tasked the pardons staff with getting cases through the pipeline so we could have hearings. Many busy days ensued, and many Pennsylvanians changed their lives.

We were also warehousing prisoners who had been rehabilitated. The Board of Pardons had the authority to recommend to the governor the commutation of life sentences. This was rarely done because of the Gerald McFadden fiasco. McFadden had been sentenced to life in prison in 1970 for robbery and homicide, but in 1992, the Pardons Board voted to commute his sentence. Lieutenant Governor Mark Singel voted in favor of the release and would later regret it. During Singel's gubernatorial campaign in 1994, McFadden murdered two people and kidnapped and raped a third within ninety days of his release. When the news broke, Singel's opponent, Tom Ridge, transformed the campaign into a referendum on pardons, leading to Mark's bitter defeat. Pardons and commutations went into a deep freeze that lasted for decades.

Singel's fiasco had inadvertently distorted the process and kept good people behind bars. McFadden was far too dangerous to even get a hearing, and my safeguards blocked dangerous offenders from the process. An applicant had to have been a secondary offender with decades of service and education while incarcerated. I would never consider anyone who wasn't unanimously supported by prison authorities. Nonetheless, I believed we could be smarter on justice and save taxpayers millions. We had a geriatric population behind bars that had paid for their crimes and threatened no one. The inmates were costing taxpayers millions in health care and wasting away. Giving the prison population a spark of hope made for better safety. Corrections officials assured us that inmates who thought they had a chance at freedom were much better behaved and less of a threat to guards. Hope was therefore a compelling tool. Prison officials informed me that hope was spreading like wildfire.

I visited a lot of prisons across the state before coming into office, and I met a lot of young Black men who had become old Black men. They had struggled their whole lives because of a stupid mistake in their youth. A group of these guys captivated me at a closed-door session at a Northwest Philadelphia playground. The top dog stood up and said, "With all due respect, sir, now is the time for you to listen." They said they would support me if I promised to do something about the waste of human life in the African American community. Politicians made promises. I could deliver. During my four years as chairman of the Board of Pardons, we commuted five life sentences, including the first female commutation in Pennsylvania history. The most notable, however, was the first.

* * *

Thurmond Berry marched into the prison community room, holding the American flag. He joined the line of veterans who wore pieces of military uniforms and stood at attention. He was part of the military honor guard at the Graterford Prison, the maximum-security facility that housed 3,400 prisoners, including many on death row. In 1976, as a nineteen-year-old, Thurman had been an accomplice in an armed robbery gone bad. When his cohorts fled, he knew he was in trouble. He drove the car anyway. A man was killed. His mother said that God would forgive him, she would forgive him, but he had to turn himself in. The young Black man was given a life sentence without the chance of parole. The actual shooter had already been released, which had been a source of incredulity. However, Thurman was a model prisoner and mentor, yet the board repeatedly denied his commutation. He was pleased to meet me, a state senator who purported to care, but skeptical that I'd be able to do anything.

The chains jangled as he entered the dingy room with metal tables and cold brick walls at Camp Hill Prison. The slender microphones were gratuitous because he was right in front of us. We spent two hours asking questions about his rehabilitation. This was my first time going to prison with the board. I was surprised when Berry remembered me from my visit years back at Graterford. That's when I asked him to pray for me, that I would have the courage to do the right thing. Maybe his prayers would be answered. Dark-skinned, gray-haired, and perspiring, he was now seventy years of age. But his adversary was a woman with long brown hair and ice in her veins.

The former rising star attorney general Kathleen Kane stood defiantly in front of the jailhouse door. "What do I tell the victims?" she asked in the two hearings where she voted against commutation. It was a good question, and she was a tough lady who almost had it all. I watched her inauguration from the front-row seat under the capitol rotunda. She was the first woman attorney general. Then it all came unglued when she stooped into the gutter. The ego-driven cage match with Philly district attorney Seth Williams spiraled into much worse. She chose not to prosecute corruption cases against three African American state representatives and publicly feuded it with her top deputy, Frank DeFina. To make a long story short, after Williams successfully prosecuted the cases, she leaked grand jury testimony and was indicted. She was facing trial around the same time Thurman Berry was facing her.

He remembered her and was better prepared this time. The victim's family no longer opposed his release. He asked for and received their forgiveness. Kane rolled her eyes; tears streamed from his. The next day we gathered in the supreme court chamber and listened to the testimony of family members of the man who had died that night in 1976. They wanted to set Berry free. But how would this institutionalized man live in the outside world? His gentle sister agreed to take him in and he had a commitment for employment. He had been a model prisoner for decades and a mentor to younger inmates. He came to realize the futility of anger and found peace. Kathleen Kane remained unconvinced.

Matt Franchak emerged from the majestic conference room outside the supreme court, looking disturbed. He had tried his best but couldn't get her to budge. "It's going to be up to you, Governor," he said.

I shrugged. "What do you want me to do?"

He chuckled. "Go to work and flash those baby blues." I was surprised at his misogyny as I dabbed cologne and straightened my hair. I couldn't believe she was still so tough on crime after all the unfairness she experienced. There was no way a woman of her talent should've ended up getting charged. Enemies had a way of coming out of the woodwork and orchestrating ruin. She would never have been stopped had they not stopped her. Politics was a bloody business and she had been stabbed. She had rivals just like me waiting in the weeds, but she could help somebody else who was hurt, maybe find peace. If the victim's family could forgive, why couldn't we?

She waited at the table wearing a cobalt suit with a tight skirt and black heels. Her long brown hair looked perfect, but wrinkles surrounded her eyes. I slid into the big leather chair at the head of the table and almost fell out of it. I chose one of my oldest techniques of persuasion. I begged. She knew I was a law-and-order guy who grew up around cops. We needed to do something different rather than warehousing young men until their death. Thurman Berry posed no threat. He was rather an example of perseverance and hope. Only people like her and I could boost that inspiration.

Then I gazed into her eyes. "Please do it for me."

After a long silence, stress fell away from her face. She smiled. "All right. Since you asked so nicely, I'll do it for you."

We went back out and voted unanimously to set the man free. The supreme court room exploded in applause; better than any movie I ever saw. That's how it was done. That's why I ran.

That was public service.

Pathway to Pardons was born, and Berry triggered a firestorm of hope. We toured the state, talking about the pardons process and showing people how to use it. We unlocked the bureaucratic mystery of government. Matt Franchak coordinated with the Department of Corrections, probation officers, parole officers, and ex-offender organizations, and we assembled panels and did workshops. We had to stop the waste of human life, and criminal justice reform was needed everywhere. The issue was anathema to being conservative or liberal, Black or white. Large audiences in conservative areas where everyone was light-skinned and Republican were as common as diverse audiences in Philly. Second chances were what America was all about. No amount of education or job performance would erase the shame and disruption of a criminal record. The taint always became punitive. We were punishing them and ourselves by preventing folks from getting decent jobs, volunteering, teaching, and being full family members. The cost to taxpayers in additional social services was exponentially higher. Senators from both parties asked me to bring Pathway to Pardons to their districts, and over two years, we had traveled the state and made a palpable difference.

At Drexel University, Dylan McGarry slipped from the audience to the stage. A special guest was in the hall and wanted to say hello. Halfway through my speech, I pivoted. "Folks," I said. "One of those lifers is instead with us tonight." A hush came before Thurman Berry rose, eyes welling, body shaking, and joined me on the stage. The smattering of applause became thunderous as we embraced. That was as close as it came to *Mr. Smith Goes to Washington*. Thurman joined us at other forums, and we had incredible momentum on criminal justice reform. My do-nothing job that wasn't worth spit was going great. I didn't know what could go wrong.

\* \* \*

My grandfather, the congressman, warned that they kicked you when you got down in politics. Later, my father, the ward leader, got kicked in "petition gate." I was the Stack on the fast track and thought the hard times were over. The sky was the limit, but I could fly slowly and carefully and help Tom Wolf while learning. Obvious ambition had killed the cat many times. Guys like Budd Dwyer got talked about for governor, then targeted for prison. It was a game where you got kicked if you fell. I wanted to stay on my feet, not end up pointing a gun at my own head. But I'd come too far and got noticed by too many people.

Ambition was a magnet for enemies. Success triggered jealousy. I tried to keep my guard up but didn't expect to be attacked by my own governor. At the halfway point of our first term, Tom Wolf accused me of mistreating staff and members of the state police detail at a well-attended press conference. It was a punch in the gut. Casey had been agitated with Singel. Rendell treated Catherine Baker Knoll like she was Mrs. Doubtfire. Corbett didn't love Cawley. But none of the governors went nuclear. I was the first lieutenant governor who received a full-frontal attack utilizing all the ornaments of the most powerful office. And for good measure, the governor dragged in my wife.

In the political arena, dad said how impossible it was to disprove a negative. You defended yourself and the lie was repeated; sometimes that's all people remembered. Mayor Rizzo had taken the catastrophic step of submitting to a lie detector. If someone accused you of beating your wife, it was ridiculous to answer, "I don't beat my wife." The headline was always the denial. The presumption favored spousal abuse. It's human nature to presume the worst, and the media and slick politicians take advantage. I chose to stay out the fray and not be defensive or argumenatative, despite my emotions.

\* \* \*

I executed my duties to the best of my ability and was honored with unique tasks. I was urged to represent Pennsylvania at the Great Lakes Conference of Governors in Quebec during the summer of 2017. Governor Wolf wasn't interested in making the trek, but I jumped at it. I was passionate about international trade and building relationships with other countries. We needed to create more jobs, and Canada was our leading trade partner. I learned a few appropriate French phrases from a senatorial aide who was fluent, and I joked about the Eric Lindros trade to the Philadelphia Flyers from the Quebec Nordiques. A burly minister of commerce listened patiently to my cumbersome French, then suddenly busted, "Oh, I hated that guy!" The trade minister wore the same cobalt-colored suit as me, and we signed an agreement to increase trade between our states amid flags and diplomats. Cameras flashed and people applauded, and I was on Fantasy Island.

Governors Jeff Snyder of Michigan and Scott Walker of Wisconsin and I joined the prime minister of Ontario for further meetings. I had spent my career being blocked from important meetings or minimized. Now there was a place reserved with my name tag and sparkling water. The two governors, Snyder and Walker, had been villainized by my party, but I found them friendly and generous. I asked Walker what it was like running for president. He said, "It was fun!"

I was just trying to have fun and do a good job. I wasn't trying to upstage anybody, but I found it curious that Governor Wolf passed on important events. As I stood in the crowd at a DNC welcoming reception hosted by Independence Blue Cross, CEO Dan Hilferty asked me to speak on behalf of the governor, who hadn't shown up. I was happy to do it, but my detractors would antagonize the governor, claiming I was stealing the limelight. But I was respectful and extended the governor's warmest welcome, and the remarks were appreciated.

"You really saved us," said Dan. He was one of the most successful businessmen in America, yet he started off as an assistant to Saint Joseph's University president Father Rashford and as an unsuccessful candidate for lieutenant governor.

I gushed about his achievements. "Who would've thought the guy who finished ninth for lieutenant governor would become such a big success?"

He stopped smiling. "Ninth? No."

The next day, he called and said he had checked, and I was right. He was significantly more successful than me and a millionaire. But nobody liked to lose. Those who made a joke out of any public office aspirant, including lieutenant governor, never had skin in the game. Teddy Roosevelt saluted those in the arena whose faces were "marred by dust and sweat and blood, who spends himself in a worthy cause," instead of "those cold and timid souls" who only criticized and judged.

My two years were filled with action, and the detail clung to me as much as I to them. They made dinner reservations and attended parties. They drove

Tonya to board meetings, movies, and concerts. We couldn't shake them when we went to the shore or on vacation, but they were also a fun part of our lives. We encouraged them to enjoy themselves, which probably got them in trouble with their bosses. That trouble would eventually come to us.

At 2 A.M. on the third day of the convention, we attended a Snoop Dogg concert at the Fillmore Theater. We were escorted to a VIP balcony because a police officer friend of mine from Northeast Philadelphia knew the owner. Smoke wafted from the stage—it was the Democrats and Snoop, after all. The state police were fearful they would fail their drug tests in the line of duty, but it was only fake weed smoke. Dylan McGarry approached me with a big grin. "Guv, the owner wants to know if you mind being joined by Katy Perry and Orlando Bloom up here." They never showed. But Snoop asked to meet us and the troopers.

After Snoop's amazing performance, we got to hang out with the tall, funky hound and couldn't believe how down-to-earth he was. He danced and rapped about how cool it was hanging with the LG. He paid special attention to Tonya, who was a lifelong Snoop Dogg fan. We got an amazing picture of the two of them smiling at each other. But the best one was the six straight-laced cops posing with a top gangsta rapper. We learned through the grapevine of gossiping cops that Sergeant Nelson was not amused. Some Wolf staffers were irked because they hadn't been invited. All they had to do was call. But I never saw any of them or received any guidance regarding what the governor wanted.

Cops loved to talk about things they weren't supposed to. They'd say things like, "You didn't hear it here," or, "If anyone asks, I'll deny it." We got all the inside scoop on the detail from Greg Dietz. He was Tonya's favorite because he was like her—blunt as a hammer. Before joining the detail, he had seen the worst cases of sexual assault and rape. He was a Trumper before Trump won. He didn't like many people. But he liked us because we were always going someplace. Dietz sensed danger and was the perfect cop. Tonya requested that he be assigned to us more often. Sergeant Nelson may have considered that being bossy.

I had heard the stories about governors disliking lieutenant governors in Pennsylvania. I heard about acrimony from other lieutenant governors at the National Lieutenant Governors Association. Usually, it was the staff who found the junior member intolerable. Mark Singel received hostility from Governor Casey's staff but maneuvered around it. When I became the subject of similar gossip, I didn't perceive any danger. I kept about my business. I never had a curt word with any of the governor's staff. I sat next to the governor at several emergency management drills, and he seemed satisfied. But I could sense people were saying unkind things about me. So I requested a phone conversation with him once a week just to make sure everything was copacetic. For three weeks we chatted for about a minute on each call. Then he stopped answering.

I continued to stay busy and try to help other groups. We created a veterans task force, and I chaired the Military Base Enhancement Commission. Serving veterans was an honor, but they struggled with homelessness, mental illness, and addiction. Our task force tackled those issues and made progress on finding employment and treatment. Many of our policy suggestions were adopted by local governments. We also improved the economic viability of our military manufacturing base and increased opportunities for trade and sales around the world and our country.

I tried to make Pennsylvania a film Mecca like Georgia. As a senator, I supported the film tax credit, but we needed to do more. On a trip to Pittsburgh, I visited an old steel manufacturing plant that had the potential to become a major movie studio. The owner and his partners had renovated the area to attract Hollywood. They were soliciting offers, but nothing had been locked in. I made friends with them and promised to help. Several months later, the Pittsburgh film office recruited me to help in negotiations for a Netflix show called *Mind Hunters*. The owner of the Pittsburgh site had cold feet. He was open to talking to me because we had a good rapport, and against his better judgment, he trusted me. The deal looked like an absolute winner. I reassured him it would bring hundreds of new jobs and be profitable for him. I was glad to help and honored that he trusted me enough to go forward. *Mind Hunters* became a long-running show that generated millions of dollars for the Pittsburgh economy and many jobs. I'm still bitter that I wasn't cast as an FBI agent like Netflix promised.

Tioga Marine Terminal was located in my senate district and offered more opportunity for economic growth and job creation. Our port facilities were world class but had been neglected. Just as I had done as a senator, I obtained funding for Tioga and Packer Avenue terminals to upgrade the massive cranes and infrastructure. It was also a priority of Governor Wolf, and in the fall of 2016, I learned of his press conference to announce millions of dollars of state investment. I wasn't invited. Maybe it was an accident, but I remembered that my old man had always said just show up and act like you belonged. I had chased Wolf around on the campaign trail and knew the drill. Matt Franchak called the executive director of the Port Authority, who arranged for a seat on the stage and got one for Larry Farnese too.

The moment I walked onto the senate floor, I saw Farnese pacing near his desk. "Those sons of bitches didn't invite me!"

I put my hand on his shoulder, "Don't worry, my friend. I got you on the stage next to me."

Farnese smiled. "Stack!"

* * *

There was nothing more disrespectful than not inviting senators to events in their own districts, but governors did it all the time. Ridge did it, but he was a Republican. Rendell did it and blamed other people. Wolf looked surprised when I entered the hotel lobby, looking like Johnny Fontane from *The Godfather*. I always remembered what Rendell had said to Fumo. It wasn't important that I wasn't invited, just that I was there. Wolf rode the escalator with union leaders panting and fawning, scurrying after him. A gaggle of thick-necked men gathered around a pink-faced, silver-haired celt who may have wanted me excluded. I waived enthusiastically to Johnny Doc, and his eyes erupted into contempt and surprise.

The star of the Philadelphia security detail was Sergeant Colleen. She was about five feet tall with short, wavy brown hair, a black pantsuit, and a gray Glock. She was a South Philadelphia police officer who could handle herself. The curly wire hung from her ear as she led me to an elevator ahead of a crowd. My staff accompanied me with a couple members of the protective detail. There was no room in the elevator for Dougherty or his troops when they tried to board. The petite sergeant put her hand out. "No!" Doc stopped in his tracks and went from pink, to pale, then straight to purple. I could almost smell the smoke. An uncontrollable smile broke across my face just as the doors closed in slow motion, and I saw his murderous eyes. It was just another straw on the camel's back.

The port executives seated Farnese and me in the front row next to Governor Wolf, who seemed uncomfortable. He and Doc embraced like old friends as the union boss introduced his cohorts. Doc had been Wolf's biggest contributor through his union PAC after Schwartz lost in the primary. No one ever held a grudge against him for supporting their opponent if he bought the cash. He formed the SuperPAC in 2018, raised unprecedented sums, and garnered undying affection.

The vibe in the room was a mix of positive energy and foreboding. The sparkling Delaware River could be seen through the giant windows over the governor's shoulder. Wolf was compelled to mention us casually, but the port executives were effusive about our long-term assistance. Larry's nerves were frayed because he feared intimidation or disrespect from Doc's people. They would never get over their defeat, and the number of Doc loyalists indicated this was a Wolf-Dougherty show. He had imitated Fumo, become port commissioner, and stacked the board. But it was a great day, and I was heartened by the state's investment. We needed the investment to become a world-class port. We could compete with Norfolk and New York City and get the big boats to unload in Philly.

* * *

A few weeks after that elevator closed on Doc's humiliated face, Gary Tuma pushed my office door open a crack and peered cautiously through to see if I was in. He was a veteran spokesman in the capital with a thick silver mane and salt-and-pepper beard that conveyed grizzled wisdom. As a former spokesman for Senator Fumo and Governor Rendell, he brought more experience than my humble office required. "It would be a coup to get him," Fumo advised. Matt Franchak helped the negotiation by finding extra salary. Now I had one of the best press hands in Harrisburg but with the taint of a disgraced senator.

"Can we have a confidential talk?" Tuma cleared his throat. "I feel funny about it. I don't want to offend you, but there are rumors going around."

I waved my hand for him to continue.

"That you're going to be indicted by the FBI." I didn't know the FBI indicted anybody. But the pitter-patter in my chest beat like a big brass drum.

Tuma slid into a leather chair at the conference table and shared that he'd been getting inquiries from reporters for weeks. He didn't want to upset me, but they were relentless and sounded like my arrest was imminent. I hadn't heard anything. The FBI came to my house in 2014 while investigating Congressman Chaka Fattah.

That sunny morning, Tonya woke me by whispering in my ear, "This is not a joke. There's an FBI agent at the front door."

I rolled over. "Tell him I'm not here."

She made coffee, and we sat in the living room, talking to the agent. Senator Hughes was a suitemate, and his secretary had signed a car loan for Fattah. My secretary had notarized the form. The agent was a tall, friendly guy and was just verifying information. He said if I was in trouble, they would've been there at the crack of dawn, wearing FBI windbreakers. There had been the Beach Street probes and some other whispers but no real investigations.

Back in my office, Tuma rubbed his beard and gazed at the chandelier. Then he leaned forward. "We need to do something proactive to stop this nonsense." He proposed an *Alice in Wonderland* plan for me to deny the rumors.

Having a press conference to announce I wasn't being indicted wouldn't work. I'd look like a guilty idiot and trigger an actual FBI investigation.

Tuma wanted some time to think about it but proposed "maybe giving an exclusive interview to one reporter." The reporter would tell all the others the rumors were false.

Tuma was worth his weight in gold because he knew the media war horses. He had been at war with legislators for decades. Brad Bumstead was the vexatious, sweating, indignant reporter out of classic movies. He wore thick spectacles and polyester pants pulled up high to constrain a prodigious stomach as he chased down slimy politicians. His pencil-thin mustache made his lips look even thinner. He was that guy who exposed legislative greed, abuse of perks, and junkets that we laughed about until we were the subject. He'd ripped me over excessive car wash reimbursements a few years earlier, but he mostly tortured others.

Tuma said he would pitch him, and we would hope for the best. As he was going out the door, he said, "Try to call the governor—he's probably hearing the same thing."

Wolf hadn't been taking my calls for a while, but for some reason he answered. Maybe he hoped I was calling to resign. He was exasperated. "I've heard the FBI raided your office."

I was right down the hall. Wouldn't everyone see them? I chuckled at the absurdity. "I can assure you, Tom, the FBI is not and hasn't been."

It was all made-up Philly turf war stuff. I had a plan to end the gossip. Wolf probably believed me. But the damage was done. Whether I liked it or not, I had become controversial. Wolf was obsessed with appearances—mostly his own. His administration had to be above reproach.

What did Fumo think? He was nonchalant. "It's an old South Philly trick. Now everyone will stay away from you."

"Was it Dougherty?" I asked.

"Of course!" he blurted. "I didn't think that job was worth spit, but maybe you've turned it into something. You've obviously made an impression." Fumo thought Tuma knew what he was doing but was wary of trusting reporters. "In the end, they always screw you."

Tuma respected Bumstead from the old days. He was the elder statesman that the new kids looked up to. Bumstead savored the Starbucks coffee from a PCN mug, my parting gift from appearing on the news show. He would later criticize me for serving such an expensive brew at taxpayer expense.

Our session was more like confession. I never got to speak to reporters and just be myself, and this was a relief. Usually, I was forced to avoid them or have aides deliver the message. I followed that advice grudgingly. I thought I knew how to keep my foot out of my mouth, but I wasn't always right. I gazed into his eyes like they were Kathleen Kane's emerald orbs and assured him there was no investigation. There were people in Philadelphia who were jealous even though this was supposedly a do-nothing job, and the source was a prominent union leader, but I didn't name him. I should've but still hoped for a de-escalation of the feud.

Bumstead listened intently, almost kindly. He relished the intrigue of our mysterious, gritty city and the access to its treacherous mechanisms. He must have been convinced there was no investigation. Bumstead carried the message back to the henhouse and the rumors dissipated.

The smear campaigns had gradually become supercharged. Maybe it was ignited when that elevator door closed on Johnny Doc's crimson mug. Maybe it was 2008, when I helped Farnese humiliate him. It could've been when I beat his guy, Salvatore, with the help of his mortal enemy. The water was under the bridge, but it didn't matter. He would never stop, and he was gifted in igniting the hateful rumors, and not just in Harrisburg. Wolf would take his side because he needed his money and clout. This is what we believed. It might be considered speculation, but from where I come from, you know what you know. The rumors went everywhere he went, including the conference room of the Philadelphia Port Authority. Soon members of the Wolf administration were echoing the lies that would soon become self-fulfilling.

\* \* \*

I recommended Whitney White for appointment to the Delaware River Port Authority Board. He had served as a trade advisor to President Clinton and was from Philadelphia. He had the right résumé and a gregarious personality. He was a tall, athletic-looking African American from the same neighborhood as board chair Ryan Boyer, AKA Black Doc. They disagreed on port business. At the third meeting, White invited Boyer outside. After things calmed down, Wolf's deputy chief of staff, Obra "Opie" Kernodle, advised him to stay away from me because I was being investigated.

The governor's budget address was the greatest show in Harrisburg, filled with pomp and majesty. The raucous house chamber was filled with cabinet members, distinguished citizens, legislators, and the media. I banged a Paul Bunyan-sized gavel to bring order and summon Wolf to the dais. All eyes were on me for the moment, and then the rambunctious rumblings retreated, and I introduced his excellency the governor and reclined to a high-back chair perfectly positioned behind the governor and in front of every camera known to mankind. Without uttering another word, I appeared in every front-page photograph and news video across the commonwealth. I'd spent years jostling to get into photos in the local paper. Now my earnest mug was effortlessly ubiquitous.

During Governor Wolf's first budget address, his call for tax increases received boos, cackles, and hisses. We wouldn't pass a budget for another ten months. A supplemental budget funded government programs until the second budget address. By then Wolf changed his tune, declaring that citizens were exhausted from tax increases and that it was time to live within our means. Government was either no longer broken or we had found a different way to fix it. He did the same thing in the next two budgets in exchange for increased public and higher-education funding, which Republicans wanted anyway. It became crystal clear that Governor Wolf wanted the same thing as most politicians—another term.

The happiness I had felt in the early days of the administration had given way to feeling like I was walking on dangerous ground. Wolf did not want to corroborate or even communicate. There was a rumor going around that I said I'd hoped he would die after a prostate cancer scare. His staffers reportedly now hated me. My stylish dress had become an issue of contempt. I knew I was in big trouble after the second budget address, when a PCN commentator said, "Forget about what's in the budget . . . let's talk about Lieutenant Governor Michael Stack's electric-blue suit."

I continued to help constituents from my senate district and advocated for other projects around the state, utilizing my office. Members of the executive detail asked me to push an amendment that would classify them as emergency responders, and I asked Joe Scarnati for assistance. An opportunity to advance cures for cancer arrived through Dana Dornsife, a passionate advocate for expanded clinical trials. Her charitable foundation provided funding for minority participation by reimbursing travel and living expenses. By convening meetings with Republican leaders and Senator Dinnamin, we crafted legislation that helped encourage more clinical trials and increased the chance of curing cancer. Important senators accepted my invitation to meet because of the power of my bully pulpit. Kim Ward, Lisa Baker, John Gordner, and Joe Scarnati were amazingly kind and effective. I had always known them as the worthy opposition but learned they were even better allies.

Just before Christmas in 2017, I received a disturbing phone call from Governor Wolf. I was just about to attend a holiday party for my former law firm at Normandy Farms in Blue Bell. The air was icy, and the governor was irate. I jumped back into the SUV, and a trooper listened to the conversation. I had never heard Wolf sound belligerent.

"Are you running against me in the primary?" he asked.

This accusation was startling. I stuttered at first. "Absolutely not!" I imme-diately thought of my old friend, the poisoning electrician, who was at it again. "This is why we should talk more, Tom. People make stuff up."

I could hear him breathing heavily. "You're not going against me?" He asked one more time.

"Of course not, Tom." I felt sweat drip down my back as I walked through the deep freeze. I knew the relationship was over. I made my way through multiple parties in the complex and found John Elliot. He was surrounded by well-wishers at the bar. I smiled tensely and shook a few hands, then tugged on his pinstripe jacket. I whispered. "I think I've got a serious problem with the governor."

# CHAPTER THIRTEEN

# THE BEGINNING OF THE END

There had been some logistical issues with the detail and minor tiffs over preferred personnel, but there had not been any substantial problems with my staff. Matt Franchak and Dylan McGarry were resolving the remaining issues with Wolf staffers. It turned out they were using a stall tactic to prepare a decisive attack.

I needed to get away from the capital. My happy place was a small apartment on the Inlet in North Wildwood. The salty sea air cleared my head. The seashore was desolate during winter, and I could run on the boardwalk and think of summer.

Trooper Rob Brown was as tall as an NBA swingman with a shaved head and slender build. We were shooting hoops under the lights at the Avalon Recreation Center, talking about the show *Power* that he loved. His jump shot was falling, so I rebounded and kicked it back. We got into the black SUV, and I saw a missed call from Tonya. It was just another night in the frozen ghost town until I heard her voice. She was terrified.

"I'm under investigation by the inspector general." She had received a letter that afternoon. It didn't make any sense. The agency investigated fraud and waste by commonwealth departments, not civilians who didn't even work for the state. And she was the second lady, for God's sake! I tried to calm her down and called Matt Franchak, who sighed.

"You got one too," he said. I remember that moment vividly. I was a little kid in the pitch-black dungeon filled with screeching demons. That's what it was like. As I write about it today, the healing is almost complete. But at the time, it was excruciating and terrifying. I'm about to take you with me through the most insidious frame-up I ever experienced.

\* \* \*

I couldn't get the senate to provide an attorney like in the past. I couldn't ask the governor's general counsel for assistance because she had helped orchestrate the investigation. I needed counsel fast, and my kitchen cabinet of Franchak, Dylan McGarry, and Marty Marks recommended Mark Sheppard, the dismally dark but highly competent attorney who had represented me in the Beach Street probe. He was also expensive—I would scramble to find the money. Matt asked John Elliot to help, and the meetings were being scheduled. I could hardly breathe when I hung up.

Rob Moore had been sitting at the steering wheel the whole time, listening like he'd done for two years. When I looked over, he said, "I'm so sorry, Guv." He was a good cop and knew about the investigation from the beginning. Somebody had told him to keep his mouth shut, and he followed orders. They all had. They had jobs to protect and families to feed. Governor Wolf was the most powerful man in Pennsylvania, so who could blame them for changing from protectors to spies?

I desperately tried to get a meeting with Wolf, who had notified the media of the investigation. His staff fanned the flames with rumors of horrendous conduct. I didn't know what to do. I thought he was going to try to bleed me to death by building enormous controversy. John Elliot advised me to go ballistic and call out the governor on his accusation that I was planning a primary run. I was hesitant to take such action because it was unbecoming and would destroy any chance of reconciliation. I wanted to neutralize controversy and get the governor to suspend his violent course. I violated the rule that had helped me through controversy in the past. Instead of keeping my mouth shut, I proposed a press conference.

I hadn't thought of Budd Dwyer in a long time. He must have felt completely alone as he rambled through a defensive speech, pleading to reporters who didn't give a damn about him. My ornate office was packed with hungry reporters, clicking cameras, and glaring lights. The doors to the balcony were open, and the gentle breezes softened the stultifying, stressful air. Hundreds of citizens had visited my capitol suite, where I encouraged school kids to sit at my desk and pose for pictures. I followed the example of Lieutenant Governor Catherine Baker Knoll, who was an unofficial tour guide and one-woman welcoming committee. They called her Mrs. Doubtfire, but she was more like everyone's favorite grandmother. Our visitors spent time and saw the scenic vistas of the Susquehanna River and our ancient grandfather clock. The only reporter to visit was Brad Bumstead. It was hard to get the media interested in criminal justice reform or veterans' rights, but the smell of blood was magnetic.

Senator Fumo wasn't in favor of the idea. "You're crazy! Do you think you're JFK and they're going to listen politely? They're animals!" I knew it was a long shot and perhaps a big mistake. But I calculated that Wolf would torture us to death. He was going to drag out a long, shameful scandal and bleed me into resigning. He might even want me to pull a Budd Dwyer. He had gone to the extra effort to drag Tonya into it. The Wolfies were circulating salacious lies, and I knew it would get worse, the usual misogynist slanders against women. They didn't know her. Anyone who did loved her.

# CHAPTER FOURTEEN

# A LADY SECOND TO NONE

I noticed the feisty brunette at the Main Line picnic because of all the people listening and laughing around her. My sister thought she looked like Pocahontas because of her petite stature, long brown hair, and tan skin. Her honesty was in your face, but also like a cool glass of water on a hot day. If you don't want her straightforward opinion, don't ask or be in her vicinity. When I opined that politics would complicate our relationship, she said I was just trying to avoid a commitment. There was only one exception to her no-holds directness. After we got married, she confessed, "I was abused as a child, and we're not going to talk about it." I was Irish and brought up in secrets, so it was no problem.

One time, a big-mouthed labor stooge reproached me for some innocuous vote. As I began an explanation, she stepped from behind me. "Stop talking to my husband."

The yappy official froze.

"He's the best labor senator there is and has more important people to talk to than you, so beat it."

His mouth hung open. When he gained his composure, he asked, "Is this the wife?"

I nodded.

"Oh, I like her! You should bring her around more."

He wasn't the only one. Women flocked to her after I joined the ticket, and they wanted photographs. She didn't like Dougherty and said so, sometimes on social media. When state representative Kevin Boyle glowered across the table at a charity fundraiser, she felt menaced. She dealt with it by throwing a cup of Pepsi on him. He rushed to the media, and Chris Brennan wrote a sympathetic story about poor little Kevin. The consultants called it bad publicity, but after that, more women than ever wanted to meet her. "Women know when they're being menaced," Tonya said. She stood up to bullies like second nature, and she rarely got it wrong. In 2023, Boyle was locked out of his house caucus for violating a protection from abuse order and stalking women staffers.

After we were notified of Tonya being under investigation, I entered the press conference from the balcony with rolled-up sleeves and sat behind a desk overflowing with microphones reminiscent of Budd's last day. I wasn't facing a prison sentence but something horrible and dangerous with some kind of ruination lurking. There were a bunch of hearsay rumors, but it was official that Wolf was assembling a list of accusations he could pour onto a public fire. Unlike Dwyer, I was in control and sane and knew how to accept blame for "whatever the investigation is about." I must have done something to offend the governor and wanted to atone. To this day, the amount of groveling I did was stultifying.

Wolf was a better actor than me and had established the facade of the good-natured, honest millionaire fighting for decency in government. Calling him a liar or idiot wasn't going to work. I answered every question patiently and articulately for over an hour. There was only innuendo and rumor—none of the reporters had any names or evidence of specific incidents. It was a whispering campaign better than Salvatore had ever concocted, except for the glaring, radioactive letter from the inspector general's office.

When I was asked if I knew what it was about, I said, "It's above my pay grade." I apologized for ever raising my voice or being impatient with anyone, and I offered that Tonya and I "would do better."

Tony Romeo, the portly reporter who attended Budd's conference as a younger man, asked if I had angry moments. I stupidly answered I had "Stack moments," which became a punchline. I had hoped that this public display of self-flagellation would put the controversy to rest. Hope was the thing with wings that flew out the window.

Dylan McGarry, who had a perpetual five o'clock shadow and perspiring forehead, offered, "If it works, you beat back a governor who is trying to kill you."

The next day, I was on the front pages of every newspaper from Bradford to Bucks, in front of the microphones, looking defiant or sad. Texts poured in complimenting me for being a stand-up guy.

Bill DeWeese, the former Speaker of the House who went to prison for Bonusgate, texted, "The optics show a compunctious remediation and remuneration." I still didn't understand what he was talking about, but he sounded positive.

A snowdrift silence followed the press conference for three days. Reporters admitted that the source of all the rumors was the governor's office, but crackling ice signaled the avalanche, and down came a storm of negative stories. "Unnamed sources in the governor's office" accused me of everything except murder.

Every perk and expense of the lieutenant governor's office had been abused in extravagance and excess.

The protective detail was a limousine service for Bonnie and Clyde, who brought mayhem and madness everywhere they went.

State House was like a Hollywood mansion for wild parties.

Even the Starbucks coffee served to constituents was a gratuitous entitlement.

Nobody cared that our office had spent far less than the last two lieutenant governors. The predisposition toward political leaders was negative, and Wolf and his "unnamed sources" fanned the flames. They knew what they were doing, had an excellent plan, and executed it masterfully.

Wolf's office scheduled a meeting for the following week, and I hired Mark Sheppard to deal with the inspector general's investigation and Dan Fee for public relations. Fee's shaved head and soft voice gave him the appearance of a kind of monk. His personal connections in the administration might enable us to find out why Wolf wanted to kill us. Furthermore, I wanted a way to amend the relationship and put out the fire. I knew Wolf wanted to kill me, but I wanted to talk him out of it. McGarry and Franchak tried to handle the press after Tuma's untimely retirement. Campaign advisor Marty Marks recommended Sheppard and Fee, but their pessimistic personalities provided a grim outlook, with Fee calling the crisis "existential." I was disgusted and in shock that the survival of my career could be on the line over the petty whims of hateful staffers and a spiteful governor. But I put my ego aside, knowing they were trying to hurt Tonya as well. She never ran away from a fight. I've been in numerous campaigns where the way to win was to shut up. That wasn't her style, and her anxiety was becoming overwhelming.

The working group discussed options. Tonya had complained about being forced to ride with certain troopers. She wanted to make some changes in staff but hadn't been belligerent. In any event, we could've withdrawn her protection willingly if that would've been helpful. We both knew how to drive. Nonetheless, she had been more anxious in the last year from the political battles with Dougherty, and the public nature of Wolf's investigation had activated early childhood trauma. I was forced to disclose these personal facts to the group and then to Wolf. She had begun repeating herself and falling into crying jags. She was convinced that Johnny Doc was coordinating a slander campaign with Wolf. She was overwhelmed by the governor's crushing authority and his intention to destroy her. She wasn't sleeping and was terrified. These were the exact symptoms of someone who had suffered assault as a little girl, and it led toward a breakdown. An adult far bigger and stronger had her under his complete dominance.

I was incredulous that she'd been targeted as a private citizen, not a state employee. If this was a political feud, decency demanded the exclusion of spouses. The inspector general didn't have authority and was being used as a weapon, one they seemed to use gleefully and gratuitously to inflict fear and humiliation. But Sheppard jabbed that no one cared about the origins of their authority, just that they were investigating a high public official and his wife. The agency wasn't an independent investigative entity but an agent of the governor and would give him whatever he wanted.

We needed a strategy for the meeting with Wolf. Fee and Sheppard saw the problem through rose-colored glasses and were naive. They had bought into Wolf's good-natured, Jeep-driving nerd image. They thought I could appeal to his decency. I thought they were wrong, but I was good at following a strategy if I had a consensus. We agreed that I should go to the meeting and beg for forgiveness. Sheppard believed that once the mental health issue was revealed, Wolf would be sympathetic. They prepared a long, contrite email where I disclosed private details of my marriage and our recent struggles with anxiety. We were getting help, and there wouldn't be any trouble. I followed the script perfectly.

The governor usually acted bemused and friendly, if detached, but he suddenly turned appallingly unsympathetic and aggressive. Wolf scoffed about Tonya's anxiety issues. "Yeah right!" It was a disheartening, disrespectful, and disingenuous gesture unbecoming of a governor. I held my breath and couldn't believe it. Suddenly he was Mr. Tough Guy. I'm sure his staffers had bolstered him as they hid quivering and giggling in the next room. The Jeep show was over.

* * *

The next part of my story consists of my recollection only. It was a frightening time in my career. Fear affects perception. I don't believe there were any other witnesses, but it was a terrifying time because I was clueless as to why he needed to batter me and my wife so intensely. I could never quite figure it out.

I had tussled with some tough people in my challenging climb through the bloody path, and I had tasted the bitter pills of rejection and defeat numerous times, but there was always a semblance of respect between me and my opponents. Not from Governor Wolf. The level of disrespect had my head ready to explode. There was no time for incredulity and hurt pride. Lunging for his skinny, sweaty little neck wouldn't get us out of this terrible quandary. Outwardly, I remained calm and apologetic, groveling while feeling horrified and sickened.

A palpable vibe of sadistic confidence emanated from him. "I'm stripping you of the detail and State House staff and announcing it to the media."

I asked if we could just do it quietly because it was something I'd wanted to do anyway. I wanted to restore privacy to our relationship. I hoped he didn't want to ignite a public scandal at this most vulnerable moment. I would do whatever he wanted but implored him to leave Tonya out of it.

He went out and had a press conference and brought her name into it. He even had the audacity to state that he had tried to help us. This gentleman, who had won a single election in his entire life, would show a veteran like me how to behave. He had a smirk on his face and chuckled as I departed from the meeting.

"What a dick!" cried Marty Marks, or words to that effect.

"You're kidding, right?" asked Dan Fee when I returned to the office.

"Nope," I said. "I wish I was."

"You told him about your wife?"

He didn't care. Sheppard became alarmed that Wolf intended to spill the inspector general's report to the mass media, creating a tidal wave of irretrievable scandal. Interestingly, the governor had compiled a draft of the report that was filled with exaggerations and lies before announcing an investigation. Citizens were never thoughtful or fair during controversy. The report was a Pandora's box that had to remain sealed. Otherwise, we would need to spend every waking hour denying lies or explaining the appropriate context with little chance of success. I wasn't a rookie. I knew what they were trying to do. There would be no way to undo the damage, and Sheppard's priority became the prevention of that public fiasco. It was maddening and disturbing to do everything in one's power to prevent a person in authority from distortion and destruction. My fundamental trust in the fairness of our democratic system was shaken.

After finally beating Salvatore in 2000, I had won every election since and had been the first Philadelphian in history to win lieutenant governor. I remember standing on the hardwood floors by the fireplace at State House in 2015, thinking my winning streak would never end.

When Fee called the situation existential, I still didn't grasp it. In my 2000 campaign, Neil Oxman thought the insurance fraud attack was "possibly fatal." Back then, I endured several nauseating days in a mental funk, and then snapped out of it and dug my way to victory. I always came off the ropes fighting. I kept thinking I would snap out of it and find a path to safety. The blows I took were severe, coming from the most powerful man in the state. He was trying to ruin us. By talking that trash to my face and being proudly belligerent and uncaring, the governor demonstrated he would go all the way, and he wanted to get Tonya too. He was getting away with it. He acted like he was just the voice of decency against horrendous people. And there is no way he believed it.

You can't disprove a negative, as my dad said. Nonetheless, there wasn't one obvious lie to retort. According to the report, an "unnamed trooper" carried my intoxicated derrière home every night from Harper's Tavern, a watering hole near the residence. Many lieutenant governors had enjoyed a drink at that place, but not me—not once. Maybe the inspector general was thinking of somebody else. As a lawyer, one lie made a witness's entire testimony unbelievable. Here *was* one. But if that report got out, I'd have to do an item-by-item denial every day.

The Wolf folks dangled the report to the media, making their mouths water. The administration spun it with a shameful aura, as if our shamefulness was just beyond imagination. But they encouraged everyone to use those imaginations. Interestingly, not one individual filed a grievance or complaint or lawsuit, any of which might've resulted in a financial windfall from the state. Nor had a single state employee contacted a reporter. In fact, David Fillman, president of the employee's union for state workers, performed a thorough probe. That's why he backed my reelection and was one of our largest donors.

The whole story originated from the governor's office, and his anonymous staffers poured fuel on it. It was one thing for me to be vilified as a professional politician who had been in the public eye for years, but to witness an impending breakdown, my beautiful wife in pain, and then to be rebuffed and ridiculed was beyond the realm of shabbiness and savagery. As I predicted to the governor, she had a breakdown, and she courageously sought help. She flew to Sierra Tuscan, terrified of living in her own state, to sort out childhood trauma issues that had haunted her and been ignited by this attack.

Frankly, we could've flipped a coin or gone as a couple. Instead, I buckled down and wrestled the grizzly bear. Our strategy was to do what worked for me in the past. I worked like a maniac. I presided over the senate with renewed energy. I smiled until it hurt. I traveled the state and stayed in the public eye. My colleagues saw I wasn't dead yet. The working group coached de-escalation at all costs. That's not what Tonya wanted, and I was glad she was safe. I expressed the unpalatable sentiment that Wolf and I were working it out to reassure my base.

The wretched stories kept coming, but I never read them. I noticed a cartoon of me as Rocky Balboa accompanying a Chris Brennan story ("Remember When Lieutenant Governor Mike Stack Was in *Rocky II*?"). They had the right cartoon—I would fight until the final bell. If Wolf wanted to get rid of me, he could've been more tactful. He could've said that the relationship wasn't working, I wasn't his choice, and he could've offered an exit strategy. His destructive staff probably guaranteed him resignation in weeks.

Some of my staffers wanted to shift the blame to Tonya. Somehow, speaking her mind was insanity under their definition. I think she pegged it accurately when she said that other treacherous forces were behind the violence. She wanted to go to rhetorical war, confident the truth was on our side. Maybe it wouldn't have resulted in our public decimation, but I doubted it. But she was the bravest girl I ever met. Other politicians had thrown their spouses under the bus. There was no way I would do it.

I visited Fumo at his mansion to seek guidance. Bob Brady, who still called Tonya Pocahontas, joined us as Fumo talked to me like one of his children who was always making mistakes. "I told you to get rid of that detail. I knew Wolf would leverage you."

Brady asked how much money I had in my campaign fund. Since Wolf had accused me of preparing a primary run, maybe I should do it. But it would take multiple millions just to strike back against their taxpayer-funded smears. Brady and Fumo were appalled at the terrible advice regarding Tonya.

"She'd kill you! And you'd deserve it . . . with all due respect," Bob said.

"She's crazy, not nuts," Fumo said. He thought my high-priced advisors were clueless. They believed what they had read instead of what we were telling them.

I ended up with three people—Fumo, Brady, and my mother—who I could talk with about my wife. They didn't think Tonya was a mental case. The scandal wasn't her fault, even if they were gunning for her. Frankly, I had no intension of taking the bad advice but was taught to listen to advisors before making tough decisions. Sheppard and Dan Fee were incredulous that I wouldn't follow their plan. I was grateful to have friends like Brady, Fumo, and Mom.

I kept hoping some significant person would rush to our defense, but the cavalry never showed. Other friends and politicians endorsed me for reelection, and I appreciated their support. I had friends on both sides of the aisle, but politics is feeding frenzy of rivalries. More than a few competitors weren't shedding any tears for me.

The political philosopher Edmund Burke stated, "I am convinced that we have a degree of delight, and that no small one, in the real misfortunes and pains of others." Therefore, I learned to be reasonable in my expectations. I stopped thinking of myself as a victim. I was in the frying pan and scrambling to find a way out.

Let's keep it real. I had a radiant title and had been elected by a million Pennsylvania voters. I was privileged to serve, but politics is a hard business. It was my turn to struggle because "into each life some rain must fall," Longfellow wrote. "Some days must be dark and dreary," and I had been handed a valuable learning challenge. Once I put the pity aside and postponed my own breakdown, things got easier.

# CHAPTER FIFTEEN

# THE MOST IRRELEVANT JOB SUDDENLY BECOMES RELEVANT

The parade of opportunists came marching down Broad Street like the Mummers. Seven candidates announced they were running for lieutenant governor as Democrats. Rarely did an incumbent lieutenant governor even get a challenge. Ed Rendell had once endorsed Congressman Joe Hoeffel against Catherine Baker Knoll in her reelection, then withdrew it the next day and endorsed the incumbent. There were sometimes tensions between governors and lieutenant governors, but since 1968, the governors stuck with their partners. My situation was unique, and the Democrats blindly followed the governor and rallied against me. Many of the candidates, including John Fetterman, campaigned on issues that had nothing to do with the office, like the legalization of marijuana and ending fracking. Pennsylvania Democrats loved female candidates, and male electeds dreaded them. Three bold ladies vied to make this the year of the women. The race veered to the need to have a female lieutenant governor. When the other candidates talked about relevant issues, I wouldn't get any credit for my accomplishments on pardons or veterans. They wanted to "restore dignity" to the office, and I wanted to cringe.

All I could do was attend every forum and be the most prepared. I knew the job and was good at it. The other candidates proposed criminal justice reforms that I'd already done. I talked about Pathway to Pardons and received restrained applause. I outclassed them all as I had done four years before. Regardless, I couldn't get my wheels out of the mud. My mother watched the forums and complimented me on my performance and how smart the women were. "Mom!" I complained. "They're trying to kill me."

She smiled sweetly. "Oh dear, I don't think so."

My winning political calculus had flipped from the previous election. In 2014, I was the only candidate from the east. I had Philadelphia and the surrounding counties to myself. The western opponents split that region's vote, and two others shared central and northeast Pennsylvania. I was the only lieutenant governor candidate on TV in southeastern Pennsylvania, and I won in a landslide. Now everything was different. I had three opponents in my backyard. Fetterman had all the fanfare of a big-top clown with his towering height, hoodie, and shaved head. But he had a big problem—Aryanna Berringer, an Iraq veteran (and a darling, according to my mother) who also proclaimed herself a poor woman, unlike wealthy Fetterman. If he could take care of that pesky combat soldier, he would have the west all to himself.

Every strategic move I made was counteracted by Wolf and Dougherty. How do I know it was Dougherty? Supporters claimed they couldn't help me because Doc said it would be embarrassing to the governor. They also said that staffers from the Wolf administration had called, and Doc was supporting Fetterman and Nina Ahmad in Philadelphia, furiously trying to split my vote. Wolf's proxies recruited Fetterman, and John admitted he wouldn't have got into the race without Wolf's ascent. In 2016, he had unsuccessfully run for the United States Senate and needed a road to another shot. The mayor of tiny Braddock fashioned himself as a blue-collar hero with a Fu Manchu beard instead of the WWF Jesse Ventura. Lieutenant governor was a stepping stone to Washington.

The talking heads on *Inside Story* in Philadelphia were baffled. Why was Wolf doing this to the guy from the city with all the votes? But there were plenty of rivals in Philadelphia that were happy to see me sweat. Johnny Doc encouraged the building trades to back state representative Madeleine Dean against me. I respected her qualifications, and she offered me the most trouble. My mother thought she was particularly intelligent.

As the deadline for petitions approached, we developed a three-pronged strategy. First, convince Madeleine Dean to run for Congress instead of lieutenant governor. Second, keep Aryanna Berringer in the race against Fetterman. Lastly, we had to keep that damn IG report private.

Madeleine Dean served in the state house and had more intelligence than the average representative. Her auburn hair and stylish suits gave her a fresh, almost complementary appearance next to me. She probably sensed the slurs weren't true and might have even been sympathetic. Her electoral base in Montgomery County was sizable and adjacent to my former senate district. Our rapport was warm and respectful, and she knew one of my staffers. Dylan McGarry worked behind the scenes to convince her to run for Congress. There was an open seat, and she could be a much bigger player as a woman in Washington. With darling Aryanna giving Fetterman fits, I would have only Chester County Commissioner Kathi Cozzone as a female opponent. I might be able to capture enough of my base to slip by Fetterman as he split the west.

Dylan McGarry's perpetual five o'clock shadow had become a six o'clock one. But he was earning it. Two days before the filing deadline, McGarry phoned with the good news. "Madeleine Dean is officially out, Guv. They can't stop you now!"

I was relieved for two minutes. I would have Philadelphia to myself and wrestle with Cozzone for the blue-collar county votes. Just before deadline, Nina Ahmad, a millionaire woman of color who had announced for Congress against Dwight Evans, switched to run for lieutenant governor. Her media advisor, Ken Snyder, was the guy who talked me into running for the first time and turned down a request to work for me in the reelect. The next day, Aryanna Berringer withdrew, leaving the west to Fetterman. And I had big trouble in my own city.

Ken Snyder claimed responsibility for my lieutenant governor victory and my senate victory fourteen years before that. He said he was sitting out the lieutenant governor's race in 2018. Then he got the call from Dougherty explaining that Nina Ahmad would spend $3 million for an office no one cared about.

In the meantime, Mark Sheppard and Dan Fee got large sums of money from my campaign fund to get us out of the crisis. Out of the frying pan and into the fire I went. I was behind in campaign fundraising with dim electoral chances. Wolf and his proxies intimidated my contributors, but many solid friends hung on. Dougherty claimed, as usual, that my victory would hurt labor. He helped both Ahmad, who hadn't attended a single forum, and Fetterman, who he showed how progressively pragmatic he was by accepting Bernie Sanders's endorsement around the same time. Fetterman was against fracking and in favor of it in the same week.

* * *

When I was sworn in as lieutenant governor in 2015, I wished my dad could've been there to see the culmination of all our hard work together. I missed him even more. He may not have anticipated dark days like this, but he would have been ready with guidance. He would have found a bright side and joked about similar treachery in his adventures. He might've said that at least we'd have something to write about in the book. I'm sure he would've scrolled through his weathered brown book, looking for someone to call. The more I thought about him, the less worried I became about losing. He would've loved the danger, the pulsating perilous romp of it all. What a glorious challenge to tango with the big boys!

My fundraising organization was in shambles, and we couldn't find a consultant to get us organized. I was left by myself in a dingy office with a cell phone and a yellow legal pad. I called anyone I could think of and asked confidently for help. Solid people stepped up, and fair-weather friends floated away on breezy clouds, never to be heard from again. That discovery was platinum. Dave Fillman of ASCME District Council 21 remembered a dinner at State House and our affectionate rapport with those who served us. He told them to call if I ever acted it up. He hadn't heard anything, so he wrote us a big check. Bobby Henon of the Steamfitters Union didn't care about incurring Wolf or Dougherty's wrath. He didn't care who he pissed off—that was his livelihood, what stood him apart from the followers of Philadelphia. He was Good Bobby Henon as opposed to extortionist Bobby. Once, I mistakenly called the other Bob Henon.

"Is this the good Bobby Henon or the bad Bobby Henon?" I asked cluelessly.

Johnny Doc's crowbar answered, "It's good Bobby Henon!"

Whoops.

But through all this mud, I was lucky to have some loyal friends. I raised enough money to produce a strong commercial about my military service and gratitude for veterans. Not much had gone right, but I'd try to win this fight.

It was unreasonable to expect privacy in today's politics. Tonya and I worked through the trauma together via video conference and quick visits. Nonetheless, an unidentified source in the state police leaked a story indicating her whereabouts. The negative stories were hitting but hadn't killed us yet. The source was trying to inflict more damage but got greedy. Suddenly even the heartless media were horrified that someone who was trying to get help was being tortured. I couldn't believe it took so long for decency to appear. The front office was shamed into shelving their burn book. Even bloodthirsty reporters like Angela Couloumbis, who had baited us to come and tell our version early on, conceded as much. We had probably stopped the long-term damage to our reputations, but in the short run, a cloud of amorphous suspicion hung. And even after Wolf's lawyer, Denise Smiler, stalked Tonya in treatment, his staff criticized my stepson for working in the senate and living at the State House. But Justin considered it a badge of honor to go through the battle with us, and he became my emergency driver and crisis companion.

# CHAPTER SIXTEEN

# WHO ELSE WANTS TO FIGHT? LET'S GO!

The good times were gone and weren't coming back. I knew how to rumble and got my fair share of punches in, usually in grudgingly fair fights. But this was a gang fight, one on twenty. Nina Ahmad's ubiquitous commercial proclaimed she'd ban assault weapons and make every dream of soccer moms come true. Her unicorns and gummy bears campaign sidestepped a lack of public service record or a workable plan. She emphasized that she was the only woman of color running and we were long overdue. My staff and friends were certain of victory, but I had a bad feeling. I wasn't impressed by Fetterman and didn't think he was a major threat. Nina was on TV three times more than us and pandered to diversity over accomplishment.

Months of sidling up to Wolf, begging him for mercy, wasn't how I usually campaigned. The accusations had taken me out of my game. They had us tied up on the railroad tracks and the train just kept coming, blaring its horn, not letting me think. I had won races and battled the Republicans in the senate, and this pointy-headed menace and his thug aide de camp were tearing it all down. We both knew there'd be no reconciliation if I won. He must have been desperately afraid I might just do it.

I made it back to the fishbowl conference room at the *Philadelphia Inquirer* building, where I had appeared every four years since my twenty-fourth birthday. I recalled the nostalgic days when Neil Oxman bolstered me to barge in and blow those ivory tower bastards onto their butts. I don't even know where I found the guts as a damn kid to even show up, let alone tango with Pulitzer Prize winners. But I had already scooped the endorsement of the *Daily News* against a titan senator. Twenty-something years old, and I could either wet my pants or win. Let's see, which would it be? I was tougher than I knew, though petrified, a special combination. My central nervous system blasted steam, but my eggshell psyche was armor-plated. Just go in there. That's all I had to do. But that was ancient times and felt like seconds ago. Now I was in with the clowns and would never see things the same, not this silly periodical or America.

The elevator doors opened, and I could taste the dust and smell the asbestos. The white elephant on North Broad Street had been the epicenter of Walter Annenberg's empire. But they didn't make them like they used to. Once a beehive of journalistic activity in 1988 and 1992, where the spirits of Woodward and Bernstein and journalistic heroism pinged off the walls, it was now a dusty old ghost town with tumbleweeds rolling past an ancient, crumbling cathedral. Empty desks and cardboard boxes took the place of Coronas and rumbling presses. But there was one remnant of greatness in Signe Wilkinson, the Pulitzer Prize-winning cartoonist was still there, seeing my fingers clutching dirt as I dangled from the cliff. She scribbled a good one of me. She made me look younger with nice hair exploding off the top of my head, blowing my stack after the big press conference.

She was okay in my book, a petite, bookish-looking woman approaching retirement, hoping she had enough money. Her portrayal wasn't cruel, just witty, intelligent, and intuitive. Our eyes met as I swam toward the bowl. Her smile was warm.

"Your cartoon of me was pretty good." I forced a little chuckle. "I can always brag that I've been the subject of a Pulitzer Prize winner."

She leaned closer, grinning like she was my favorite aunt. "You survived it." She was authentically impressed. "That's the important thing."

Chris Brennan led the editorial board interview, which was interesting since he'd written so many negative articles about me. I should've worn my old school sweatsuit with black knit cap and entered to the theme of *Rocky*. Instead, I strutted in wearing dark pinstripes and sapphire silk. Surprise and dismay made him quiver and quake. He had a face for newspapers, that giant pumpkin perched upon those slouching shoulders with rivers of sweat streaming down the temples. The pretend eyes and crimson cheeks made him passable as a living, breathing human being, but he lived under a bridge.

Brennan announced that the board never interviewed lieutenant governor candidates. "We are making an exception because there's unusual interest this year in the office." He said that I would've been reelected easily if it were not for "the issues that Governor Wolf has with you." Other than that, everyone agreed, "You've done a good job." But that was Brennan. He would set you up and try to make you feel safe before dropping a piano on your head.

At the Pennsylvania Society in December, he had cornered me and said I was the odds-on favorite for the time being to win renomination, then he let go of the ropes, asking about my reaction to Ed Rendell's endorsement of Fetterman in Philadelphia that day. Instead of spewing profanity, I responded calmly, as my heart contorted like *Alien* in my chest, that my countless endorsements came from folks who were "currently serving." Ed was a great guy for being a treacherous has-been, but it was a free country.

The editorial board session was as predictable as a stick in the eye. The questions meandered into rainwater runoff and local income tax, and then drifted down the creek to where the elephant waited. The inspector general's report was no longer a big issue. The controversy had run out of destructive steam. It had ruined more than a year in Tonya's and my life but started to gather dust. However, Brennan wanted to kick some more back into my face.

Should the report remain private? The women who had watched Tonya get savaged through innuendo finally found some decency and agreed it should be private. Maybe they saw my polling numbers and thought I wasn't a threat. The *Inquirer* endorsed John Fetterman instead of either women from the east or the hometown kid. It had to be a fix. That kind of thinking was why we were in a warehouse.

* * *

Judge Eugene Maier spoke at my dad's funeral in 2012. On that sweltering July day, 1,327 people lined up to bid farewell. Many were politicians of significant fame, but others were boyhood friends who knew him as Mickey. The watchman of my journey from boyhood to the capitol went to assist God in making deals. The judge's wit was as dry as dust, and his disposition sometimes grim, except when he was in the company of dozens of children and grandchildren and our family as we celebrated the Mike Stack Annual Treasure Hunt.

Gene once said that the one word to describe my father perfectly was "kind." William Naghey described my dad as a beloved politician, but his obituary talked more about his painting and writing than his king-making. Judge Maier had been a hanging judge but ultimately kind like my dad. He witnessed my battle throughout the year and had confidence I could pull it out. He had been in the trenches with Fumo when they feared police commissioner Frank Rizzo would have them killed. Gene handed the envelope across the table as we ordered the early bird at the Cape May Courthouse Diner. Mom had that blessed Mother Mary vibe about her, like I was the martyred son.

The judge was optimistic. "This is only the beginning, not the end." He patted my forearm gently. "I'm not kidding."

I spent the rest of the weekend trying to avoid Nina Ahmad's commercials while watching sports. But they just kept airing. Snyder must have convinced her she would win if she would just buy enough commercials. She was Dougherty's vehicle, whether she knew it or not. They knew she was siphoning my votes in Philadelphia and Allentown. I'd had bad feelings in other elections, but this one was thick and unrelenting.

I was grateful to reach election day and appeared perky, even if mentally exhausted. I never stopped working, but the bitterness was suffocating. I just couldn't get out of the mud. Every time I made a little progress, another wrench fell into the engine. I was filled with venomous contempt for my own party. All the attacks came from Democrats. They were worse than all of Salvatore's whispering campaigns combined. I never got a chance to counter-punch because Wolf was on the phony high ground.

Nonetheless, I won Philadelphia in a landslide. It was an incredible feat, but my margins of victory were far less than four years before. I lost votes to the ladies I'd needed badly, and Fetterman won the west because he was their only candidate. Statewide voters were notorious for detesting the word "Philadelphia" under candidates' names. I had overcome that in 2014 with overwhelming commercial superiority, but not in 2018. I received over 130,000, a substantial total, but would not be renominated. There was no bright side except that we had taken a huge public scandal and made it a non-issue. At the end of the day, I lost a competitive election against several qualified candidates. The media and John Fetterman played it up like he was special, but I had won something big. The governor came after me with lethal intent and failed. He never even thought I'd make it to election day. He wanted me to resign in disgrace. Dream on, little dreamer. And he did me a big favor by letting me know how tough I was.

Brennan should've never done that goof about me being Rocky. I used it as inspiration. I had gone the distance and knew that I wasn't just some bum from the block. Now I wanted to scoop up my little Adrian and get the hell out of there.

# CHAPTER SEVENTEEN

# THE HARDEST PART IS OVER . . . EXCEPT FOR THESE NEXT HARDEST PARTS

I was both disgusted and relieved when I walked into my capitol office. Franchak joined me with folders in both arms.

"What are you doing with those?" I asked.

He smiled patiently, as if he were waiting for the joke to be over. "We've got a lot of Pathway to Pardons work to do, Governor. People are counting on you."

I gave him ice. We had the largest number of applications for pardons in decades, and we needed to review them. The program we started a couple of years ago had grown exponentially. At one joint meeting with Senator Street at John Bartram High School, two thousand ex-offenders filled the auditorium. Criminal justice reform affected thousands of lives. People were counting on us, darn it!

Seven months was ample time to make a difference. Everybody in the fishbowl of the capitol knew I'd lost. They'd be waiting for me to cry and stamp my feet. They could wait until the cows came home. I presided over the senate with an ulcer-causing grin, showed up early, and left late.

Even though I was punch-drunk and traumatized, Fumo and others urged me to run for city council against incumbent Brian O'Neill in Northeast Philadelphia. I won the council district resoundingly in my recent loss, so my support was solid. It's hard to believe I could muster up another campaign after the excruciating experience with the governor. I explored the possibility of becoming a college president, but maybe it was time for a break from leadership. Tonya enjoyed Los Angeles and wanted to get out of Pennsylvania. I had spent sixteen years in Harrisburg and was happy to go, but I wanted to keep my hand in politics in Philadelphia. I had the option to return to practice law with John Elliot at the end of the term if nothing better came along.

Franchak had me on the phone for twenty-five minutes with agenda items after saying he only needed five minutes. We played this game for years. No matter where I was or what I was doing, he only needed a couple minutes. I gazed at the ocean from my little Wildwood deck. The longer the call went, the more likely bad news was hiding at the end.

"Why are you torturing me?" I commented. "I'm going out of office."

Matt chuckled. "I only have one more thing." The worst had already occurred, so I wasn't worried. "Governor Wolf has invited you to his swearing-in."

My gut churned.

"He wants you on stage, and he's going to thank you for your service." He had a lot of nerve. He must've wanted to appear magnanimous. By not accusing him of perfidy over the last year, I looked like a good guy.

I had a history of sucking it up. Mom loved my concession speeches in 1988 and 1992 more than my victory speeches. As an Irish mother, she thought humility was next to divinity. I didn't pass on blame or let them see the disappointment. The old man had taught that today's enemies might be next year's friend, so we should be gracious to all. I had always turned the other cheek in the interest of winning later. Even with Dougherty, it was a one-way fight. Over the years, we had sit-downs over cups of coffee where I apologized for the wrongs he had envisioned. "You're OK with me, Senator," he would say while crossing his fingers. He'd start rumors and undercut my support, and I'd have no choice but to smile.

The next week, Franchak quipped, "The governor's office called again."

It was more calls than the last couple of years. "I don't care." They wanted to use me to feel better.

Franchak never held a grudge, and he appealed to my better nature. In fact, his kindly nature was a secret weapon. "You'll be the bigger man, like always." When I brought him into the caucus, senators were compelled to trust him and hated me for it. He would explain the legislative intent, and if Franchak believed in it, it must be good and decent.

I was sick of his damn decency. "Your brand has always been perseverance. Why not sell your brand?"

Russ was the burly capitol policeman I greeted every day as lines of visitors went through the metal detector. He would stop and salute. He knew I'd been an Army captain and saw me battle every day. I snapped a return crisply. He was the only thing I still liked about the capitol. We never noticed each other until it was hitting the fan. But he was something to look forward to, even on that last day.

The frigid air and gray sky captured my mood perfectly. For decades, I'd gone into tough rooms and won people over, even as a young kid without a prayer. I went where I wasn't invited, first with my dad and then by myself.

They thought I had a lot of nerve for a guy who was about to lose again. I had acquired a taste for it. I had lost so much that I came to know its truth.

Churchill called defeats the stones on the path to victory, and that bulldog was right. Russ knew this was the last time we would see each other for a while. He was already welling up. Franchak and McGarry escorted me along the polished cobblestone under the dazzling rotunda, down the escalator, and to the rear plaza. The montage played through my brain like a 1980s movie. As a young punk, I was battered by Salvatore. In a trudge and a blink, I stood with arms raised, confetti falling like an impossible dream.

I had graduated from the MasterClass. One of my key mentors was the chairman of the most formidable party machine in America. "When you smile," Bob Brady said, "it kills them." Time and again, over the years, that was his advice. It was too simple and difficult.

"Let's go talk to Brady," my dad would say.

"What did Bob say?" Tonya would ask.

"He said, 'smile.'"

I could follow orders.

I sat in the front row on the stage among the former governors and first ladies. Dad had always pushed me to get up front, to act like I was important and belonged there. Now there was a seat reserved. I could feel the wind trying to move my long, gelled hair. I scanned the crowd for people I knew. People were watching me and smiling back. My pals from the senate waved, Democrats and Republicans, women and men, assembled in the front rows. They were relishing it, couldn't believe their eyes how I was coming off the ropes, firing.

*Oh, Chris Brennan, you are my muse, mocking me as Rocky and inspiring my inner strength.* I rose with the bell when introduced by John Fetterman, my opportunistic successor, who was dancing on my grave right in front of my face. I gave the crowd my pistol fingers and smiled so hard, acid was coming off my teeth. Oh, the pain, the melting agony, the memories of four years before with Tonya and her beautiful brown mink and radiant smile, and Justin a little shy by my side.

Wolf turned during his speech and had a confused expression, like he couldn't believe I was standing there. He coughed as he said my name. He saw in my eyes what he couldn't take away. The cameras clicked and flashed, and applause grew into thunder, louder than four years ago. I milked it and waved both hands, pouring salt in Tom's wounds and thus healing my own.

If this all sounds like grandiose trash-talking, so be it. We who win find ways to claim victory. I didn't rush off the stage when the band started to play. I shook Wolf's hand longer than he wanted and chatted with his family. I wanted everybody to get a good look at me. The new lady senators embraced me as I came down the steps. Katie True was already giving Jay Costa a headache. I was happy to see them. We needed them in our caucus, and they would transform the ladies auxiliary into something stronger.

I used to beg people to knock on doors with me or attend civic meetings. Then in 2000, I had an army. Everywhere I went, I was surrounded by supporters and staff. After coming off the stage, I walked alone back to where Russ was waiting near the metal detectors. His cheeks were wet and his eyes red. He suffocated me with a bear hug, then saluted again. It was absolute waterworks. My black Cadillac was just outside the door in the best parking spot on the planet.

"Dad, check out this spot!"

I started the engine.

# CHAPTER EIGHTEEN

# I CAN'T GET NO SATISFACTION . . .
# BUT I TRY.

Mick Jagger received millions of dollars to write a memoir, but he gave the money back. He didn't want to revisit the pain.

For a long time, it was hard to go through it again. I hung out at our family home a few days after leaving. I bumped into all kinds of friends around town who thought I was still in office. They congratulated me and sent good wishes to Governor Wolf. I sat in the chair at the head of the long, oval table in the kitchen, where Dad had held court. Framed newspaper stories about him hung on the wall, including his obituary, which called him "a political influence far beyond" Northeast Philadelphia.

"Well, they won't be able to take shots at me anymore," I sighed.

My mother chuckled. "Oh yes they will." Maybe that was a good thing.

\* \* \*

A few weeks later, I opened a letter from former senator Jim Ferlo, the guy who thought I wasn't serious enough to be leader and who had worked against me. Now he praised my "amazing work on criminal justice and pardons." He predicted I wouldn't get the "credit you deserve." He didn't like Wolf; thought he'd been reprehensible to me. Then Ferlo asked for help for a friend who needed a pardon.

Ferlo was a progressive from Pittsburgh who didn't like Fetterman. Yesterday's enemies were today's friends. I called Matt Franchak, now Farnese's chief of staff, and asked him to help Ferlo's guy. He probably got a pardon. Jim passed away four months later. In retrospect, he wasn't that bad of a guy.

\* \* \*

I love action movies, but the two best helicopter camera shots I've ever seen weren't in the theater. They were in the beautiful blue skies of Philadelphia.

One was at 542 feet above the ground, rotating around the observatory deck of towering Philadelphia City Hall. Under the feet of a thirty-seven-foot iron sculpture of William Penn stood a quivering Councilman Rick Mariano, a Johnny Doc protégé who was threatening to jump. There was only one man who could calm him down. Ricky was on the phone asking Bob Brady what to do. Bob feared heights but waited on the inner steps, trying to bring Rick in. He embraced another Philly politician on the way to the pen.

The other superb helicopter shot was from two hundred feet and eyed two rowhomes in South Philadelphia that were being raided by the FBI. In August 2018, the agents in the blue and yellow windbreakers seized boxes of evidence as a ruddy-faced John Dougherty paced and yammered along the sidewalk in cargo shorts and a bad-fitting Sixers hat.

\* \* \*

Soon after I left office, John Elliot hired me back to the firm and encouraged me, saying, "We'll keep our powder dry and look for targets of opportunity." The gray day after my loss, he remarked, "You got mugged." He had wanted to attack the governor but changed his mind. "You were in an impossible situation but did everything you could." It didn't make me feel better.

That Christmas, John Elliot and I attended the firm party at the Westmoreland Club in Scranton. An elite, power player who will remain nameless noticed me sitting with Elliot and came over. The tall, elegant attorney with salt-and-pepper hair raised money for presidents. I could never get him on the phone when I was running because I wasn't big enough. He moved briskly past Elliot to shake my hand and leaned in like he would tell me where Hoffa was buried. "I watched you at the inauguration. It was extraordinary." He didn't think I needed to do it. "But you were so gracious."

My gut churned.

"If you didn't know what had happened, you would have thought everything was great between you and Wolf."

I just nodded.

"I'm not the only one who noticed." There was no crying in baseball. I understood it better than ever. "Whatever you're running for, I want to support you." I hadn't tried to impress anyone, just behaved as a man of dignity and honor. But it was gratifying that a smart guy recognized mettle and wanted to back me in the future.

I believed that day would come again. But now it was time for something completely different. Tonya suggested that I go to Hollywood and become a standup comedian and actor. I'd been the lead actor in community theater productions and had done standup before winning the state senate seat in 2000. I was a political animal, not a junkie. A break was in order. But how in the world would I just show up and start performing in the entertainment capital of the world? I applied the same principles as running for office—you don't get elected if you aren't on the ballot. You can't get booked without going to auditions and doing standup on stage.

I enrolled at the Los Angeles School of Comedy and started developing an act. Then Tonya put a casting app on my phone, and we submitted for parts. Almost instantaneously she said, "You've got an audition at UCLA Film School for the role of All American Father tomorrow and, two hours after that, at the Steven Spielberg School at USC for Mean Father." I had wanted to act in film for a long time. Now I was doing it. She acted as my driver and navigator to make sure I showed up.

My spine-tingling performance in *The Bottle* got me murdered by my son. The movie was only five minutes long, but I was in it with a juicy part. For years I sat in my senate office, longing to get into the creative activities. We fought for budget dollars to help fund the arts. It was a painful route but I may never have had the chance if not for the tiny little fall. Since then, I've done twenty films and recently starred in a feature called *Money and Greed*, shot on location in Kentucky. I got my Screen Actors Guild card in 2010 from an online series called *Finders Keepers*, but I never had the chance to use it. Now I'm on my second agent and almost booked a Hallmark film. Some of the directors predict I will do a reverse Schwarzenegger: go from being a politician to a movie star.

I took up surfing shortly after my dad's passing. He loved the ocean, and it made me feel closer to him. My hair developed some blond streaks a few summers ago, so Tonya took me to the salon to finish the job. Philly Mike transformed into a California surfer dude overnight. But even as I strutted down Sunset Boulevard in sandals with a winning grin, the aftershocks of stress and anxiety crashed like hurricane waves. I didn't want to live in the past. I had seen so many candidates who lost races and couldn't let it go. I had been pummeled, but I was okay now. Tonya guided me to calmness by proclaiming we were free, and advising me to smell the roses of my accomplishments. Her recovery enabled her to face her demons and move forward positively. She passed on her wisdom.

My mom was right about them taking shots. The old rivals and media clowns had fresh fodder. My comedy teacher Sunda Coonquest got me ready for the stage by rehearsing potential routines. Some of them were crude and incomplete but only practice. I put one on a casting site to demonstrate standup ability. Not long after that, I got a text from Chris Brennan.

"I saw your standup. Doing a story for *Clout*."

My old buddy had followed me to Los Angeles. Stalk much, Chris? Doc must have put him onto it because Brennan wouldn't have known where to look. Call me paranoid, but that's how lightbulbs operated. Someone uploaded my act onto YouTube and Brennan saw it. His story slanted toward how I'd gone nuts. A Harrisburg TV station also did a smarmy story that made me look human. That was the characteristic that consultants wanted to show—humanness. I received many compliments from folks back home, particularly younger ones. I relished the idea of the front office people wishing they could put my off-color quips into a secret report.

Doc's little plan boomeranged, so he sent the footage to John Elliot, who found it offensive to our clients. We decided to part ways. The man who had been a mentor since childhood just couldn't take my jokes. Nobody could poison like Johnny Doc. But one person's poison was another's punch.

Tonya exploded in laughter. "He knows he hasn't beaten you, and it's killing him!"

The Crazy Man couldn't let it go. He was obsessed with me and my happy life. She thought that was the biggest compliment he could give and that I should be so proud.

I must admit it was flattering to be stalked all the way to the West Coast. Nonetheless, Sunda remarked, "That Brennan guy was trying to hurt you, but we'll use him." She urged me to spell her name right and "make sure he mentions The LA School of Comedy." Brennan acted like my publicist and wrote another story about my luxury home show, where I chose between three seven-million-dollar houses. The show was scripted, but Tonya loved the exposure. "Those idiots will make you a star!"

After all that, the pandemic hit. I read every book I could get my hands on. Reading quieted my mind. Writing in a journal helped reduce my anxiety. I'd been under assault for so long that it was hard to calm down. My exciting political career had waylaid abruptly. The blanket of accomplishment helped conceal the pain of many years. I had always thought victory in 2000 would be the balm to heal all wounds. Instead, it concealed them. The dam broke and I was overwhelmed with shame for my learning and political failures. Accolades had been my opium. I had a ridiculous number of plaques, awards, and trophies and a résumé of certified victories. But suddenly, without my fancy title, I was standing naked in the rain.

The healing came more rapidly as I looked back in awe at all the hurdles I'd jumped. I was an awesome dude, regardless of title. This simple recognition of self-love was something I had missed. Many people do the same as they rush through life to achieve things. But they sweep past the most important thing—the unique creation in the mirror. I learned to drop the rock of impossible expectations and relish the rarest treasures of my life, those that I loved and who loved me. I reached out to family members and healed old wounds and stupid grudges. God had given me the grace to face adversity head-on. My trials and tribulations were opportunities for future success. Even though I was technically defeated, I persevered until the end of my last election. What a gift to get the chance to struggle and fight for a worthy cause. I knew that it was okay to ride off into the sunset and try new things.

I thought about my dad every day during the Wolf crisis. What a dangerous situation like the ones in his books. But what could be more thrilling than reality? He loved crisis or else he wouldn't have ended up in it so much. He would've opened the brown book and looked for someone to call. He might've found somebody from an ancient campaign who knew Wolf. He would've been okay losing and urged me to get ready for the next one. But I had to get out for a while. That job had become a prison.

When the pandemic ended, I returned to standup. Audiences provided the energy that I had loved in politics. Introducing President Obama in 2014 as the lieutenant governor nominee before thousands was like skydiving. I strolled aimlessly down a dark runway to get to the curtain. Then the man with the walkie-talkie pointed to a plank over the crowd toward the podium forty yards away. I prayed the microphone would work and words would come out, that I wouldn't fall into the crowd. The president was going to put us over the top in that amazing moment. Most of the people in the audience rooted me on, guys like Pedro Cortés, who would become secretary of the commonwealth and then be fired. There was no envy, only joy. Little ole Mikey from Somerton was going to be lieutenant governor. It was a once-in-a-lifetime opportunity, and nothing could change its magnificence.

But the habit of self-sabotage came back in LA. Nothing was good enough. I had to climb higher. The unrealistic expectations frustrated Tonya. She raved at how far I had come and the parts I got to do. I walked into auditions alone, without staff; just me and my blond hair and my damn gumption. I even got to star in a hip-hop video playing a Maury Povitch character who revealed the results of the paternity test. "You are not the father, Jamal!"

The gold-toothed gangster danced for joy, and the music kicked in.

My nephews raved, "Uncle Mike, you killed it!"

Was it gubernatorial? Sure, if you like eclectic and different and, dare I say, fresh.

I examined whether I wanted to be in politics again. I had survived, but was I still viable as a candidate? When my former senate seat became vacant, I decided to dip my toe in and drove around my district and chatted with constituents. My rivals were terrified. They thought they were safe because I was doing a little acting in Los Angeles. Somebody ran to Brennan, and he produced a front-page story announcing, "STACK IS BACK!" He used two appealing photographs: me in a tailored suit with a beaming smile. Larry Farnese raved that people were running for governor and mayor yet "they're writing about you!" The governor and his pals had done "everything but kill you, and you're as viable as ever."

I didn't want to go back to politics and my old senate rivals, but I did want everyone to know I wasn't dead and could strike at any moment. My former campaign manager Marty Marks said, "Obviously you can get press whenever you want it." He was right. I didn't need a media advisor anymore. Whether I liked it or not, I was famous. I was getting my sea legs back like I had decades before. I almost quit in 2000 when Dad encouraged me to go one more time. That was going to be my last run. I couldn't envision myself on the trail ever again, and yet there I was. The last setback had been almost unbearable. I tried to snap my fingers and wake up from the trance. I learned that I don't dictate it. The healing comes when I'm healed. I gave myself a break to let God do the directing.

A few weeks after Wolf's attack, a man in rags approached me as I pumped gas. The guy was about my age and had more problems than me. He asked, "Are you lieutenant governor Michael Stack?"

I put the pump back. "Yes, I am."

With all the sincerity in the world, he said, "I'm sorry for your troubles."

I reached into my pocket, but he waved me off and patted me on the shoulder. Big deal. I had some hard times, but it was nothing.

\* \* \*

I kept up the momentum on a trip to Egypt. Our tour group began as strangers, but soon folks talked about their lives. During a cruise down the Nile, sixteen-year-old Elizabeth from New York asked, "What's up with you, Philly Mike? You're like a secret agent."

Our group of twelve waited for dessert at our usual table. They looked at me like I was E.F. Hutton. "I was a four-term senator and lieutenant governor of Pennsylvania. Now I'm an actor and tech CEO."

Elizabeth screamed, "I knew it! It's the charisma."

She made me laugh. One either has the charisma or doesn't. It cannot be hidden. It's funny how that threatens some people. Most are inspired.

No one had access to the internet, so I know they hadn't googled me. But two days later, at the Cairo Marriott, as we celebrated our last night, Steven, a

UCLA professor, asked for a photograph. "My wife googled you back home," he gushed. "Holy crap! We couldn't believe it. You're a comedian and an actor and lieutenant governor. We're fans!"

The rest of the group pushed in for photographs, including Inas, the Egyptian tour guide, "in case you become president." Somebody needed to call Brennan—Stack was back!

Tonya recovered faster than me. She moved on in an Old Testament sort of way—you know, God's wrath coming down to destroy evil. She believed justice would be done. She had kept the card of the FBI agent who visited our house on Wayside Road a decade before. "Let's just say I recommended they take a closer look at the Crazy Man." Did her actions lead to that spectacular helicopter shot of the federal raid on Two Street? I wouldn't rule it out. She wasn't just Pocahontas but Xena, Warrior Princess. Those who offended her shouldn't sleep soundly.

\* \* \*

Little Xena was looking for work. One day, she walked into our Los Angeles apartment and asked, "Would you think I was crazy to become a roller guard?" She was offered a job at Moon Light Skating Rink, the famous venue of Hollywood films. I learned that she was a roller queen in high school. She did twirls and skated backward along Venice Beach Boardwalk.

I laughed at her question. "You'd be crazy not to."

Two weeks later, she had glitter in her hair and on her face and a brand-new pair of purple skates, a tight, sexy referee shirt, and a whistle. My Roller Derby Queen swept around the rink, keeping law and order and protecting amateurs and children.

\* \* \*

I always felt I needed more experience as a business leader to be a better politician. This would never happen while I was a senator or lieutenant governor. I didn't take any action. I was just standing there with a surfboard under my arm. One of my old friends who worked for a start-up technology firm called. His Israeli founder, who had visited the senate years before, wanted to talk.

"The day he met you," he said, "he wanted to hire you, but you were wasting your talents in politics."

Professor David Hold eventually convinced me to become the CEO of Telenet Doctor, an amazing company. It was just one more freaky development that wouldn't have happened without the fall. We might transform the world and provide care to the underserved. The challenge has been breathtaking and unexpected. And there's a surprise guest who wants to help and maybe make a fortune. My old mentor, Senator Vincent Fumo, has a bunch of people who owe him. Once again, we can make a difference.

I didn't know if I would ever gain back my political magic. I watched the murder rate soar and lawlessness become rampant in Philadelphia. I wanted to step forward and be counted as a voice for change. There were ten candidates for mayor, including two multimillionaires. I decided to go to the city commit- tee meeting on Spring Garden Street, where candidates would seek support. The rickety old building on Walnut Street was sold a decade ago, and the new headquarters is named after Bob Brady. Could I walk into a crowded room and claim it, like my dad always encouraged?

Chris Brennan stood in the lobby, jotting down notes in his pad, sweating as usual. "Hi, Governor," he stuttered, startled. His eyes widened. "Are you running for mayor?"

I leaned on the wall like James Dean. "I'm thinking about it."

"Will you let me know as soon as you decide?"

I was back in my suit, looking tailored, fit, and ready, as if I never left. Chairman Bob Brady sat at the head of the table. He was older, with less hair, but still big-chested. Indicted councilman Bob Henan sat near him. Familiar ward leaders joined the city committee. I never said I was running; I just told them what I would do. I appreciated the opportunity to speak. They clapped like thunder.

My phone blew up the next morning with congratulations. Several texts included a link to the story. Chairman Bob Brady confirmed I was running for mayor. The story by Brennan included things I didn't say. The photograph was nice: five years earlier, me grinning and confident in front of a banner with my name, hair brown and short. But who cared? They spelled my name right, as Aunt Betty used to say. They still didn't care what was true. They wanted to write something about me.

I attended eight forums and performed well. I never even opened a cam- paign account. No one asked a question about Tom Wolf. Folks remarked how great it was to have a former lieutenant governor in the race. It would cost millions to compete in the anarchy. I accomplished what I wanted. I showed myself and them that I could do it. Brennan's next article had the headline: "STACK LEAVES THE STAGE WITH US WANTING MORE." And one way or another, they would get more.

I liked the idea of becoming a political talking head. That mysterious path required guidance. In the summer of 2023, I put aside any animosity for past assaults and called Dennis Owens from ABC in Harrisburg. He was friendly and excited. "I've got some ideas, but first let me ask you for something. We're bored covering the budget stalemate."

That was the groundhog day of my Harrisburg career.

"How about we do an interview with you about what you've been up to?"

Maybe he wouldn't hijack me.

"In an hour?"

I knew better.

A minute into the interview, he jabbed about my "historical" loss and skepticism about anyone voting for me again. What did I expect? Nobody cared about the past except the bored media. Owens asked about Wolf and "some controversy with the state police." It was like old times. I didn't show it, but I was frazzled and slightly cut. My mother guaranteed they'd take shots again, as predictable as the change of seasons. It didn't hurt as much as the excruciating old days. Maybe I'll never have the thick skin they say political leaders need to have. I'm a little tougher now but still sensitive. My healing has continued incrementally.

* * *

John Dougherty stood on his front porch in shorts and a wrinkled button shirt as FBI agents carried boxes to the sidewalk. His face was flushed as he jabbered in his usual incomprehensible manner. When the microphone appeared, his words were from a different reality. "I'm good. I'm good. Okay."

He wasn't.

He was convicted of multiple counts of extortion, bribery, and corruption along with his codefendant, councilman Bobby Henon, on November 16, 2021. Bobby acted like a victim until eventually taking his medicine. Doc incited Bobby to threaten Children's Hospital of Philadelphia officials to use Local 98 electricians on their MRI machines or get shut down. CHOP was considered a divine agent here in Philadelphia, the savior of poor, sick little children. There was no line of decency for power-mad Doc. The wiretaps revealed the gangster rantings of a megalomaniac disconnected from human suffering and decency. Guys like John McCullough, Steve Traitz, and Joe Dougherty all worried about their piece of the pie. Two of them died in prison, and one at the hands of an assassin.

I liked Bobby Henon when I endorsed him in his maiden campaign. He had the talent to be an excellent public official, but he couldn't shake the ten-thousand-pound gorilla. He was sentenced to less than three years and went to prison shortly after he was sentenced.

Dougherty hadn't yet been sentenced and was active in Local 98's election to get a new leader. He switched allegiances several times, and his candidate didn't win. But it wasn't a landslide. His legacy of fear remained. He fired his lawyers and was inexplicably given leave to find new counsel. But the former electrician's boss was convicted of embezzling more than $600,000 from his union to enrich himself and his family in yet another trial. It was his second conviction in as many years. A looming trial on extortion charges "could complete the hat trick," said an *Inquirer* editorial. The hat trick didn't come because there was a hung jury. The feds could still retry him, but his codefendant nephew pleaded guilty and is going to jail.

\* \* \*

Mobster Whitey Bulger was revealed to be an FBI informant since 1975. Bulger provided information about the inner workings of a crime family and other rivals in Boston and Providence, Rhode Island. His federal handler, John Conley, ensured that his Winter Hill Gang was ignored by police investigations. Beginning in 1997, press reports exposed various instances of criminal conduct by federal, state, and local officials with ties to Bulger, causing embarrassment to the FBI. Bulger was finally indicted for murder and racketeering but fled after being alerted by his FBI handler. Fumo and Brady always believed Dougherty was the Whitey Bulger of Philadelphia. Unlike district attorney Seth Williams, a Black guy who was whisked off to prison immediately after conviction, Dougherty went through a third trial without ankle bracelets.

Prosecutors caught Dougherty on tape threatening to sue, "heat up," or "run over" potential witnesses against him. He used millions of dollars to elect governors like Ed Rendell and Tom Wolf and unleashed the five-thousand-member union army to help turn out the vote on election day. In the end, the union dues paved the way for Dougherty's rise and fall. He took control of Local 98 in 1993 and, two years later, helped electricians union member Rick Mariano to city council. In 2006, Mariano, who appeared in the helicopter shot, was sentenced to six and a half years in prison for taking less than $30,000 in bribes. Doc then helped elect John Street as mayor where his union members used thug tactics to harass and disrupt his opponent's campaign events.

Vince Fumo believed his case was spurred on by the Crazy Man. Brady was investigated for bribing a congressional opponent to get out of the race. Two of his aides were convicted. But Bob survived and thought Doc was behind it.

Larry Farnese was our anxious housemate at the lieutenant governor's residence when he was indicted for allegedly buying the vote of a committeewoman to remain Democratic ward leader. The trial took place in January 2017. We listened to his nervous rantings around the clock and feared his conviction. After his acquittal, I welcomed him back to the senate from the dais. I banged the gavel and offered congratulations to the senator "for beating the rap." We all believed it was Dougherty who spurred on that case, too.

Nonetheless, shortly after Farnese's acquittal, I learned that Tonya and I were being investigated by the state inspector general. Dougherty was one of Governor Wolf's largest donors, even after his 2018 indictment. I hired Farnese's attorney, who had been Fumo's attorney and mine on the Beach Street controversy.

Among the happiest times of my life was sitting by the fire at State House with Tonya, Larry, and Justin, discussing all the potential dangers and all our exciting adventures. People in the administration hated us, and we couldn't figure out why. We knew our old friend from Two Street could instigate acrimony in any situation. But there had to be partners on the other end who would stir the poison even more. He never did any damage by himself, but we could always laugh because we were going through it together. We hoped that one day the Crazy Man would get his.

I was escorted to the dance of a lifetime by the most powerful politician in Pennsylvania. Senator Fumo had been convicted by a jury in 1978 on fifteen counts of mail fraud, but on the day of his sentencing, a federal judge overturned the conviction. He went on to become the prince. He was completing his second term when Budd Dwyer called his press conference. The blood never stopped flowing after that day. A jealous protégé of the brash young senator became his most bitter enemy.

After the first conviction, Johnny Doc was unrepentant. "What Councilman Henon and I were found guilty of is how business and politics are typically and properly conducted." As a historical note, federal prosecutors in Philadelphia have convicted more than one thousand people of public corruption over the last forty years. Over the last decade, Philadelphia ranks ninth in federal corruption convictions. One study found that malfeasance across the state amounts to a corruption tax that costs about $1,300 per resident. But guys like Lightbulbs got help. And he wasn't in leg irons and a jumpsuit like the rest of them. African American district attorney Seth Williams was whisked to solitary confinement moments after conviction.

After Doc was convicted, Tonya waited every day to see him enter prison. Maybe our Whitey Bulger was offering up others so he could avoid the can.

"Don't worry," I said. "He's going away."

She connected him to much of the mayhem in our lives. He and others were like the demons of her childhood. She had a hard time sleeping, knowing he was out terrifying people. On October 1, 2024, John "Johnny Doc" Dougherty reported to federal prison in Lewisburg to begin a six-year sentence. Pocahontas had a restful sleep.

\* \* \*

My story is sometimes too crazy to tell. I've often feared people wouldn't believe me. Yet I told a bunch of men at a church in Pacific Palisades my story last year. "Everything was going great until I got caught up in a big public controversy. I chose my sixteenth year in elected office to have a meltdown."

One could hear a pin drop.

"It was a lot of made up stuff, and I assure you I was framed. But when you're framed in politics in Philadelphia, no one gives a shit."

They erupted in laughter. My mortification lessened, and then I was relieved. Thunderous applause followed, and I finally let go of the past. Grandfather Stack and my old man joined the laughter from up above.

\* \* \*

My endorsement of Allan Domb for mayor of Philadelphia got some coverage. His field organizer, Gary Masino Jr., remarked, "It's just like old times, Guv. Let me know what you want to do and I'm in."

I wasn't interested in running for state treasurer. Rob McCord resigned from the job after pleading guilty to extortion, yet another case Dougherty had spurred on. Rob was so overwhelmed by the millions Tom Wolf was spending on the campaign that he threatened contributors to give more. Johnny Doc had once bragged as we stood in the locker room at the Philadelphia Sporting Club that McCord was "being looked at." Allyson Schwartz was supposed to be a shoo-in as the first female governor of Pennsylvania, but she couldn't keep up with Tom Wolf's spending. Joe Torsella, who had lost to her for Congress, captured McCord's old job. He may have been one of my rivals for governor if I hadn't gotten jammed up with the inspector general and he hadn't lost for reelection. Somehow attorney general Josh Shapiro was unopposed in the Democratic primary for governor in 2022.

Over coffee, I thought Torsella was messing with me when he said he'd been acting and singing in community theater productions and short films. When I asked him about his ambition to one day be governor, he said, "I thought I wanted that." His priorities were different now. He liked taking care of his family and being creative.

John Fetterman stole Governor Wolf's thunder. He didn't wear custom suits like me or joke with senators while presiding; instead, he wore a hoodie and gym shorts. He cared more about marijuana legalization than balanced budgets. Senate protocol forced him to wear a suit while holding the gavel, and then they stripped him of that role for failing to follow the rules in a blowup with Jake Corman. The Republicans suspended him for a couple weeks until he agreed to behave. Things moved fast in the senate, and he was likely confused. He hadn't spent years learning how to do it.

My friend Senator Camera Bartolotta, a conservative Republican, texted, "MISS ME NOW?!" with a link to the story. I felt bad for the guy. He's like many Democrats—they think they know everything, or they don't care about substance and traditions. Their ambition suffices for credentials. His carried him to the United States Senate despite suffering a stroke along the way.

The shaved head and tattoos served as his blue-collar costume. The circus was on. No one cared that he was a trust-fund baby who was supported by his parents. Doctor Oz was such a bad candidate that it didn't matter when Fetterman froze in front of the camera worse than Joe Biden. The stroke had affected his brain. He was in favor of and against fracking. But he still won election.

Shortly after being sworn in, he was hospitalized at Walter Reed for depression. The United States Senate nearly changed its protocol to allow Fetterman to wear his big-top costume. Now he's a heroic advocate for mental health. Several news stories reported that he dissuaded Kamala Harris from choosing Josh Shapiro as a running mate. He cautioned that Josh would try to outshine her. Fetterman also visited President-elect Trump at Mar-a-Lago and advocated for United States occupation of the West Bank.

* * *

Over the years, I've maintained contact with all the amazing characters who ran Harrisburg. Republican John Perzel rose from a Mayfair row home to become Speaker of the House. Republican attorney general Tom Corbett secured a conviction against him during the Bonusgate scandal. Perzel allegedly used taxpayer money to create a computerized voter outreach program. He only cared about votes. After being stripped of everything and sent to prison, he was joined in the cell by his old Democratic nemesis Bill Deweese. You can't make this stuff up. They worked out together and pulled strings and did their time joyfully. Perzel is now a successful consultant who espouses the uselessness of the past yet routinely recites the deficiencies of his conviction. He thinks I may need a letter from the state police saying I really was a good guy and that Wolf made it all up.

Bill DeWeese was also Speaker. He was the guy who just wanted to have a look at me in case I won in 2000. As a frequent guest at State House, he espoused the injustice of his case but bragged about how many chin-ups he could do and what a good rapper he'd become. His lovely girlfriend, Senator Camera Bartolotta, was his companion, always laughing at his jokes. We watched the Eagles win the Super Bowl by a crackling fire as DeWeese threw down rhymes.

Larry Farnese was Fumo's unlikely successor. He was always underestimated and usually overachieved. As my top lieutenant during the leadership battles, he routinely completed tough tasks. Perpetually sweating and anxious, he walked into the flames. No one thought he would beat the feds. He won acquittal, but the trial damaged his reputation, and his timing, which had always been flawless, got compromised by the pandemic. Then the Crazy Man endorsed his opponent, a socialist named Nikki Savell. In a perfect storm where Larry's voters didn't come to the polls, John Dougherty got some revenge.

Daylin Leach transformed from enemy to friend and joined me on the stage during my 2014 victory. On the senate floor as I presided, he was baffled by the problems with Wolf. He and fifteen other senators endorsed me for reelection. Later, he was accused of sexual harassment. Jay Costa commissioned an investigation, and Leach's scandal led to defeat. Daylin's voicemail still regales, "I'm out there making the world a better place. It's just what I do." He seemed envious of my standup comedy adventure. Leach claimed his worst vote was for Costa against me for leader. John Yudichak, another vote against me, joined the Republican caucus in 2020. John Blake left the senate in 2022 after failing to get Costa's support for a leadership position. Those three would've given me the leader's job. In my 2010 concession speech, I predicted they would regret it. My dad's advice about today's enemies becoming tomorrow's friends often came to fruition. Jay advocated for my primacy in the Wolf administration, then, when things turned bad, tried to help. He led an endorsement press conference of sixteen senators when I was hanging by a thread. We've stayed in touch, and he's been an advocate of my start-up company and a mentor to my stepson, Justin.

\* \* \*

After I was out of office, I traveled to Colorado with my mom to say goodbye to her nephew Peter, who was going to commit suicide. He was one of eight from her sister Mary, who passed away twenty years ago. Her husband, Ralph, had been ambassador to Chile, and the kids had a tumultuous upbringing. They were wild hippies who were intense and intelligent. We loved them as kids but were intimidated. She didn't support his decision to take advantage of legal suicide in Colorado. But her niece Missy needed her support. She explained some of the reasons why Aunt Mary had mental health challenges. Missy was still looking for answers. I watched them have the conversation quietly and learned a little bit more about my mom.

My mom was always the one to hold things together. I learned that she lost her mother when she was seven. Her dad may have been in his cuffs, and family members attempted to separate her from two sisters and a brother. They needed to make the family look stable so they could stay together. She took on that responsibility as a little girl. Maybe that's why it was natural to keep my dyslexia a secret and to try to de-escalate the situation with Wolf. Every family has secrets. Sometimes the best way to hide is by being out in public. I started asking more questions after going through the wringer with the governor. At the end of the day, our crises teach us how to survive and maybe how to improve. I worried about our family's honor and how everything would look.

After the pandemic, I returned to the premier event of the Philadelphia Democratic Party, the Jefferson Jackson party I had attended in my teens with my father. I retrieved my cobalt suit from the Batcave. I embraced old friends and adversaries, some who thought they saw a ghost.

"Let's go, Guv! Whatever we're running for, the Duckman is in!" said Mr. Birts, an old stalwart and friend of my dad. I had forgotten about that nickname. Not Ducky, Guv. It's all been worth it just to get that nickname. My dad would've used it all the time and driven my siblings crazy. Every time I talk to Farnese, he says, "they did everything they could to kill you, and after all these years, you're standing there with that title. It kills them." Good.

The hall wasn't as crowded or twinkling as the old days, but it was splendid. The men with dreams who wanted to meet my dad had been replaced with new dreamers. The dirty looks and scoffs were there and always would be. They knew I wasn't dead, even though it felt like it for a while. My mother was in the crowd and gushed, "How nice it is that so many people are happy to see you."

Years later, I think I understand what I had been feeling. Politics had been my love, with all its warts and foibles, and after being stripped, all my hard work and advancement in politics gone, I was crestfallen. I had a broken heart from the loss of a vital relationship. And I was bleeding. There was no one to write a note to. But now I was almost healed.

\* \* \*

At the Board of Pardons meeting a week after the loss to remain lieutenant governor, Josh Shapiro asked me if I saw it coming. "Of course! The governor ran a negative campaign against me for two years. It would've been a disaster for him if I won." I was a little hot. I told Josh this wasn't my first loss. He was surprised. I inflicted the punishment of my perseverance story on him, the same one I told here, the same one I told to school kids, my three losses and the thank-you notes I was forced to write. "I always come back stronger than before." His eyes widened. I acted confident but wasn't sure I believed it. Maybe I had the same doubts as Lincoln. Or the desperation of Bobby Kennedy that turned to hope when he recited Aeschylus. "Pain which can not forget falls drop by drop upon the heart until, in our despair, against our will, comes the awful grace of God."

The depression lasted longer than my senate losses. Time heals all wounds, and over the last years, the value of the struggle, the car wreck of a public fall, and the reemergence of optimism have energized my life. One must be a big dog to draw that kind of violence. I knew I wanted to survive to fight another day. Each year, the ache of the past has dwindled. Lots of folks have had challenges far more severe. Health crises, death, and homelessness shatter lives. Our stuff is a little punch in the nose. I'm not angry with Tom Wolf or John Dougherty or anyone. Staying angry doesn't work for me. It's like Senator Williams said: People like nice guy Mikey better, including me. Resentment is like drinking poison and expecting others to die.

A journalist who covers politicians listened to my story. It was kind of a random conversation in California. "So, what!" he said. "It's blood sport. All you guys get cut."

Angels show up when you aren't looking. I was terrified when Tonya was dragged into Governor Wolf's investigation. She needed her own lawyer, and Michael Quinn came to the rescue. He had just gotten home from work and jumped back in his car, driving two hours to see us. He had come to her rescue many times before. "This is a blip on the screen of your life. No one will remember this." It was different for her than me. I was used to getting tarnished but she was a civilian.

Tonya recently confided she thinks Quinnie was right. He passed away suddenly at the age of sixty. Life is too short, and it was way too short for Michael Quinn. Having a friend like him makes me feel rich. He didn't charge us a nickel. Quinnie had been an all-American rower at Temple University. The president of the university decided to cut the sport because it wasn't a real revenue provider. I was one voice to help save crew. Michael always gave me credit for being the one who saved it—he said it out loud everywhere we went. Other people helped too. Sometimes we get credit, sometimes we don't. Once that's not important, freedom comes.

I've gotten to do amazing new things that guys my age rarely get to. I've got another standup show in Hollywood. I'm in rehearsal for a feature film. I appeared with Tonya on *Let's Make a Deal* dressed as Julius Ceasar and Cleopatra. I've created and co-written a pilot about my adventures with Senator Fumo and the crazy times in the city of blood. I've done this book and let people get to know me. A friend who followed my political career remarked, "I'm amazed at how you're putting yourself out there."

So am I.

When I was a little kid, I had a great imagination. I would tell stories and people would think they were made up. What I've told you in this book is from my recollections. I've referred to newspaper articles and done some web searches, but a lot of this is how I remember it. I do not say my recollections represent stone-cold facts, just precisely how I recall them. I was blessed to actually be there and experience these exciting moments. Of course, there are three sides to every story: mine, yours, and the truth. Governor Tom Wolf has diminished in his relevence as the years have passed. Johnny Doc is innocuous now that he is behind bars.

* * *

I spent a recent Christmas and New Year's with my mom and siblings. Judge Stack left the bench years ago, but people think she's still there. She was always fair and kind. We all try to be kind. My little struggles are nothing compared to those folks unjustly imprisoned or in desperate poverty or living with the fear of death. All my loved ones are in my life. My stature, reputation, and record of service are intact.

It's just like when I was a kid with dyslexia and thought I was a freak. I was the only one in the family who wanted to run in the crazy world of politics. When I was nine, I thought I must've done something wrong to be so confused in school. The grownups were harsh and told me I was doing it on purpose. I had the same notion with the most powerful person in the state. That was some exquisite gaslighting. His team rivaled the nuns at Saint Chris, but only the nuns were uninformed. My sisters and brother often asked quizzically, "What the heck is Michael doing?" I must've been crazy running for office and getting up on stage. They still scratch their heads about all the things I'm doing. For the time being, I'm swimming with different sharks, the ones in La La Land, maybe someday the real ones who make the TV shows. I charge into auditions like they're ward meetings or union halls. And I'm never walking without my dad, remembering to sit in the front row so they know I'm important.

I haven't given up on my political dreams, just expanded the field to include so much more. I was recently on the campus of the University of Southern California, Los Angeles, to rehearse for a horror movie called *Monstrum*. I met a sophomore who was studying molecular biology while I searched for a T-shirt store. She was kind enough to walk me there, and we discussed her future. She wasn't sure what she was doing with her career path or what her future would hold. I told her part of what I've told you in this book. "Don't worry," I said. "You can reinvent yourself over and over again. Look at me." The young rocket scientist looked relieved.

Tonya spent the holidays in Los Angeles with our dog, Peaches. It works for us. She wasn't coming back to Philadelphia until John Dougherty was in prison but no longer has that excuse. But there are others like him in our great metropolis that's caught in a time warp. His mistress, Marita Crawford, conveyed Doc's orders to Bobby Henon, but she cooperated and got only a few days in prison. She was recently hired as the legislative director of a Philadelphia city councilman and was honored by the Italian American Society of South Philadelphia.

Some may interpret that as a stamp of approval for guys like Johnny. Philadelphia is a strange place that can't seem to stop the violence against itself. Our long history of corruption and destruction continues as kids die from gun violence and hopelessness. But our great city can reinvent itself too. I aspire to be a part of it. I'll never be able to let go of my call to service.

I recently performed at a soldout show at The Ice House in Anaheim, California. I was one of the comics sandwiched between the headliners. For the first time, I tried my material about being the former lieutenant governor of Pennsylvania, the biggest do-nothing job in America. "I worked so hard for the chance to do nothing." The line got laughs and I got relief. "Soon the governor became obsessed about exactly what I wasn't doing." More laughs. The road to laughing has been long but beautiful. It took what it took to to get well. Laughter was the best medicine.

* * *

Recently, I pitched a gentleman from a giant health insurance company about my telemedicine start-up. I knew him from my days as a public servant. I don't know what will happen; probably something amazing. Anything could happen. Whether the business takes off or not, it already has. I'll return to LA to complete some postproduction work on a science-fiction film called *Chomp*. It was nominated for best thriller at the Micheleux Film Festival in Los Angeles. Tonya and I sat in the front row, watching me on the big screen, looking scruffy and crazy. I played a child who dramatically aged from an experimental drug and became my current age, which is seven years younger than Tom Wolf at the time of our election. Sometimes I feel like I took a drug that increased my wisdom exponentially. Once, it dropped like trickles of blood; now, it cascades upon me like a waterfall. I've learned so much in such a short time.

I tell young people that their struggles will make them better. It doesn't always seem like that, but they will get through it and learn lessons that will make them happier in life.

* * *

I traveled to the shore recently because a rainstorm was coming. I love being at the shore in a storm. I went to Wawa, our amazing convenience store where you press buttons on the screen and delicious hot food appears. I strolled over to the newspapers like a burglar casing a joint and saw the *Inquirer* and *Daily News*, the tormenting poison ink pulsating like arterial blood. I hadn't read them for years, not wanting to get burnt by a hot stove. But the pain was over, and I had forgiven everyone. I gave myself permission to read their fiction. Hands trembling, I turned back the front page of the sparse and tiny *Daily News* that, in a different era, was bulky and filled. It now took minutes to read instead of hours.

Chris Brennan announced he was leaving the paper, and this was his last *Clout*. He was only a few years late. Farnese thinks he's got a job with Cherelle Parker, our new mayor. She got 66,000 votes to win in a landslide. I had over 130,000 votes in my loss. Doc had a lot of friends in their camp, but Chris won't have the Crazy Man to write his stories anymore. Tonya thinks he may have some attention from the people in the windbreakers. Who knows? She's been right before.

John was rumored to be "giving everyone up" to get a shorter sentence. The chatter is on the streets. We like to hear things rather than read them. Some are speculating he'll take the coward's way out. They did the same with Fumo, who would've never given them the satisfaction. No one mentioned Budd Dwyer, who took it all too personal decades ago and was so proud and indignant that he couldn't accept that it was only blood sport, nothing personal. We always speculate on the death of others in a city that's filled with blood, violence, corruption, and endless hope.

I never read the stories, just the headlines. I'd look for my photograph or one of my friends. Reading was like handing my "good friends" a rusty knife to turn in my gut. But on that rainy night, the opening sentence from Brennan's last story read: "If the *Clout* column had a Mount Rushmore, which four faces would you expect to see carved in the granite up there?"

You've got to be kidding! A photo of yours truly, with long blond hair, looking thoughtful and confident next to the legendary Bob Brady, our titan and the longest-serving big city boss in America. Milton Street, the former senator, mayoral candidate, and fellow inmate of Vince Fumo, looked ready to rumble. Completing our Mount Rushmore with the beehive hairdo and iron disposition was Marge Tartaglione. Bitter and resilient, she dominated in a man's world for decades. I promised my dad on his deathbed that I would take care of family business and send her to retirement, and then I'd get in the mix for governor. Wow, what an honor to be included with those legends, those he revered and talked about from the time of my boyhood. Was Brennan going for one last cut, or was he trying to make amends on the way out?

\* \* \*

We were the stars of a show about politics from the city of brotherly blood. The story continues. The other headline was "A look back at *Clout*'s top moments as its lead reporter says goodbye." I outlasted him. What a breathtaking trip it's been so far. Those other icons are much older than me.

I wouldn't have written it this way. It's simply too sensational to be true, so many twists and turns and surprises and agonizing struggles. I prefer a happy ending. Maybe it is or could be. Let me take some more time to reflect and maybe write some thank-you notes. It's been a fantastic adventure.

My dad would've loved it.

# ABOUT THE AUTHOR

**MIKE STACK** received his GED from Villanova Law School in 1992 and has been a member of the Pennsylvania Bar for decades. He was elected to the Pennsylvania Senate in 2000 after three losses. While enlisted in the US Army in 2007, Stack competed against people decades younger and served as an officer and Judge Advocate General until 2015. He was the first Philadelphian elected lieutenant governor, and served until 2019. He is the global CEO of Telenet Doctor. As member of the Screen Actors Guild, he's appeared in dozens of films and is a featured standup comedian at the Ice House Comedy Club in Pasadena, California, and the Comedy Chateau in Hollywood among other venues.

www.ingramcontent.com/pod-product-compliance
Lightning Source LLC
Chambersburg PA
CBHW011154090426
42740CB00018B/3391